State -Society Relations in Nigeria:
Democratic Consolidation, Conflicts and Reforms

Published by
Adonis & Abbey Publishers Ltd
P.O. Box 43418
London
SE11 4XZ
http://www.adonis-abbey.com
Email: editor@adonis-abbey.com

First Edition, August 2007

Copyright 2007 © Kenneth Omeje

British Library Cataloguing-in-Publication Data
A catalogue record for this book is available from the British Library

ISBN: 9781905068579 (HB), 9781905068586 (PB)

Printed and bound in Great Britain

State -Society Relations in Nigeria:
Democratic Consolidation, Conflicts and Reforms

Edited by

Kenneth Omeje

Dedication

This book is dedicated to all those who risked or lost their lives fighting to forestall fraud and malpractices in the April 2007 elections in Nigeria.

Preface

Given its large population and oil-rich economy, as well as its significant military and diplomatic clout in the regional scene, Nigeria is recognised as one of Africa's most influential countries. But the external influence often commanded by Nigerian leadership in regional politics and elsewhere hardly translates to greater respectability, legitimacy and support of the political regime at home. From one regime to another, the history of post-independent Nigeria has been ridden with political instability, centrifugal pressures, developmental retrogression and multifarious conflicts of varying intensities.

The democratic transition of the fourth civilian republic in 1999 - earned at a costly prize of popular resistance against corrupt military dictatorships - came with great hopes and promises of proactive reforms and change. The road to reforms and change has been uneasy, provoking considerable criticisms, conflicts, challenges and opportunities.

The edited book is an assemblage of well-argued contributions that explore the problematics of democratic consolidation, conflicts and reforms in Nigeria's contemporary political history. It analyses the history, structures and dynamics of low intensity conflicts, the conflict management strategies, the neo-liberal economic and political reforms, the war against corruption, as well as the challenges of democratization, good governance and development. The controversial April 2007 national election – why and where it went wrong – is also critically analyzed.

The book adopts an integrative methodology based on a trans-disciplinary, multi-track, and empirically-grounded analytical framework. The integrative conceptual and methodological approach adopted in the various chapters of the book is partly a reflection of the rich scholastic and professional diversity of contributors. On the strength of a dynamic interface of social theory and empirical realities, the contributors offer useful functional guides to Nigerian policy makers and local and international stakeholders concerned with the challenges of helping to rebuild Africa's most populous and largest oil producing state.

Kenneth Omeje

June 2007

Acknowledgements

This book would not have come to fruition without the motivation, commitment and support of many key persons. I wish to gratefully acknowledge the professional support and understanding of the Editor of *African Renaissance* (*AR*), Dr P. C. J. Adibe. It was my reading the various articles on contemporary conflicts and reforms published in *AR* and debating them with the Editor and other colleagues that provided the initial intellectual inspiration for this project. Three of the contributions in this volume were developed from the original *AR* articles that helped to inspire the book project. To all the contributors and reviewers, I say a big thank you for your critical insights, commitment and professionalism.

I am grateful to my colleagues in the Africa Centre and the University of Bradford for their encouragement and goodwill – Dr David Francis, Prof Nana Poku, Prof Paul Rogers, Dr Joao Porto, Dr Usman Tar, Caroline Nwagwu, Grace Maina and Fatoumata Tambajang – to name a few.

I am indebted to my loving wife, Ngozi, and daughters, Rejoicing and Chibia, for their unflinching support and understanding. To my parents, in-laws, family members in Nigeria and Christian brethren in Bradford and elsewhere, I convey sincere thanks for your prayers and solidarity.

Table of Contents

Chapter 1

Introduction:
Reappraising Contemporary Political Developments in Nigeria

Kenneth Omeje

This book primarily explores the problematic of state – society relations in Nigeria and its consequences for democratic consolidation, conflicts and reforms. Nigeria's post-independent history has been extraordinarily turbulent. Efforts at state-building have been truncated by a spiral of centrifugal pressures and ethnocultural hostilities, which have plunged the country into a major civil war and a variety of low intensity communal violence and political insurgency. The euphoria, enthusiasm and hope of building a virile African state that characterized the attainment of political independence and the early years of self-rule have been ostensibly displaced by a palpable cloud of despondency, disenchantment and disillusionment with the Nigerian project. Frustration and apathy, poverty and crime, lawlessness and violence, tend to have risen to unacceptably high levels, with the result that, since the 1990s, Nigeria has consistently produced a much larger volume of internally displaced persons (IDPs) and [economic] refugees compared to many war-torn, post-war and collapsed states in the global South. From the perspective of key stakeholders, compatriots and sympathetic observers, the exodus of different population categories from conflict-prone Nigeria, is to say the least, a highly devastating and worrying trend.

But as the nexus of government reform measures since the inauguration of the fourth civilian democratic republic in Nigeria in 1999 suggests, there is a smattering of hope capable of inspiring deeper political thinking and policy [re]engineering. The road to reforms, as a number of contributions in this book demonstrate, has been a mixed grill, provoking considerable criticisms, conflicts, challenges and opportunities.

9

This introductory chapter is divided into three sections. Section one examines the reforms and contradictions of the Nigerian fourth civilian republic. In section two, an attempt is made to operationally conceptualize the state and society as basis for analyzing state-society relations in contemporary Nigeria and the spate of dysfunctional political conflicts that tend to undermine the country's fledgling democracy and development. Section three presents a review of the various chapter contributions in this book, highlighting the key intellectual/practical concerns and policy alternatives emerging from the contributions.

The Politics of Reforms and Contradictions

Nigeria's enormous human and material resources have, by fortition or design, conspired to cast a spell or curse on national development. Being Africa's largest oil producing country, Nigeria has earned over US$400 billion as economic rent over the past 50 years (1956-2006) of oil production (*Daily Trust*, 16.11.06). More than 95 per cent of this amount was earned after the first 15 years of oil production and export (i.e. from the oil boom period of the early 1970s onwards). The huge external revenue from the country's abundant oil resources have over the years funded a spending spree on unsustainable white elephant development projects and a bewildering mode and scale of prebendal accumulation by the hegemonic elites that have in recent decades earned notoriety for the country as one of the most corrupt countries in the world. Negative internalities like prebendal corruption, bad governance, lawlessness, crime and violent conflicts have not only crystallized to a development-impeding proportion, but have also significantly ruined Nigeria's international image. Mass wellbeing, human security, basic social services and public infrastructure have suffered a devastating blow.

The democratic transition of the Fourth Civilian Republic inaugurated in May 1999 after 15 years of unprecedented military dictatorship and decades of political instability and economic plunder provided a great opportunity to rekindle the Nigerian dream by giving the country a fresh start. Political and economic reforms aimed at positioning the country on the path of enduring stability, growth, development and security were among the top priorities of the fourth republic civilian regime and political leaders. Diverse reform measures have been implemented, especially at the macro-economic level. These include banking and financial sector consolidation reform, implementation of the Extractive Industries Transparency Initiative (EITI) marked by the publication of monthly oil revenue distributed to the three ties of government, public service reform aimed at injecting efficiency by curtailing waste, redundancy, corruption and extravagant perquisites associated with top public offices, and anti-corruption campaign. These reforms are all part of the National Economic Empowerment Strategy (NEEDS), a short-term macro-economic restructuring and development programme for the country promulgated in late 2003. NEEDS is the Nigerian version of the World Bank Poverty Reduction Strategy Papers (PRSP) believed to have replaced the ill-fated Structural Adjustment Programme (SAP) imposed on many developing countries (Nigeria inclusive) by the World Bank. The new programme (NEEDS), which is credited to be a home-grown policy, is premised on the rhetoric of wealth creation, employment generation, poverty reduction and value reorientation (see Omeje, 2006:29). The economic restructuring agenda focuses mainly on strengthening and expanding the private sector, public sector reform and anti-corruption campaign. With limited support from the international donor community, the National Planning Commission (NPC) encourages the various state governments to develop their own, State Economic Empowerment and Development Strategies (SEEDS) to compliment NEEDS at the sub-national levels. SEEDS was launched in early 2004.

An Appraisal of the Reform Programmes: The Macro-Economic Portrait

It seems early days to do a comprehensive empirical assessment of some of the reform programmes but what is most apparent is that with the end of President Obasanjo's second and last term in office in May 2007, the so-called dividends of democracy desperately expected by Nigerians seem to have been slow at materializing, if ever they will – to echo the sentiments of many critical observers – not withstanding the much publicized growth of the national economy. Available macro-economic indicators suggest impressive trends between 2000 and 2005 in external revenue, balance of payment profile, Gross National Income (GNI) per capita, GDP [growth], and foreign reserves (cf. The World

11

Bank, 2006; UNDP, 2006) – thanks to the fantastic appreciation in oil price due largely to the disruptive effects of instability and wars in the oil-rich Arabian Gulf. Fiscal responsibility and financial management, especially at the federal government level tends to have relatively improved during the second term of President Obasanjo's administration (2003 – 2007) – thanks to the team of dynamic technocrats drawn into key economic and fiscal positions, including the President's national economic planning and management team. However, the observed positive trends do not give much room for celebration but apprehension for at least four important reasons. The first is that following recent reports by leading international development institutions such as USAID and the World Bank, human security statistics remain abysmally disturbing. About two-thirds (70 per cent) of the country's citizens live in poverty subsisting on less than one US dollar a day; unemployment rate remains high, with up to 40 per cent of urban youth population being jobless; half of the adult population is illiterate; close to four million Nigerians are HIV-positive; infant mortality rate remains high with 20 per cent of children dying before the age of five; life expectancy at birth is 43.7 years, and corruption is endemic, with Nigeria still perceived as one of the most corrupt countries in the world based on the annual Corruption Perception Indices published by Transparency International (cf. USAID, 2004, 2005; The World Bank, 2006).

Levels of Government, Politics of Intrigue and Contradictions in Reforms

The second reason for apprehension over the present reform project is that the reform-induced improvement in economic management is, to a large extent, limited to the federal level (i.e. federal government ministries and, to a lesser extent, parastatals). Fiscal responsibility hardly exists in the political lexicon of most state and local government administrations for whom nothing has practically changed. The nature of power distribution in a federally constituted presidential democracy, whereby the federating subnational units enjoy relative autonomy and are not strictly accountable or answerable to the centre in matters of fiscal responsibility serves as a convenient alibi for the hegemonic subnational elites to perpetuate the neopatrimonial aggrandizement and appropriation of state resources.

12

The controversial immunity clause in the 1999 constitution which unduly protects executive office holders from prosecution on abuse of public office, including charges of corruption, strengthens the predisposition of many governors to prebendal corruption and the constraints of responsible federal agencies to institute and actualize effective probe or prosecution.

Prosecution of corrupt Governors is only possible after they have been impeached and thrown out of office by the state legislatures but in reality, impeachment proceedings have mostly been instituted against governors who in addition to charges of 'gross impropriety' have lost favour with 'consequential power brokers' (CPBs) such as political benefactors or God-fathers instrumental to the governor's electoral installation, the federal government or powerful politicians at the federal level, party chieftains and, most crucially, the state legislators. Impeachment proceedings, which are usually not without substantial evidence of impropriety (e.g. monumental stealing of public funds, money laundering, electoral fraud) as demonstrated by the recent removals of the governors of Bayelsa, Anambra, Ekiti, Oyo and Plateau states, and the failed impeachment attempts in other states like Enugu, Adamawa, Lagos, and Abia states, for instance, have always been preceded and instigated by the governor's loss of favour with CPBs. In the circumstances, state government legislators become the expensive bride in the pendulum of power tussle between the governors and the CPBs. Without doubt, the spate of impeachments, vicious factional conflicts and associated state of emergencies imposed by the president to manage the crisis have worrying implications for democratic consolidation and political stability in Nigeria.

Similarly, some of the impeachment procedures raise constitutional queries. A typical example is the case of Plateau State where only 6 out of the 24 members of the State House of Assembly convened and got the embattled Governor Joshua Dariye impeached and the decision was upheld with his deputy Michael Botmang sworn in as Governor (*This Day*, 13.11.06). The constitutional provision for an impeachment to be legal is a quorum of two-thirds of members of the state legislature. Because the state governors do not control the security forces (the President does), it has become possible to impeach a governor by unconstitutional means and have the unlawful decision enforced using federal government security might. Thankfully, some of the unconstitutional impeachments including that of the governors of

Oyo, Plateau and Anambra states have been reversed by the appellant court. Not withstanding the controversial questions of constitutionality in some of the impeachments which usually provoke prolonged legal battles, it is apparent that the governors by their gross political misdeeds, which include efforts to control, weaken, dominate and manipulate the state legislators, have often been the architects of their downfall. Because of their relatively weak power position and reliance on the generosity of the state governors for accumulation of prebendal spoils, many members of the state legislature do not hesitate to seize any opportunity of discord between their governor and an aggrieved / powerful external CPB capable of backstopping the legislators with prebendal largesse, to institute impeachment proceedings against the governor.

The outcome of the impeachment proceedings, will, among other things, depend on how the governor and his formidable adversaries play the politics of swinging the decisive legislators to their side of the pendulum. As a matter of fact, there are usually no scarcity of charges of 'gross impropriety' or 'impeachable offences' to level against a serving governor and any other elected executive public office holder in Nigeria for that matter. For instance, the federal government main anti-corruption agency, the Economic and Financial Crimes Commission (EFCC) recently announced that at least 32 of the 36 state governors have serious cases of corruption against them, and that it had plans to prevent the governors concerned from escaping the country before they hand over power in May 2007, when their executive immunity from prosecution also seizes (*New African,* 2006:67). 15 of the alleged corrupt governors have been indicted in a report submitted by the EFCC to the Senator in September 2006 while at the time of writing investigation was not yet concluded on the rest. It is unnecessary to delve into the speculative territory of what could happen to the large number of allegedly corrupt governors with cases to answer when they leave office. The import of the EFCC revelation on corruption among governors in relation to the impeachment politics is that many governors charged with or implicated in cases of 'gross impropriety' (impeachable offences), can and do prosper in their offices essentially because they retain the blessings of the CPBs. This political practice reinforces the apron strings of prebendal corruption and patron-clientelism. It is interesting that as at the time of going to Press in June 2007, the EFCC had not apprehended any of the alleged corrupt governors, neither could the anti-corruption agency redeem its boast of preventing the governors from disappearing before their handover dates. Seven of the supposedly indicted governors were already at large by the 29th May 2007 official handover date and as such did not feature in the handover ceremonies. Most of these ex-governors were suspected to have fled the country.

The local government administration presents another intriguing narrative under the prevailing democratic order. Lacking in constitutional autonomy by reason of being made appendages of state governments under the 1999 constitution, the local government administrations are more or less run as fiefdoms of the executive state governors. The executive state governors supervise the election of the local government council members through their various state electoral commissions, disburse and manage – until recently - the federally allocated revenues of local governments, dismiss the elected local government council and appoint a caretaker committee almost at his will and ultimately manage and supervise prebendal corruption at the local government level oftentimes to their own advantages. Even though, the federal government has recently reverted to the pre-1999 method of disbursing local government revenues directly to the local council authorities, the latter have not been able to significantly break the clientelist subjection to the state governors, most of whom have continued to demand patrimonial tributes and homage from the local council authorities. Most of the local government chairmen recently indicted by the EFCC were in connection with making irregular transfers to their governors and colluding with the latter to siphon away local government funds (*Vanguard*, 28.09.06). In effect, prebendal corruption remains rife, especially [but by no means exclusively] at the subnational levels of government where the phenomenon persists at a magnitude that greatly impedes development.

Limited Political Will and Deepening Contradictions in the Anti-Corruption Campaign

The third reason for apprehension over the Nigerian reform project is the limited political will to drive the core aspect of the federal government reforms on fiscal responsibility and anti-corruption with the required vigour. It is apparent that despite the fact that the fiscal accountability and anti-corruption campaign of the Obasanjo's administration was quite late in coming because Obasanjo's first term in office (1999 – 2003) was a continuation of the old order in terms of the scale of unaccountable rule and prebendal corruption, with the exception of a few high profile scapegoats, the government has not demonstrated the political will to enforce accountability and anti-graft measures across the board in spite of the multiplicity of reports and allegations of staggering corruption that have taken place among members of his administration and beyond. Even the presidency is not free from the widespread sleaze. Both President Obasanjo and his deputy Atiku Abubakar have been implicated in cases of financial impropriety.

On his part, Vice President Abubakar was indicted in 2006 by the EFCC and subsequently, by a federal government ministerial panel for diverting about US$125 million of public funds into personal business interests (*New African*, 2006:68; *BBC News*, 10.10.06). Much of the allegations of corruption are in connection with Abubakar's handling of the Petroleum Technology Development Fund (PTDF) supervised by his office. Abubakar, however, dismisses the charges as politically motivated to prevent him from running for president in the 2007 national elections. Political discord between the Vice President and President Obasanjo was aggravated after the former threw his weight behind the national assembly to block Obasanjo from changing the constitution to seek a third term in office. But following the conclusion of debate and final adoption of the report of the Senate committee on PTDF, the Nigerian Senate in a controversial decision on 10 May 2007 reinforced the indictment of Vice President Atiku Abubakar regarding the alleged complicity in misappropriation of the Petroleum Technology Development Fund. The Senate's indictment was, however, only with regards to the approval which the vice president gave in respect of the $20 million additional fund requested by former Executive Secretary of the agency, Yusuf Hamisu Abubakar, for some projects earmarked by the agency – money that eventually was unilaterally placed in a commercial bank (*This Day*, 11.5.07;).

President Obasanjo, on the other hand, has been variously indicted by the media and opposition politicians for allegedly using his office to unduly benefit Transcorp, a business conglomerate incorporated in Nigeria under Obasanjo's tenure and in which the President held major equity shares in 'blind trust'. Under very controversial circumstances Transcorp was sold some public companies like Nigeria's largest hotel

Nicon Hilton (now Transcorp Hilton) in October 2005 for $105million and the Nigerian Telecommunications Limited (NITEL) in July 2006 for $750million, under the privatization programme of the federal government (Ajobolu, 2006; *New African*, 2006:69). The company has also received many controversial privileges, presidential waivers and government contracts since its inception, including award of offshore oil blocks, license to build a 400,000-barrel per day refinery in Lekki Free Port Zone in Lagos, license to build an independent power plant in Nigeria, access to the federal government cassava project for the construction of cassava processing exports facility, etc (cf. *New African*, 2006:69; Galadima, 2006). When it was revealed in the media that Obasanjo held more than 200 million shares in Transcorp through a blind trust, the President ordered his corporate representative, Obasanjo Holdings Limited, to divest from the company. Many of the President's cronies, including top federal government officials, are also reported to have acquired more than 400 million equity shares in Transcorp (*Newswatch*, 29.08.06).

The assessment of the progress made thus far in the anti-corruption campaign in relation to the scale of the problem by Nuhu Ribadu, the head of the government leading anti-corruption agency, the EFCC, attests to the apparent insignificance of the present efforts. According to Ribadu, since gaining political independence, corruption has cost Nigeria 220 billion pounds (about $500 billion) of development funds, which have been stolen by past leaders (governing elites and their collaborators); he lamented that in the three years of government's anti-corruption campaign (2003-2006) only 1 per cent (about $5 billion) of the loot has been recovered (*Daily Champion*, 18.10.06). It is pertinent to observe that given the structural pervasiveness of prebendal corruption and perverse accumulation in Nigeria, public finance of all categories - oil and non-oil revenues, development aid and balance of payment support loans – have over the years been essentially treated as lootable economic rents. Because of its unwillingness for a surgical sweep, many critics have accused the anti-corruption campaign of the Obasanjo's administration as both selective and witch-hunting, being ostensibly manipulated to blackmail, discredit and subdue opponents of the president. Many critics further argue that President Obasanjo's controversial securitization of corruption is a sheer grandstanding measure orchestrated to launder the notorious corruption-centred image of the Nigerian government believed to be the major obstacle to the administration's international diplomacy for the forgiveness of Nigeria's external debts. The Obasanjo administration, however, deserves some credit with respect to debt relief, having achieved forgiveness of about 60 per cent of Nigeria's external debt owed to the Paris Club of Western creditor states and used part of the windfall revenues from oil exports to finance a debt exit strategy outlined by the Club. The reassignment to foreign ministry of the government's ebullient Finance Minister and an ex-World Bank Vice President Ngozi Okonjo-Iweala whose international diplomacy was key to the debt forgiveness partly lends credence to this viewpoint. Subsequent events that followed the reassignment of portfolio, in particular, the discourteous removal of the ex-Minister as head of Nigeria's Economic Intelligence team by President Obasanjo compelled her to resign her ministerial post and return to the international financial community.

At another level, it is apparent that government anti-corruption campaign glosses over the massive structure of perverse accumulation by private citizens, especially the high incidence of advance fee fraud, code-named 419 after the applicable criminal code in municipal law. '419' as it is popularly called Nigeria is the internationalization of accumulation by impersonation, deception, forgery and fraud mostly by young Nigerian jobless school leavers who target vulnerable western audience through advantages provided by globalization of high-tech communication and financial transactions. Using the Internet, for instance, 419 conmen send deceptive emails asking for help to spirit looted funds out of Nigeria into their victim's bank account and subsequently request the willing victim to make fund transfers to settle local tax and administrative charges. Whilst the defunct military dictatorship of General Sanni Abacha made some bold strides in trying to combat 419 and drug crimes, the Obasanjo regime seem to have only excelled in proactively tackling the problem of drug, in particular, fake pharmaceutical drugs.

Under the dynamic leadership of Dora Akunyili, the federal government food and drug regulatory body, the National Agency for Food and Drug Administration and Control (NAFDAC), has been exemplary in ridding Nigeria of sub-standard / lethal food and drug products. NAFDAC has vigorously pursued this policy objective through uncompromising public enlightenment campaign, border control, blacklisting of many notorious local and foreign corporate sources of fake food/drug products, raiding of markets/manufacturing companies and destruction of counterfeit products. The result is that from about 41 per cent of all available processed food, pharmaceuticals and related products in the period preceding the appointment of Dora Akunyili as NAFDAC Director General in 2001, the volume of fake and sub-standard food, cosmetics, medical devices, chemicals, detergents and packaged water and imported drug products in Nigeria dramatically fell to less than 16 per cent in 2006 (*Daily Champion*, 6.11.06). Dora Akunyili has earned dozens of international honours for her robust and effective approach to the fake drug problem, which until 2001 was a seemingly insurmountable national predicament. The real challenge of NAFDAC and the federal government is how to ensure the sustainability of the progress made in the post-Akunyili and Obasanjo era. It is significant that Dora Akunyili has on repeated occasions narrowly escaped blasting assassination attempts supposedly masterminded by aggrieved stakeholders in the food and drug counterfeit trade whose livelihood has been adversely affected by the sweeping reformation of their industry. The lesson from the positive story of the woman nicknamed 'Nigeria's drug warrior' by the international media is that given the breadth and depth of the structures of predatory and perverse accumulation in the country, serious reforms cannot be possible without uncompromising political will and readiness for great personal prize, which may not exclude paying the supreme prize.

The markedly successful story of combating fake food/drugs in Nigeria does not, however, extend to the 419 fraud industry, which the federal government has not seriously securitized apparently because its physical impact is largely on the outside world. In a recent survey report published in November 2006 by the London-based Chatham House, a highly-regarded independent research network, Nigeria topped a UK poll for Internet scams, credit card fraud and money laundering. The report estimated that 419 scams said to be carried out by fraudsters of Nigerian origin cost the UK residents and agencies more than £150 million annually - with average losses per victim amounting to about £31,000 (cf. Peel, 2006; *Business in Africa*, 21.11.06). Thousands of Britons have been reportedly conned out billions of pounds in the last 10 years through scams supposedly originating in Nigeria. According to the Chatham House report, an analysis by Dutch-based consultancy Ultrascan concluded that the total losses from advance fee fraud to British companies and individuals in 2005 was £275 million, an amount only superseded by that of the United States which was US $720 million (about £380 million) that year (cf. Peel, 2006; Jones, 2006). Even though Nigeria is said to top the poll list, it is important to state that Nigeria is not the only source of the scam. Advance fee fraud is a fast growing industry in many West African and Latin American countries. Because the scams directly affects sections of the international community, the phenomenon not only greatly damages the international image of Nigeria, but also feeds negative stereotypes on how ordinary Nigerians are often perceived and treated abroad.

The fourth and probably most significant reason for apprehension over the present reform project is that the fiscal responsibility and anti-corruption campaign of the Obasanjo administration is spearheaded by a team of professional technocrats that are essentially external to the ruling People's Democratic Party (PDP) and have remained a recurring source of irritation and worry to the latter. This raises concerns about sustainability in the event that the biblical proverbial 'Pharaoh that knows not Joseph' comes to power in Nigeria. Thankfully, the fear of policy continuity and reform sustainability tends to be eased with the 'victory' of Obasanjo's chosen candidate and PDP flag-bearer, Umaru Musa Yar'Adua in the April 2007 presidential election. Yar' Adua's presidency is not likely to unravel the diverse reform measures initiated by the Obasanjo regime. Nonetheless, it suffices to observe that in an essentially neo-patrimonial system where the personality dispositions and clientelistic networks of the political office holder supersede political institutions and, to a large extent, shape their behavioural and policy outcomes, the alienation of the party in the implementation of Obasanjo's reforms is both unhealthy for democratic consolidation and sustainability of the reform programmes. One can only hope that the PDP government of Yar' Adua will work hard enough to, not only expand, institutionalize and consolidate the reform measures, but also to achieve sufficient buy-in of the party's rank and file regarding the reform programmes. This will help to ensure that whatever positive reforms achieved will not be as short-lived as similar measures introduced by past populist military regimes, including ironically the anti-corruption crusades of Obasanjo's first leadership spell (the Murtala/Obasanjo regime of 1976-79) and the Buhari/Idiagbon regime (1984/85). Whereas President Shagari's administration (1979 – 83) derailed the gains of the relative fiscal discipline achieved under the Murtala-Obasanjo's military administration, the seven years dictatorship of General Babangida completely ruined and eroded the economic containment and anti-corruption (the famous War Against Indiscipline) policies of the Buhari/Idiagbon regime in preference for the most virulent package of neo-liberal reform and its associated neo-patrimonial profligacy.

State-Society Relations and Political Conflicts in the Fourth Civilian Republic

From civil militia insurgency to pro-Sharia fundamentalist violence, from the revival of separatist nationalism to the proliferation of criminal violence and ethno-cultural hostility, the Nigerian fourth civilian republic has witnessed an explosion of political conflicts to a magnitude and scale that completely defied the crystal balls of the most informed political thinkers. The multiplex conflicts that have rocked the fourth republic have not only fractured state-society relations but have also tended to accentuate the fractionalization of the state's hegemonic elites and fragmentation of society.

For analytical reasons, it is important to try to operationally conceptualize the state and society as a prelude to contextualizing the dominant nature of political relations within and between the matrixes. Coalescing the dominant discourses of the state, Ismail (2007) proposes a trifurcated conception of the state focused on institutional, functional and relational components. On the institutional side, that state is a set of interrelated governmental institutions responsible for making rules, controlling and regulating social relations; functionally, the state is a set of public institutions established to accomplish specific objectives, such as provision of security and welfare for people under its juridical domain; and relationally, the state is a set of relationships and interactions among social classes and groups that is maintained, organized and regulated by political power.[i] Based on the nature of its oil-dependent political economy, the entrenched culture of patron-clientelist relations, and the profuse patterns of predatory accumulations propagated by the hegemonic elites, the Nigerian state has been variously described as 'a rentier state', 'a neo-patrimonial state', 'a prebendal state' and 'a predatory state' (cf. Joseph, 1987; Omeje, 2006).

With regard to [human] society, most conventional definitions have tended to underscore such sociological attributes as 'mutual or common interests', 'distinguishable social networks and patterns of organization', 'distinctive culture', shared institutions', 'a sense of common identity', and 'shared territoriality marked by intense social interaction' (see Giddens, Duneier & Appelbaum, 2005). These defining characteristics could be more or less true for different societies but do not necessarily have to agglomerate in an ideal structure as a *conditio sina qua non* for any community of people to definitionally qualify to be called society. Sociologists tend to classify human societies in both historical and spatial dimensions, on the basis of which they delineate a range of typologies that should not necessarily engage our attention in this study. Even though society historically preceded the state, it is significant that the state as a juridical and territorial entity has emerged to partly provide an organizational framework for the conception and classification of society. Hence, in a world that is essentially structured into sovereign territorial states, society exists at different corresponding levels, namely local or subnational, national and international levels. With special reference to this study, the conception and analysis of society will be limited to the local and national levels.

Within the reflexive parameters of the state system, the society is the sphere of human organization, relationships and interactions that are distinguishable from the institutional state and its agencies. Given the complexity and interface of formal and informal social relationships and networks within contemporary political communities, it is important to note that a clear-cut demarcation between the state and society can be analytically tricky. In fact, the problem of a clear-cut distinction is a lot more problematic in neo-patrimonial systems where the neo-Weberian modernist dichotomy between the sacred and secular, the traditional and modern, and the private and public are complexly blurred, with the result that social and political actors are hard-put within this mosaic of post-colonial realities.

The organized and more consequentially activist face of the society, which articulates the interests, aspirations, grievances and sentiments of the society, is the civil society. To a large extent, the civil society in Nigeria embodies and reflects some primary characteristics of the larger society, not least in terms of ethno-cultural heterogeneity, intense primordialism and political fragmentation (cf. Osaghae, 2005;

22

Ukiwo, 2005). Similar characteristics and attributes tend to be more or less shared by the various factions of the hegemonic elites.

Conflict Production and Prosecution

Focusing on the essentially dysfunctional conflicts, it is apparent that conflict production and prosecution in contemporary Nigeria have largely taken three major (but by no means mutually exclusive) forms. The first is elite politics marked by the often manipulation and politicization of ethnocultural issues and identity, as well as the mobilization of sections of the populace for political violence usually to maximize some self-serving advantages. Mobilization of the subalterns by members of the political (politicians / public office holders) and traditional (community and religious leaders) elites have increasingly featured dysfunctional activities such as recruitment/arming of thugs for personal security, intimidation of opponents, confrontation and fighting of opponents' private/official security, electoral fraud and malpractices; deployment of hired assassins on specified political targets, and incitement to primordially-motivated violence. Most of the high and low profile political assassinations, inter- and intra-party violent clashes, election and impeachment-related violence and religious riots that have accentuated the incidence of political instability since the return to civilian democracy in 1999 fall under this category of conflict.

The second category of conflict is the non-elite instigated, largely spontaneous, intra-society mass conflict. This category of conflict is broadly related to the interaction of structures of primordialism, 'environmental scarcity' (Homer-Dixon, 1994) and socio-economic deprivation, especially among the youths populations – the main conflict protagonists. Conflict triggers include communal (sub-ethnic) land disputes and the correlated resource struggles, religious bigotry, and historical animosity between proximate communities. There is a sense in which this category of conflict intersects the structures of elite dysfunctional politics, hence, majority of the non-elite instigated and episodic conflicts are context-specific. Examples include some of the vendetta and bloodletting that have erupted in the Ife-Modakeke communal dispute, and also in the Aguleri-Umuleri community crisis. A number of recent religion-related killing of Ibo migrants in northern

Nigeria and the reprisal killings of Hausa/Fulani migrants in the Ibo southeast falls into this category of episodic, spontaneous, mass revolts.

The third and arguably most intense category of virulent conflicts in contemporary Nigeria is the civil society-led conflicts. Even though the civil society played a major role in the termination of military dictatorship in Nigeria and continues to play a leading role as government watchdog, it is evident that there is 'an emerging construction of civil society as a vanguard of ethnic militancy marked by violent engagement with the state and other ethno-cultural groups' – a phenomenon otherwise conceptualized by Ikelegbe (2001:20) as 'the perverse manifestation of civil society in Nigeria'. Capitalizing on the libertarian opportunities offered by the present democratic dispensation amid the profound institutional dysfunctionality and failure of the state to provide significant development support and dividends of democracy to the populace, the civil society has spawned an avalanche of 'civil groups' that, to a large extent, champions exclusivist primordial causes using violent means. As a result, there has been a proliferation of zonally contextuated civil militia groups championing militant micro-nationalism, separatism, ethnic chauvinism, anti-establishment and anti-oil predatory insurgency, anti-crime security vigilantism, and religious fundamentalism in different regions of the country. The disruptive impacts of these militia activities for democracy, development, national integration and state-building are so far-reaching that many analysts and critical observers label the leading militia organizations 'uncivil societies' as a way of distinguishing them from the more constructive civil groups. Some of the militia groups concerned with the divisive and disruptive activities include the Oodua People's Congress (OPC) in the southwest, the Bakassi Boys and the Movement for the Actualization of the Sovereign State of Biafra (MASSOB) in the southeast, the Taliban Nigeria Movement and other pro-Sharia groups in the north, the litany of natural resource-based militias in the oil-rich Niger Delta - the Niger Delta People's Volunteer Force (NDPVF), Movement for the Emancipation of the Niger Delta (MEND), Pan Niger Delta Revolutionary Militia (PNDRM), Federated Niger Delta Ijaw Communities (FNDIC), Movement for the Survival of Ijaw Ethnic Nationality (MOSIEN), Delta-Bayelsa Freedom Fighters, etc. Most of these militia groups are well equipped with small arms and light weapons and often operate as [sub]ethnic armies. As ethnic armies, they not only confront and attack the state and its agencies (including, in the case of the oil-rich Niger Delta, facilities and personnel of joint venture oil multinationals perceived as collaborators with the state), but they also spearhead communal and inter-ethnic wars, including offensive, defensive and retaliatory killings of members of rival groups. The state has increasingly securitized the need to combat the various militia groups leading to intensified military crackdown and occasional stand-off. It is significant to note that as opposed to ameliorating or curbing the situation, the state's military solution tends to compound the militia-related violence. Another significant point is that because the militia activities have intense ethnic import and primordial linkages, a large number of the civil militia groups are tacitly supported, funded and armed by some of the ethno-political elites. Consequently, the civil militias are often recycled individually and as groups for political and electoral violence by some of their ethno-political elite patrons. It is the complex elite connections and support of the civil militia groups that mostly complicate the efforts of the state to stamp out or curb the phenomenon.

Democratic Consolidation, Conflicts and Reforms in Nigeria: An Outline of the Book

Ethnic Conflict

In their everyday conversations, the majority of Nigeria's tend to blame the malaise of the federation on the ethnic bogey. Ethnic consciousness and its structural externalities of chauvinism and ethnocentrism, stereotyping and politicization, discrimination and recrimination, offence and defense, and attack and reprisal, are believed to be deeply entrenched in Nigeria. They also form a crucial part of the worldview and existential realities of most individuals and groups.

In chapter 2, Ukoha Ukiwo 'explores the evolution of ethnic identities and conflicts in Nigeria'. He examines the 'roles of labeling, administrative reforms and introduction of electoral politics in the evolution and mobilization of ethnic consciousness and identity politics' dating from colonial history. Ukiwo demonstrates, on the basis of three comparative studies of inter-group relations between specific Niger Delta ethnic communities, that 'ethnic conflicts were more likely in contexts of reverse domination' – that is, where historically dominant groups in [pre-]colonial era became political minorities under the [post-]colonial administrative structures. The author flexibly applied this conceptual framework to analyze the dynamics of ethnic conflicts within the Niger Delta region, on the one hand, and between the Niger Delta ethnic minorities and the Nigerian federal state perceived as an agency of major ethnic groups, on the other hand. To redress the negative externalities of ethnicity in Nigeria, Ukiwo articulates a constructive proposal for redefining the basis of state citizenship and transforming the oil-centred political economy of the federation.

Contestation for State Power, Electoral Democracy and Conflicts

Political power is by far the most coveted 'commodity' in Nigeria's post-colonial history given its instrumental value as a means for prebendal aggrandizement, disbursement of patronage, protection of the office holder and his immediate primordial constituency, as well as for liquidation of adversarial groups and opponents. This explains the collective desperation that characterizes the struggle over seizure of political power and perpetuation of the incumbent power holder in office. The use of military, electoral and militia violence are all familiar paraphernalia of this zero-sum power game. Based on a critical diagnosis of the convoluted history of electoral democracy in Nigeria, Usman A. Tar argues in chapter 3 that the underlying structures and patterns of political practice and electoral democracy in the fourth civilian republic remain strongly pitted in the murky trajectory of the volatile past. Democracy is practically reduced to multi-party elections, while the elections are held hostage by defective practices (ballot box rigging, violence and related irregularities), faulty institutions (manipulative electoral bodies, oligarchic / dictatorial party system, nebulous constitutional framework, etc) and powerful stakeholders. 'These problems', Tar submits, 'need to be overcome if democracy is to flourish in Nigeria: otherwise, the country risks autocracy or even military re-intervention.' To overcome the problems and build a functional democracy, Tar, among other things, places faith on the proactive nature of the civil society and the presence of a strong opposition party, not withstanding the authoritarian tendency of the

26

state. Above all, he recommends the need for an equitable developmental state.

Further, Gani Yoroms, in chapter 4, examines the implications of elections and electoral malpractices for democratic growth in Nigeria. The author explores how election rigging has progressively evolved in Nigeria's political history, the motivations of key actors, the tactics they employ and why the phenomenon has become highly entrenched in the political process. Yoroms argues that the methods and strategies of electoral malpractices in Nigeria's contemporary political history have become exceedingly sophisticated and impunity-bound that they make an utter nonsense of the democratic process. 'What is clear and worrisome', Yoroms observes, 'is that rigging is becoming too sophisticated as it can be done without violence and be seen to be credible.' To curb electoral malpractices and position the country on the path of democratic growth, Yoroms advocates the need for a credible, non-partisan, independent regulatory body or set of institutions to be charged with regulating all aspects of the electoral process, including the party system, political campaign, and conduct of elections.

Small Arms Proliferation and Youth Mobilization for Conflicts

The preponderance of structural violence and political conflicts in Nigeria precipitates a corresponding ubiquity of small arms and light weapons in the hands of a vast range of lawless users and protagonists. In chapter 5, Oshita O. Oshita explores the problem of proliferation of small arms and light weapons (SALWs) in Nigeria, which he argues, has 'rapidly assumed the dimension of a complex political emergency' given that the phenomenon hugely 'impacts negatively on the national economy, destroys food security, dislocates civilian populations, sustains negative peace, and compromises law and order, including the criminal justice and public safety functions of the government'. He explores and analyses the sources of SALWs and the motivations behind their menacing proliferation and use. He critics the sloppy approach of government to the problem of SALWs and proposes a strategic framework of state – civil society partnership to systematically combat the proliferation and use of illicit weapons in Nigeria.

Discussions of political conflicts and SALWs in Nigeria are incomplete without underscoring the historical role and changing dynamics of youths' involvement. The youth dimension is the primary focus of chapter 6 by Kenneth Omeje. From a 'trans-historical perspective', the author argues that 'youths in contemporary Nigeria tend to have far less opportunities, security and hope when compared to youths of previous generations of the country's history or youths in modern Western societies'. 'The vast majority of Nigerian youths were raised amidst overwhelming structures of prebendal corruption, anomie, deprivation, hopelessness and violence - factors that have, to a large extent, contributed to shaping their worldviews, including their perceptions and orientations to the state, society and politics'. It is the apparent recycling of this vicious macro-structure, which is disproportionately hurtful and ruinous of the youth populations that Omeje conceptualises as an arguably 'unending generational curse'. Omeje proposes a constructive systemic framework for solving the problem of youth violence in Nigeria. His proposal *inter alia* focuses on how to: (a) strengthen the structures of good governance, conflict prevention and peacebuilding at the level of the key state institutions; (b) significantly grow and expand the economy to create more gainful jobs for the youths; (c) expand and strengthen the capacity of the state to regulate the private sector in order to enhance the advantages of local stakeholders and political economy; and (d) rehabilitate protagonists of youth violence, especially the various militia groups operating in different parts of the country.

Politics of Neo-liberal Reforms and Institution-Building

In chapter 7, Adeniyi O. Adegbuyi reviews the evolution and social consequences of one of the leading World Bank/IMF structural adjustment policies in Nigeria – the privatization of public enterprises. He locates the privatization programme implemented in Nigeria since the General Babangida's regime in the second half of the 1980s within the programmatic framework of the neo-liberal international financial institutions' (IFIs) one-size-fits-all economic reconstruction therapy for countries of the global South. Based on a critical examination of the successive phases of privatization implemented in Nigeria during the past two decades, Adegbuyi argues that the policy is impregnated with the self-serving accumulation interests of the hegemonic rentier elites in Nigeria. He argues that the federal government has been indiscrete in its approach to privatization with the result that many hitherto functional public utility corporations such as banks, manufacturing and telecommunication companies, etc have been privatized while a number of dysfunctional firms like Nigeria Railway Corporation and petroleum refineries are not privatized. The social cost of the programme on the public, notably spiraling inflation, rationalization of work force, employment freeze and job insecurity have been palpable. To ameliorate some of the negative social consequences of privatization, Adegbuyi articulates a number of transparency and good governance initiatives, including the need to extend the anti-corruption campaign into all spheres of the [privatized] public sector. 'Proceeds of sold investments', the author argues, ' should be re-invested or used to address pressing needs and problems like food production, employment generation, education, health, water, shelter and other top social priorities'.

As part of the focus on contemporary reforms, Chukwuemeka U. Okoye and Onyukwu E. Onyukwu examine in chapter 8 the political economy of poverty reduction in Nigeria, its historical antecedents, institutional and programmatic framework, key approaches and dimensions, as well as the limitations and shortcomings of the project. The authors present a critical review of efforts at poverty reduction pursued by previous regimes in Nigeria as basis for establishing what the Obasanjo's regime have done differently under the National Poverty Eradication Programme (NAPEP) – the pivot of the government's poverty reduction strategy. The authors argue that even though the design characteristics and operational strategies of the current poverty reduction programme, NAPEP, have overcome many of the shortcomings of its predecessors, especially in the area of programme coordination, monitoring and evaluation, and people participation, the programme is still fundamentally defective because of its narrow conception and approach to the whole issue of poverty. NAPEP, the authors continue, adopts the seriously flawed physiological model of deprivation [and poverty reduction] to the utter exclusion of the ideally complementary social model of deprivation, focused on different generations of human rights and notions of social justice. Furthermore, there is a universal recognition that the state alone cannot significantly tackle the issue of poverty reduction in developing countries and as such needs to engage proactively with other agencies and stakeholders – the private sector, NGOs, community based organizations, the donor community, etc. This aspect of inter-agency collaboration deemed to be highly crucial to effective poverty reduction is one area the state has not strategically securitized to achieve both the objectives of NAPEP and the United Nations 'Millennium Development Goals'. This chapter offers a suitable framework of how to substantially revivify the federal government's poverty reduction efforts within the shortest possible time.

Writing on the Banking Sector Consolidation reforms in chapter 9, Stanley Ukeje, Chukwuma Agu & Onyukwu E. Onyukwu present a critical analysis of the 13 point programme agenda initiated by the Central Bank of Nigeria (CBN) in 2005, under the leadership of Professor Chukwuma Soludo, with the key object of revamping the banking sector to foster soundness, integrity and professionalism. The reforms were preceded by what the authors described as 'nearly two decades of reactionary banking regulation', characterized by weak capitalization, poor liquidity, policy inconsistencies, crass unprofessionalism and intense volatility of not only the banking industry, but also of the general macro-economy and polity. The reforms have helped to favourably reposition the banking sector in diverse ways. The first is the strengthening of the capital base of banks with more than a tenfold increase of paid-up capital requirement. The new capitalization requirement led to the de-registration of many banks that could not meet up the requirement and, more significantly, the 'consolidation of banking institutions through mergers and acquisitions'. Other elements of the banking consolidation reforms discussed in this chapter include 'improvement of the financial infrastructure (including laws and information systems); ationalization, restructuring and strengthening of the regulatory and supervisory framework in the financial sector,' and measures to check the 'poor governance practices of financial intermediaries that submit inaccurate information to the regulatory authorities'. In underscoring how successful the reforms have been, the authors posit that 'the sense of renewed confidence in the banking sector and the overall macro-economy is almost palpable'. 'In addition,' they further observe, 'the Central Bank has repositioned itself with increased capacity to be able to provide effective oversight to the new banking structure.' Beyond the significant measure of success recorded over the limited period of implementing the reforms, the authors conclude by identifying some of the major challenges that lie ahead.

The Anti-Corruption Campaign, Human Security Deficits and Challenges of Reform

In chapter 10, Paul Okojie and Abubakar Momoh x-ray the problem of corruption in Nigeria, its historical context and the campaign of the President Obasanjo's administration to stamp out the menace. Although corruption is entrenched at all levels of the state and society in Nigerian, the authors focus their analysis on the high profile category they described as 'grand corruption' defined as 'the systematic use of public office by the political elites for self-enrichment' through 'embezzlement, fraud, bribery and misappropriation of public funds'. The concern with 'grand corruption' or 'corruption in high places' is justified on the grounds that by virtue of its sheer scale, grand corruption greatly impedes economic development and political stability. It also undermines the moral authority of the governing elites to govern, including the authority to credibly fight corruption and be taken seriously both at home and abroad. Using empirical and statistical details from Nigeria's past history and the post-colonial history of a number of other African countries, Okojie and Momoh argue that grand corruption impoverishes the vast majority of the underprivileged classes and can trigger coup d'etat, civil war and the collapse of the state.

Focusing on the anti-corruption campaign of the Obasanjo's regime, the authors acknowledge that 'very modest progress has been made,' but argue that a more rigorous longitudinal survey is required to verify if the campaign has produced the desired attitudinal change towards corruption. Furthermore, the authors underscored the legitimate concerns of critics of Obasanjo's regime who lampoon the President for using the war against corruption and its enforcement agency (the EFCC) to target his opponents. Pointing to diverse allegations of corruption against President Obasanjo and some top members of his administration, as well as the massive fraud that characterized the April 2007 election, the authors submit that President Obasanjo has not demonstrated the integrity and political will requisite for effectively tackling corruption and ensuring good governance in Nigeria. The chapter concludes by articulating some empirical benchmarks for an effective anti-corruption policy regime in Nigeria.

In chapter 11, Habu S. Galadima examines the 'rhetoric' of reforms against the backdrop of staggering human security deficits and endemic faultlines of communal violence in Nigeria. Based on an empirically grounded review of the security situation across the various spheres of the economy and the state and society, Galadima deplores the scale of human security deficits in the country and the foreboding strategic danger of instability, insecurity and unsustainable development. He makes a strong case for fundamentally reviewing Obasanjo's reforms to meet the challenges of peacebuilding and sustainable development. Reviewing and deepening the present reforms in a much more ingenious and transparent way is imperative for the continuity and survivability of Nigeria as a coherent federal state.

Postscript – The April 2007 Elections

This book project was already at an advanced stage at the time of the April 2007 elections, with most of the chapters already completed. Some of the contributors had to recall their chapters after the elections to reflect this important history in their analysis. At the time of going to press, there was already a cloud of debate in and outside Nigeria on the legitimacy of the elections and, perhaps to a lesser extent, the new government of President Umaru Musa Yar' Adua. The handling and outcomes of the elections did not come to many informed observers as a surprise. As a matter of fact, a number of contributions in this volume that were written before the elections had logically anticipated a colossally flawed election in which the ruling PDP would retain power by hook or crook. And it happened. This is by no means intellectual cynicism. The 'high stakes rentier character of the Nigerian state' (Omeje, 2006) founded on what Michael Watts (2005) describes as the 'oil complex' almost inevitably turns electoral democracy into a chessboard of Machiavellian calculations in which outcomes at every level are determined by balance of power amongst contending actors.

Even though the federal state has the advantage of control of some of the most decisive resources (federal wealth, critical institutions and security forces), it does not by any means enjoy a monopoly of the instrumental resources. The political theatre mirrors what Nicholas Rose (1999; see also Watts, 2005) describes as volatile and unruly 'governable spaces' in which there is a ubiquity of territorialized spaces of micro-sovereignty where diverse actors, including dissidents and underdogs are capable of far-reaching intrigues, terror, manoeuvres, desperation, surprise and gain. This is particularly true at the subnational level of the governable spaces where many political chieftains in some of the opposition parties are able, as they brag in Nigeria, to match the ruling PDP 'money for money', 'thuggery for thuggery,' 'rigging for rigging' and 'violence for violence.' That is how much compromised and illiberal 'liberal democracy' could be in a dysfunctional neo-patrimonial rentier state. In his analysis of electoral politics in chapter 3 of this volume Usman Tar aptly described the Nigerian state as a 'regressive state,' implying 'a state which, in addition to demonstrating the manifest features of a failing state, spirals backwards in spite of having what it takes to develop ....' It is on the backdrop of the embedded paradigm of dysfunctionality that one can begin to make sense of the deliberate institutional laxity and extreme malpractices and violence that characterized the preparation and conduct of the April 2007 elections, an election that all major local and international observers have unanimously condemned as a travesty. The European Union (EU) Election Observation Mission to Nigeria headed by Max van den Berg reported that the polls 'fell short of basic international and regional standards for democratic elections and cannot be considered credible, free and fair,' (*Daily Trust*, 25.05.07).

The EU Observer Mission, among other things, concluded that: (i) 'the elections were deeply flawed due to poor organisation, lack of transparency, widespread procedural irregularities, significant evidence of fraud, particularly during the result collation process, voter disenfranchisement at different stages of the process and lack of equal conditions for contestants'; (ii) 'instead of guaranteeing the basic right of citizens to vote freely, the Nigerian Government and electoral officials actively colluded in the fraud and violence or at least ignored human rights abuses committed by supporters of the ruling party and others'. Following the report, the European Parliament has urged the countries in the European Union to stop financial aids to Nigeria until fresh and credible elections are held in the country (*Daily Trust*, 25.05.07). Many local and international agencies and institutions have also called for a re-run of the polls. Not less than 200 persons were reportedly killed and thousands of others injured in election-related violence on the actual polling days (Dawn, 23.04.07). In addition, more than twice the above number is believed to have been killed in the violent party primaries and electioneering campaigns in the run up to the elections. Incidents of arson and wanton destruction of properties were also rampant.

Writing in chapter 10 of this volume, Paul Okojie and Abubakar Momoh have outlined some of the major irregularities in the April 2007 elections as follows:

1. Elections materials were deliberately delayed or delivered late to many polling booths, particularly in many parts of Eastern Nigeria, where voting did not start until about 3pm. And in most cases voting took place only in towns and urban centres and not in rural areas.
2. Not enough ballot papers were sent to many polling booths.
3. Officials of the electoral agency (INEC) did not appear in many polling booths, thus preventing voting from taking place.
4. Fake/wrong voter registers were sent to some polling booths, thus preventing many people from finding their names where they registered.
5. Ballot boxes were snatched at gun point, and polling agents were scared away at gunpoint.
6. In many instances, votes were not counted at the polling booths.
7. Polling agents were forced to sign results after stuffed ballot boxes were returned by hoodlums.
8. Fake INEC Form FC 8, was given to party polling agents to sign without their knowing they were fake.
9. Thumb printing took place three to four days to the elections - a malpractice involving INEC staff and the PDP (the ruling party). Foam soaked in ink was used to stamp ballot so that the thumbprint will not be captured in case of litigation in court.
10. Polling agents of opposition political parties were not allowed into Local Government Collation centres.
11. Voting was still taking place in many states while INEC was declaring winners in Abuja.
12. In Imo state, the Governorship and House of Assembly elections held the same day and at the same polling booths. INEC, however, cancelled the Governorship election because of 'wide-scale irregularities' but approved the results to the House of Assembly election. This, it was said, was due to the fact the All Peoples Grand Alliance (APGA) candidate had won the election to the disappointment of the PDP, which having no official candidate in the governorship election backed the Progressive Peoples Party's (PPA) candidate. At the re-run of the Governorship election, the PDP-backed candidate was, as many

expected, declared winner by INEC. Imo is the only state where the ruling PDP had no official governorship candidate in the election for the simple reason that the party decided not to back the candidature of Senator Ifeanyi Ararume who won a Supreme Court ruling against the PDP as winner of the party's governorship primaries.

This listing is not exhaustive. Nigerian election tribunals and constitutional courts have been inundated with petitions associated with what could be rightly described as the most fraudulent and flawed elections in Nigeria's history. From the systematic and massive nature of the electoral irregularities, it is apparent that the entire process was deliberately orchestrated by the ruling PDP, the security forces and, most importantly, the national electoral body INEC, whose key officers are, by courtesy of a major constitutional flaw, appointees of the President. INEC seemed to have deliberately organised and presided over sloppy elections, which given the perverse political culture in Nigeria, would inevitably predispose and implicate all political parties in electoral malpractices. However, this Machiavellian machination is grounded on the fore-knowledge that if all political parties are allowed a free hand to rig, bribe, maim, and kill, the ruling PDP would without doubt emerge *primus inter pares* given the unlevel nature of the playing field. It worked. The rest is history, as they say. It is therefore not surprising that the arguments of Prof Maurice Iwu (INEC National Chairman), (ex-)President Obasanjo and the newly elected President Umaru Musa Yar' Adua in rationalizing the outcome of the elections are that: 'the elections were certainly not perfect,' 'all political parties were involved in malpractices, ' 'PDP is not the only party that rigged ...' [by implication, others were simply outrigged], 'if all the parties were involved in rigging and malpractices, then there is no basis for cancellation of the entire polls,' 'you cannot have a perfect election anywhere' (cf. *BBC News*, 20.04.07; *Guardian*, 1.05.07). These arguments are all half-truths. But as in all half-truths, the tendency for these self-serving establishmentarians is to disacknowledge or disingenuously ignore the more significant half-lie and proceed to generalise the half-truth as the only truth. In his chapter, Usman Tar has articulated the possible repercussions of the disgraceful elections for democratic consolidation and governance in Nigeria. In a nutshell, the picture seems gloomy in the short-term, with far-reaching implications for the long-term development of a stable democracy. But beyond the elections-related legitimacy crisis, which in all probability is likely to abate in the coming months, one of the greatest challenges facing the Yar' Adua government is how to more constructively reform and transparently implement Obasanjo's reform policies and programmes.

Note

1. These definitions were extrapolated by Olawale Ismail from his review of the definitions of the state proffered by P. Dunleavy & B. O'leary (1987), I. Zartman (1995) and S. Sangmpam (1993). For a more detailed discussion and references, see Ismail (2007).

References

Ayobolu, Jide (2006) 'Fawehinmi & Obasanjo's Ownership of Shares in Transcorp'. The Nigerian Village Square. http://www.nigeriavillagesquare.com/articles/guest-articles/fawehinmi-and-obasanjo-s-ownership-of-shares-in-tran.html. Website accessed on 25.11.06.

BBC News (2006) 'Nigerian Vice President in the Dock Over Graft'. *BBC News* 10.10.06. http://news.bbc.co.uk/1/hi/world/africa/6034735.stm Website accessed on 25.11.06.

BBC News (2007) 'Nigerian Leader Admits Polls Flaws'. NNC News 20 April. http://news.bbc.co.uk/1/hi/world/africa/6574869.stm. Website accessed on 6.06.07

Business in Africa (2006) 'Nigeria Tops UK Scammers' Poll', *Business in Africa* 21.11.06. http://allafrica.com/stories/200611210027.html. Website accessed on 22.11.06.

Daily Champion (2006) 'NAFDAC Destroys N14 Billion Fake Drugs in Nigeria'. *Daily Champion* 6.11.06. http://allafrica.com/stories/200611070797.html. Website accessed on 23.11.06

Daily Champion (2007) 'PTDF – Senate Nails Atiku, Clears Obasanjo'. *Daily Champion* 11.05.07.

http://allafrica.com/stories/200705110052.html. Website accessed on 11.05.07.

Daily Trust (2006) 'Nigeria: Nation Earns $400 Billion Oil Revenue'. *Daily Trust* 16 November. http://allafrica.com/stories/200611160928.html. Website accessed on 16.11.06.

Daily Trust (2007) 'Nigeria: Focus on Politics'. *Daily Trust* 25 May. http://allafrica.com/stories/200705250483.html. Website accessed on 6.06.07.

Dawn (2007) 'Ruling candidate wins disputed Nigerian presidential poll' Dawn News Agency 23 April. http://www.dawn.com/2007/04/23/rss.htm. Website accessed on 6.06.07.

Galadima, A. Anas (2006) 'Corruption Charges and Questions Trail Obasanjo's Shares in Transcorp'. *US Africa Online* 18.09.06. http://www.usafricaonline.com/obasanjo.transcorpdeal.html. Website accessed on 24.11.06.

Giddens, Anthony, Mitchell Duneier & Richard P. Appelbaum (2005) *Introduction to Sociology* (5th Edition). New York: W. W. Norton & Company Inc.

Guardian (2007) '2007 presidential election: A flawed process leads to a flurry of protest'. *Guardian* 1 May (Nigerian Daily Newspaper). Website accessed on 6.06.07. http://www.nigerianmuse.com/opessays/?u=2007_presidential_election _A_flawed_process_leads_to_a_flurry_of_protest_Victor_Onyeka_Ben _The_Guardian_.htm&PHPSESSID=a0ac5b7a14a8331f1c47338f6946100 6.

Homer-Dixon, Thomas (1994) 'Environmental Scarcities and Violent Conflict'. *International Security,* 19/1, pp. 5-40.

Ikelegbe, Augustine (2001) 'The Perverse Manifestation of Civil Society: Evidence from Nigeria'. *The Journal of Modern African Studies.* 39/1: pp. 1-24.

Ismail, Olawale (2007) 'Power Elites, War and Post-War reconstruction in Africa: Continuities, Discontinuities and Paradoxes'. *Journal of Contemporary African Studies.* Forthcoming, 2007.

Jones, Matthew (2006) 'Nigeria Scams Cost Britons Millions'. http://uk.news.yahoo.com/20112006/80-91/nigerian-scams-cost-britons-millions-says-study.html. Website accessed on 23.11.06.

New African (2006) 'Nigeria Rough Road to Election 2007'. *New African* magazine, December, pp. 66-69.

Newswatch (2006) 'The Dirty Transcorp Deal'. *Newswatch* magazine 28.08.06.
http://www.thetimesofnigeria.com/index.php?option=com_content&ta
sk=view&id=1031&Itemid=83&PHPSESSID=e1f16924491a5c766bfef4e01
7. Website accessed on 25.11.06.

Omeje, Kenneth (2006) High Stakes and Stakeholders: Oil Conflict and Security in Nigeria. Aldershot: Ashgate.

Peel, Michael (2006) Nigeria-Related Financial Crimes and Its Links with Britain. An African Programme Report by the Chatham House, London. November 2006.
http://www.chathamhouse.org.uk/pdf/research/africa/Nigeria1106.pdf. Website accessed on 23.11.06.

Rose, N. (1999) *Powers of Freedom: Reframing Political Thought.* Cambridge: Cambridge University Press. See chapter 1 on 'Governing' in:
http://assets.cambridge.org/97805216/50755/sample/9780521650755wsc0 0.pdf Website accessed on 5.06.07.

Suberu, Rotimi & Eghosa E. Osaghae (2005), *A History of Identities, Violence, and Stability in Nigeria.* CRISE Working Paper No. 6, Queen Elizabeth House, University of Oxford, UK. January.

This Day (2006) 'Nigeria: Plateau State Governor Joshua Dariye on the Run'. *This Day,* 13.11.06.
http://allafrica.com/stories/200611140017.html. Website accessed on 24.11.06.

This Day (2007) 'Senate Affirms Atiku's Indictment'. *This Day,* 11.05.07.
http://allafrica.com/stories/200705110014.html. Website accessed on 11.05.07.

USAID (2004) *USAID / Nigeria Annual Report.* USAID, 14 June 2004.
http://pdf.dec.org/pdf_docs/Pdaca038.pdf. Website assessed on 16.11.06.

USAID (2005) 'Nigeria: Budget Summary'. USAID, June 2005.
http://www.usaid.gov/policy/budget/cbj2006/afr/ng.html. Website assessed on 16.11.06.

Ukiwo, Ukoha (2005) *On the Study of Ethnicity in Nigeria. A History of Identities, Violence, and Stability in Nigeria.* CRISE Working Paper No. 12, Queen Elizabeth House, University of Oxford. June.

UNDP (2006) *Niger Delta Development Report, Nigeria.* Abuja: UNDP.

http://hdr.undp.org/docs/reports/national/NIR_Nigeria/NIGERIA_2006 _en.pdf. Website accessed on 16.11.06.

Vanguard (2006) 'Nigerian Looting and Corruption: EFCC Report Indicts 15 Governors'. *Vanguard* 28.09.06. http://www.usafricaonline.com/govngrlooting9282006.html. Website accessed on 25.11.06.

Watts, M. (2005) 'The Sinister Political Life of Community: Economies of Violence and Governable Spaces in the Niger Delta, Nigeria' in G. Creed (ed) The Romance of Community, Santa Fe, New Mexico: SAR Press. http://globetrotter.berkeley.edu/GreenGovernance/papers/Watts_Sinist erPolitical.pdf. Website accessed on 5.06.07.

World Bank (2006) *Nigeria Data Profile*. The World Bank. http://devdata.worldbank.org/external/CPProfile.asp?CCODE=NGA& PTYPE=CP. Website accessed on 16.11.06.

Chapter 2

The State, Identity Transformation and Conflict: The Case of the Nigeria's Niger Delta

Ukoha Ukiwo

Introduction

Constructivist interpretations of ethnicity have drawn attention to the centrality of the state in the evolution of ethnic identities in colonial Africa (Ranger, 1983, 1994; Vail, 1989). It has been argued that African elites were hardly onlookers but actively participated in the imagination of ethnic boundaries (Glassman, 2000; Lentz, 2000). Although 'the colonial setting was the cradle of ethnicity' (Nnoli, 1978), unequal intergroup relations in the precolonial became the template for imagination of 'the other' and *ipso facto* boundary definition. This chapter explores the evolution of ethnic identities and conflicts in Nigeria from the context of relations between coastal city-states and their hinterland. It will explore how the promotion of difference between coastal peoples and their immediate hinterland neighbours and the use of the former to administer the latter in the early colonial period led to the emergence and politicisation of ethnicity. The focus is on the experiences of three coastal communities that played prominent roles in the trans-Atlantic slave and oil palm trade and their immediate neighbours. These are the Efik, Itsekiri and Nembe-Ijaw on the one hand and the Ibibio, Urhobo and Ogbia-Ijaw on the other.[ii]

The chapter will explore the roles of labelling, administrative reforms and introduction of electoral politics in the evolution and mobilization of ethnic consciousness and identity politics. The comparative analysis of the three cases of inter-group relations suggests that ethnic conflicts were more likely in contexts of reverse domination- where historically dominant groups became political minorities. It will be argued that this context explains two types of conflicts in the Niger Delta. The first is some communal and ethnic conflicts between groups within the Niger Delta which negates effort by minority rights advocates to mobilize a pan-Niger Delta platform to challenge the Nigerian State and Transnational Oil Corporations

40

(TNOCs). The second is the 'resource control' conflicts between Niger Delta communities and the Nigerian State and TNOCs which are increasingly perceived as agents of major ethnic groups.

The Political Economy of Identity in Pre-colonial Niger Delta

The long road to eventual colonization of Nigeria began with the inauguration of commercial relations between several European trading expeditions and principal coastal states in the Bight of Biafra and Bight of Benin. Historians differ on their interpretations of whether or not these states rose in response to the trans-Atlantic trade or were already in existence before the trade (Dike, 1956; Nair, 1972). There is no gainsaying however that the trade profoundly transformed the character of the states-their social structure, their economic system and indeed their political system. These states assumed positions of influence, as they became the link between Europe and the peoples of the hinterland. Before formal colonisation, most of them were able to effectively prevent European firms from dealing directly with the hinterland.

Identity was based on residence rather than descent (Dike, 1956; Alagoa, 1963; Ranger, 1998).[iii] Given the constant need for labour in the lucrative trans-Atlantic trade, migrants who contributed to the economy and security of the state were easily integrated. Thus, it was possible for former slaves to rise to positions of prominence in the land of their captivity. For instance in Old Calabar, the relation between a slave and his owner was conceived in familial terms, as the former referred to the latter as father not master. In the Nembe-Brass area, the need for manpower led to a relaxation of rules on pre-marital sex to allow unmarried persons procreate. Children from such liaisons belonged to the parents of the girl. Kinship increasingly became matrilineal. In the Igbani-Ijaw communities of Bonny and Opobo, Igbo the language of the immigrant slaves at some point became the lingua franca. In most of these communities, integrated migrants were so loyal that they fought for their communities of residence. This explains why some European observers were astonished at, 'how clannish the slave belonging to the same house becomes. Each one considers that he partakes in the honour of the house and is zealous in maintaining it' (Goldie, 1890:57).[iv]

The success of the political integration in the pre-colonial era stemmed from the protection that all members received from the state of residence and *ipso facto* their political obligations to it. Inhabitants of such communities did not see themselves as members of an ethnic community but as citizens of a country. Thus, a cursory glance at the correspondences between earlier travellers and African merchant kings reveals that they always referred to their 'country' not tribe. Other identities discernible in such exchanges are religion and race as the kings tried to distinguish their look and ways of life from those of the European.

This by no means suggests that elements of an ethnic community such as myths of common origin, migration, shared language and traditions were absent. They were present but were hardly the defining elements of the political community and inter-group interaction. Thus in the 18th and 19th centuries, different city-states in the Niger Delta who have since metamorphosed into ethnic communities fought against and enslaved one another. For instance, the different Efik city-states at Old Calabar struggled for pre-eminence and sometimes collaborated with external agents to undermine their neighbours as changing interests occasioned (Nair, 1970). The various communities currently referred to as Ibibio, Igbo, Ijaw and Urhobo waylaid and sold their 'ethnic' brethren into slavery. It is noteworthy that the only group that did not follow this pattern in the Niger Delta and its immediate hinterland is the Itsekiri (Ikime, 1969).^v The reason for this is not far fetched. The Itsekiri belonged to a single political community under the Kingship of the Olu (Lloyd, 1963).

In any event these conflicts facilitated British penetration, as the competing city-states could not form a common front against the traders, missionaries and political officers (Tamuno, 1972). In fact, it became the ostensible rationale for colonization as the colonizers advertised the need to create an order to facilitate 'legitimate' trade. The imposition of a new political order reconfigured inter-group relations in the Niger Delta. Hitherto independent and autonomous political entities were annexed and incorporated into a new political space where they had to compete with other groups for valued limited resources.

'Bearers' of Civilization and 'Primitive' Societies: Changing Coastal-Hinterland Relations under Colonial Rule

It should be noted that integration of immigrants - voluntary migrants or enslaved peoples- was possible in precolonial Niger Delta because 'host' communities did not regard immigrants as 'inferior' people. There was no distinction between 'pure' and 'impure' blood or 'good' and 'inferior' stock. This is why the kings of the city-states cohabited with their female slaves and gave up their daughters in marriage to deserving slaves. However, the early access of coastal peoples to western goods, religion and education prompted European writers to contrast the 'civilised' ways of life of the coastal people with those of the 'primitive' hinterlanders.[vi] With the enlistment of coastal elites were into the civilization project as sundry interpreters, political agents, trading agents, teachers and catechists, the dichotomy between 'civilised' and 'primitive' groups sunk into the consciousness of all.

In the official discourse, some groups were more 'advanced' than others. The colonial subjects accepted these categories. While 'advanced' groups proudly appropriated them, the 'backward' groups mobilised to attain 'advancement'. This opened up a competition for modernization as hinterlanders craved for modernity associated with their privileged coastal neighbours. By so doing hinterlanders came under the influence of coastal elites who became agents for dispensing western education and religion. In the Cross River basin for instance,

> A completely new class of Efik elites skilled in the art of middlemanship emerged. Largely deriving its strength from the confidence reposed in it by the Europeans, it succeeded in attracting to itself, tremendous respect from hinterland dwellers who saw it essentially as a kind of club whose membership comprised only 'men of civilization' who had a lot to offer those they came in contact with (Onor, 1994: 44).

The result is what has been referred to as Efik 'cultural imperialism' as Efik teachers, catechists, traders and political agents were enlisted to 'civilise' the peoples of the area. It was not only those hinterlanders that enrolled in schools that came under tutelage of coastal elites. Through the Masters and Servants Proclamation of 1903, the colonial administration made it possible for coastal elites to acquire servants from the hinterland who served them for a certain period of time under a kind of apprenticeship scheme.

Nembe-Ijaw influence in Ogbia of central Ijaw was such that Nembe dialect became the lingua franca in Ogbia. Ogbia people adopted Nembe names and many Ogbia towns were named after the Nembe traders and political agents (Wolf 1976). However, owing to the late advent of missionary activity in the Western Niger Delta, the Itsekiri could not exert cultural influence over their neighbours (Ikime 1963). Rather Itsekiri influence derived largely from the agency of Dore Numa, an Itsekiri merchant whom the British appointed as Paramount Chief and Political Agent. He facilitated the appointment of Itsekiri chieftains to native courts of non-Itsekiri communities, a development that became a source of discord.

The advantages that coastal communities enjoyed in the early years of colonization is also evident in the appointment of Chief Dore Numa, Itsekiri chieftain and Chief Richard Henshaw, Efik chieftain as unofficial members of the Nigerian Council in 1914.[vii] The criteria for appointments were the influence and prominence of the communities of the appointees. Moreover, the native administration was initially based on the social structure of the coastal city-states widely referred to as the House System. However, while the House system was essentially non-ethnic, colonial construction of the political community as evident in the House Rule Ordinance of 1901 was *ab initio* ethnic. House Rule was superceded by Indirect Rule after the amalgamation of northern and southern protectorates in 1914 but the idea of administering people through the intermediary of recognised chiefs of their natal communities persisted.

The problem with indirect rule through paramount chiefs was that it froze the cultural exchanges among coterminous groups that prevailed in the pre-colonial period. Since the traditional rulers were appointed as custodians of culture, they sought to 'protect' their customs from 'theft' by neighbouring groups. Communities began putting patents on previously shared cultural practices and accused their neighbours of piracy. Since specific cultural forms were now tied to land, communities protested when neighbouring groups staged cultural dances in their domain. So much controversy emerged about which group invented specific cultural forms. This struggle over culture served to widen the social distance among groups and promoted the rise of ethnic consciousness. Each group regarded the practice of its neighbour as the adulterated, pirated and corrupted version of its authentic culture. In this cacophony, the colonial authorities were called upon to arbitrate and not a few district officers ruled in favour of one group against the other. Thus, in the contest of the Efik, Qua and Ibibio over the patent for *Ekpe, Obon*, and *Nsibidi*, the Efik were deemed to have borrowed the practices from their hinterland neighbours and refined them for use (Jeffreys, 1935).

Apart from squabbles over ownership of culture, hinterland communities resented the fact that colonial authorities often placed them under Native Administrations controlled by coastal traditional rulers. In the Western Niger Delta, Ijaw and Urhobo communities were drafted into Native Administrations headed by Itsekiri chieftains. Likewise in the central Niger Delta, Nembe-Ijaw and Kalabari chieftains dominated Native Administrations, which included the Ogbia, Abua and Odual communities. Such arrangements generated resentment as underrepresented or unrepresented groups claimed they were not subject to the pre-colonial coastal kingdoms. Complaints ranged from the distance it took marginalised groups to get to the native courts to the fact that customary law enforced by such courts were alien or the languages used in such courts and or councils were not intelligible. Such protests, which occasionally inspired new administrative units heightened ethnic consciousness and conflict.

With the separation came competition for development, not helped by the penchant of some colonial officers to provoke the coastal peoples by pointing to the progress of their hinterland neighbours. For instance, it became a pastime for colonial officers in Warri Province to contrast Itsekiri 'stagnation' with Urhobo 'progress' by pointing to successes of the Urhobo in running their own affairs. Such comparisons contributed to the 'politics of improvement' among communal groups (see, Pratten, 2006).

The successful penetration of the hinterland generated tensions in relations between colonial officers and coastal elites. There was a gradual change in the official discourse characterised by reports of the idleness, chicanery and aristocratic lifestyle of the coastal elites and peoples. For instance, Sir Donald Cameron, Governor of Nigeria justified the reform of the native administration in the early 1930s on the grounds that:

In Southern Nigeria in the old days when the primary consideration was to open up the country that trade and revenue might follow and allow the new dependency to be self-supporting, the Calabar government did not think of finding the real leaders of the people-perhaps they had no time for that kind of thing- and used as their medium for intercourse with the people the *loudest-mouthed ruffian* that presented themselves to their notice. As a result of this policy little was done in the way of Native Administration among the large tribes such as the Ibos and the Ibibios.[viii]

The changing official discourse followed the mass uprising against taxation in the late 1920s. Colonial officers attributed the uprising and revolts to inefficient and corrupt Native Administrations predominantly led by coastal elites. As one concerned colonial Resident commented on relations in Warri Province:

These troubles led to searching enquiries into the grievance of the people. They were connected with Native Courts and a rising wave of nationalism among the Sobo people. The Jekris, a race of waterside traders, had, in the early days of contact with Europeans and Africans, obtained ascendancy over the far more numerous and very primitive Sobos by intrigue, the power of wealth and by means of arms and powder supplied by European traders. Although British rule had protected the Sobos from excessive exploitation by the Jekris, a residual Jekri ascendancy had remained. When a small fraction of the Sobos became literate a Sobo Risorgimento movement came into being.[ix]

The coastal elites gradually lost the monopoly of influence they exercised on the colonial officers. This was as a result of three principal factors. Firstly, the people of the hinterland were producing educated people that could displace administrative staff from coastal communities.[x] Secondly, most of the cash crops were produced in the hinterland and foreign trading firms were happy to jettison coastal middlemen.[xi] Thirdly, the introduction of electoral principle showed that power inevitably rested with elites from the more populous hinterlanders.

Intriguingly, demystification of coastal elites was disguised as rectification of longstanding misconceptions about hinterland communities. For example, Jeffreys (1935:23) an administrative officer in Calabar Province said:

The initial concentration of European enquiries on the Efiks was not intentionally carried out at the expense of the Ibibio, but nevertheless the Ibibio have thereby suffered an eclipse. The first missionaries to the Cross River were invited by the Efiks and these missionaries naturally directed their first studies to the Efik language, with the result that the Efik have benefited enormously and their language has inevitably assumed a position that is not justified either upon a population or on a linguistic basis.

Jeffreys' interest in Ibibio language arose from the opposition among the Ibibio of the preference by missionaries for vernacular as language of instructions in schools. Given the strategic importance of English language for accessing employment in the colonial administration and modern economy, the Ibibio considered the policy as retrogressive, more especially as Efik was the preferred vernacular. The first major rift in Ibibio-Efik relations arose from a controversial manuscript submitted by E.N. Amaku, a teacher based in Calabar in response to a call by the United Presbyterian Church of Scotland Mission for books on local folklore. Amaku portrayed the Ibibio as slaves in the house of the Efik gentry. Some Ibibio elites pressurised the authorities to destroy the manuscript to avert breakdown of law and order in the Province. The aftermath of the event was the formation of the Ibibio State Union to protect 'themselves as a group against insult, abuse and oppression' (Udoma, 1987:x). Thus the crucible of Ibibio nationalism was Efik socio-cultural domination. For the Ibibio therefore the Efik were the ethnic 'other'.

A similar trend is discernible in the rise of Urhobo nationalism when a newspaper article published in 1934 claimed that Dore Numa was 'the recognised ruler of the Itsekiris and Sobos' and described the Urhobo as 'a hardy people, who served for several years in the capacity of slaves to their Itsekiri and Benin masters' (Ikime, 1977:81-82). The anonymous writer also insinuated that the Itsekiri were planning to restore the Olu of Itsekiri institution after an interregnum of 88 years as a rallying point against the Urhobo who had almost succeeded in catching up with the Itsekiri.[xii] The incident inspired the formation of the Urhobo Progress Union (UPU) in 1936. Thus, it could also be argued that Urhobo nationalism was born out of the efforts of the Urhobo elites to overcome attempts by Itsekiri elites to checkmate the rapid pace of development among the Urhobo.

47

The determination of the Urhobo to overturn conceptions of Itsekiri superiority found expression in another event, which almost led to violence between the Itsekiri and Urhobo. Chief Mukoro Mowoe, first president of UPU and member for Warri Province at the Western Region House of Assembly and the Olu of Itsekiri were seen inspecting the streets of Warri. This unsurprisingly attracted a group of onlookers. One Itsekiri onlooker peeved that the honourable member had a hat on his head knocked off Mowoe's hat. Mowoe's timely intervention prevented an outbreak of violence between Itsekiri and Urhobo in the vicinity (Ikime, 1977:153).

Similarly, Ogbia-Ijaw nationalism has been built around eliminating the influence of Nembe-Ijaw in Ogbia affairs (Wolf, 1976, Nwajiaku, 2005). Thus, as Okorobia (1999:208-9) aptly points out 'The fall of Brass and Nembe was a blessing to Ogbia people.' Such sentiments derived from the fact that the earlier contact of coastal peoples with western civilization created a situation where both the European colonizers and the coastal peoples themselves came to despise hinterland communities as 'primitive' peoples. These demeaning categorizations, which were rare in the pre-colonial period,[xiii] provoked a reverse cultural pride as hinterland people mobilised to challenge discourses that put them under coastal peoples culminating in the mobilization of ethnic consciousness.

It was not just reorganizations at the local level that affected relations between the coastal city-states and their hinterland. Since the coastal states attained prominence as centres of external trade, western education and colonial administration, frequent relocation of trade and administrative centres resulted in marginalization and abandonment of previous centres of growth (see, Udoh, 1967; Alagoa, 2004:67). The transformation of coastal states from centre to periphery was a blow to their economy and socio-cultural dominance. For instance, Nembe influence in Ogbia was eroded as the Ogbia people quickly renamed their villages. Igbo replaced Nembe as second language of the younger generation of Ogbia people since the new regional headquarters was in Enugu (Wolf, 1976). In Enugu, Ogbia educated elites could actually rub shoulders with the elites of coastal communities.

One Man One Vote: Electoral Principle and Tensions in Ethnic Relations

Coastal elites were forced to take a backseat as the representatives of more populous hinterland communities took centre stage with the introduction of universal adult suffrage. This change was epitomised by the change of guards in the Eastern Region in 1953 where Dr. Nnamdi Azikiwe, an Igbo, replaced Prof. Eyo Ita, an Efik, as leader of government business. The rising profile hinterland political elites can be traced to the 1946 Richard's Constitution, which provided for indirect elections to regional Houses of Assembly. This trend continued with the introduction of direct elections in the 1950s as nationalist movement intensified the campaign for self-government. The socio-political context of ethnic voting ensured that hinterland communities produced elected representatives. Consequently, the introduction of electoral principle was the last factor that signalled the transformation of city-states into what Ekeh (1996) has referred to as 'historically dominant minorities'. We shall examine the conflicts that followed this transformation in the context of relations between three sets of Niger Delta ethnic groups, and relations between the minorities of the Niger Delta and the major ethnic groups.

Efik- Ibibio Relations

The Efik-Ibibio cleavage was mediated in the colonial period by the fact that both groups had a common interest in challenging Igbo dominance. After the ouster of Prof. Eyo Ita, Efik and Ibibio elites formed the United National Independence Party (UNIP), which subsequently entered into an alliance with the Action Group. UNIP won several seats in Efik and Ibibio constituencies by mobilizing anti-Igbo sentiments. However such victories only solidified their minority status with adverse implications for access to government patronage. Efik-Ibibio cooperation was also manifest in the movement for the creation of the Calabar Ogoja Rivers (COR) State. COR State advocates however failed to convince the Minorities Commission, which submitted that state creation would not solve the problems of minorities (Colonial Office, 1958).

The request for a COR State was granted on May 27, 1967 when the military regime created South Eastern State and Rivers State as part of the twelve new state structure. Efik, Ibibio as other minorities in the region welcomed the new states as it freed them from Igbo domination. However, the euphoria that accompanied state creation did not last in South Eastern State as in other new multi-ethnic states. This is because of the emergence of new major ethnic groups and minority ethnic groups in the new entities. The Ibibio were unmistakably the new major ethnic group in the state. The military governor was Ibibio; the civil service was predominantly Ibibio; Ibibio chiefs dominated the state traditional rulers' council; and since there were more Ibibio Divisions, Ibibioland attracted more developmental projects. This development provoked an outcry among elites of other groups who claimed that it was not yet Uhuru. Igbo domination had merely been replaced by Ibibio domination. Against the background of Efik historical dominance in the region, it is not surprising that Efik nationalists began to mobilize against Ibibio domination. Ibibio dominance generated more resentment because whereas Igbo domination was administered from Enugu, the regional capital which was an Igbo town, Ibibio were 'oppressing' the Efik on their own soil – Calabar, which was proclaimed state capital in 1967. This was an unacceptable reversal of roles as the Efik were said to have derived their name from the Ibibio word 'oppress' because they oppressed their hosts in Ibibioland before their southward journey to the Cross River estuary (Hart, 1964). In this circumstance, the first strategy of Efik nationalists was to de-emphasise whatever historical and cultural links the Efik had with the Ibibio. Thus, Efik local historians began to refute anthropological and historical literature that linked them to the Ibibio and Igbo (Jeffreys, 1935; Afigbo, 1965; Noah, 1980). In place of this, the Efik nationalists claimed that they originated from the Middle East and only momentarily settled in Ibibioland (Aye, 1967, 2000; Afigbo, 1977; Akak, 1986; Roschenthaler, 2002).

Efik elites also demanded that their traditional ruler should be made the pre-eminent 'natural' ruler in the state because the Obong of Calabar and Amanyanabo of Opobo were among the preeminent chiefs in the old Eastern Region. The State Government rejected the proposal. Rather, the government raised the status of Efut and Qua traditional rulers to be at par with that of the Efik monarch. The Efut and Qua are two ethnic groups indigenous to Calabar but had been overshadowed by the Efik from the trans-atlantic trade period to the colonial era. Efik elites described the government policy as a divide and rule strategy and started mobilizing other minority ethnic groups to canvass the creation of Cross River State, which would not include the Ibibio. Efik-Ibibio rivalry lasted from the late 1960s to the mid 1980s. The Efik resisted the alleged attempt to incorporate the Efik into Ibibio cultural orbit by promoting the documentation and teaching of Efik language and culture (see, Aye, nd.) The Ibibio in Calabar became the butt of ridicule and stereotypes including the blame for the insanitary conditions of Calabar and for making churches the only industry in the state (Hackett, 1989).

The Ibibio initially opposed the proposed state largely because of fears they would become victims of another abandoned property saga.[xiv] However, as the advantages of state creation especially in elite recruitment became apparent after the introduction of the federal character priniple in the 1979 constitution, the Ibibio elite dropped their opposition to creation of states. Thus, in 1987 the military regime created Akwa Ibom State, thereby 'freeing' the Efik and other minorities from Ibibio domination. If this is what that was meant to be, the peoples of Cross River realised that not all Ibibio people were willing to leave the new state. Given the similarity of names between the Efik and the Ibibio, many Ibibio allegedly continued to claim indigenship of the state.[xv] The Ibibio still dominate federal institutions and have been involved in land ownership disputes and conflicts with several Efik communities especially over the oil rich disputed Bakassi Peninsula and Ikot Offiong. It is hardly surprising that the Ibibio are often blamed for crime, hooliganism and electoral malpractices in Calabar.[xvi]

Nembe-Ogbia Relations

Although opposition to Nembe cultural and socio-economic domination initially defined Ogbia nationalism both groups rallied together as minorities against the Igbo dominated Eastern Region Government. They championed the cause for the creation of Rivers State. It is noteworthy that the chair of the Rivers Chiefs and Peoples Conference was Mingi X, the Amanyanabo of Nembe. Though he later piped down as a result of fears of demotion in the Eastern Region House of Chiefs, the Nembe-Brass District produced the only elected member of the Niger Delta Congress, which championed the cause for the creation of Rivers State (Post, 1963). The elected member, Mr.

51

Melford Okilo hailed from Ogbia. When Rivers State was created Ogbia and Nembe found themselves in the favoured group in the evolving cleavage between upland and riverain communities. The military governor of Rivers State between 1967 and 1976 was from the Nembe-Brass axis, while Ogbia produced the governor between 1979 and 1983. Upland communities who resented the dominance campaigned for the creation of Port Harcourt State, contradicting the very basis of River State. For advocates of Rivers State had opined that:

> These various ethnic groups have historical, economic, social and cultural community of interests and are desirous of continuing this centuries old association in one new political entity. Among them no one ethnic group will be able to dominate all others and their fears as Nigerian minorities will vanish once and for all time.[xvii]

Although the Rivers Leaders of Thought may have stated the facts in 1966 the scenario changed when the Ijaw communities in Sagbama and Opobo were transferred respectively from Bendel and Cross River states in the boundary adjustment exercise of 1976. Ijaw domination became visible so much so that Non-Ijaw elements justified their calls for separation with the idea that: 'There is no community of interest between an aquatic, fishing, population and a farming population' (Wali, 1982:122). Amidst fears that the creation of Port Harcourt would lead to the eviction of the rivirine Ijaw from Port Harcourt where they owned substantial property, the Ijaw opposed the creation of the state. However in the early 1980s as a result of growing demands for new states across the country, some Ogbia and Nembe elites were active in the Bayelsa Forum, which canvassed 'the creation of a uni-ethnic state' out of Brass, Yenagoa and Sagbama LGAs (Nwajiaku, 2005a:173).

In the 1990s, Ogbia and Nembe alongside other central Ijaw played a prominent role in the revival of Ijaw nationalism in a context where the three major ethnic groups were perceived to have dominated the militarised Nigerian state. In fact, the first Ijaw youth movements such as the Movement for Reparations to the Ogbia (MORETO) and the Elimotu Movement, which spearheaded the formation of the Ijaw Youth Council (IYC) were led by Ogbia youths. The radicalisation of the Ogbia during this period derived from resentments that arose from the abandonment of Oloibiri, the site of the first commercial exploitation of oil in Nigeria. Nembe and Ogbia were two of the 7 local government areas, which were carved out to form Bayelsa State in

1996. However, Ogbia nationalism remains alive despite the trend towards pan-Ijaw nationalism (Nwajiaku, 2005b).

Itsekiri- Urhobo Relations

Unlike Efik-Ibibio relations and Nembe-Ogbia relations that witnessed moments of cooperation for the attainment of common interests, Itsekiri-Urhobo relations has been marked by perpetual conflict of interests. In the politics of the 1950s, the Itsekiri were associated with the Action Group (AG) while the Urhobo were seen as staunch NCNC supporters. Although the Itsekiri voted for 1 AG and 1 NCNC legislator, this association of the Itsekiri with the AG was born out of the Itsekiri monarch's open identification with the party. The Urhobo claim it was such undisguised support that made the AG controlled Western Region Government to change the title of the monarch from Olu of Itsekiri to Olu of Warri.[xviii] Even on the issue of state creation that united minorities across the country in the 1950s, Itsekiri-Urhobo antagonism persisted. Although Chief Festus Okotie-Eboh, an Itsekiri and NCNC chieftain was at the forefront of the campaign for the creation of Mid Western State, the Olu of Warri led a substantial group of Itsekiri to oppose creation of Miod West State (Vickers 2000). This group propagated the view that Itsekiri were Yoruba and did not desire to be separated from the Western Region. They also asked for constitutional provision that would exclude non-Itsekiri from contesting elections in Warri Division. Remarkably Itsekiri objection was one of the reasons adduced by the Commission to support its recommendation against state creation (Colonial Office, 1958:8-9).

The general feeling in Benin and Delta Provinces was that the Itsekiri frustrated the quest of the minorities in the region for self-determination. However, fears that the Itsekiri would lose out from the new region, which was established in 1963, did not materialise. This is because Chief Okotie-Eboh, who had become Federal Minister for Finance used his influence in government to inset a minority protection clause in the 1964 Mid West Region Constitution. He also influenced the NCNC controlled government of the Midwest to dethrone the Olu of Warri. The newly installed Olu of Warri never gained the support of the entire Itsekiri people. Consequently, the military governor of Midwestern State in 1967, who was Urhobo, restored the Olu to his office (Sagay, n.d.). Such a gesture however did not lead to any rapprochement in Itsekiri-Urhobo relations. When in 1976, the Urhobo led the movement of the creation of Delta State out of Bendel State, the Itsekiri opposed the proposed state owing to fears of Urhobo domination. Again in the late 1980s, the Itsekiri renewed their opposition to the creation of Delta State, which would include both Itsekiri and Urhobo. They renewed their calls for the declaration of the Warri Province as a Special Federal Protected Area or the relocation of Itsekiri with Ondo.[xix]

Since the creation of Delta State in 1991, the Itsekiri have alleged Urhobo domination because all elected governors of the state have been Urhobo. Itsekiri-Urhobo relations have been marked by several outbreaks of violent conflicts with loss of lives and property especially in the Warri area where ethnically defined communities make claims to oil-bearing land rights. Itsekiri also allege Urhobo complicity in outbreaks of conflict between Itsekiri and Ijaw communities.

The Itsekiri continue to agitate against what they consider is their 'forcible' inclusion in a Delta State where the Urhobo constitute about 50 per cent of the population. Even though the Itsekiri have historically gotten a disproportionate share of political appointments in the state[xx], the fact that Urhobo have produced and may continue to produce the governor of Delta State is unacceptable to the Itsekiri, who barely a century ago monopolised the position of the Governor of the Benin River. It is hardly surprising therefore that even though the Itsekiri were part of Delta State delegation to the National Political Reform Conference (NPRC) which was convened in 2005, the Itsekiri presented a separate memo to the NPRC, which contradicted some of the positions taken by Delta State.[xxi] According to the Itsekiri:

All Nigerians tend to accuse the tripod-Hausa/Fulani, the Yoruba and the Igbo as the cause of instability in Nigeria. To the micro-minorities, that is not true. With the recent creation of many states, ethnic monsters have emerged within them. The majority ethnic groups in the states or the major minorities in the overall Nigerian context, like Urhobo in Delta, the Ijaw in the South-South or even in Delta State, for example, do more havoc to the micro groups in their states and torment them much more harshly than the three major ethnic groups would even think of doing to others. The result is that new majority groups have emerged with their new brand of tyranny of the majority and inter-ethnic conflicts rear their heads. To the minority ethnic nationalities like the Itsekiri in Delta State local imperialism has been substituted for British imperialism.[xxii]

The reason why the Itsekiri sought a platform distinct from that of Delta State is evident in its submission that:

> Ethnic nationalities are organic and corporations in accordance with customary law. They have souls and are indestructible entities. They are in the true sense 'the federating' units in the Nigeria project, and not the artificially created states. The Nigerian federation must be an expression of the diversity of the ethnic nationalities in the country. The ethnic nationalities should be the federating unit. The cry of marginalization, fiscal federalism and resource control is expression of desire for ethnic self-determination. The artificially created states have not and cannot satisfy this desire.[xxiii]

Clearly, the Itsekiri are canvassing a fundamental restructuring of the Nigerian in such a way that ethnic nationalities will become the federating unit.[xxiv] This is understandable because under such a dispensation territorial and population size would not count and there will be no basis for Urhobo domination. They also modified the advocacy for resource control when they asked for resources to be allocated to communities where they are sourced rather than the states. Such arrangement would definitely terminate the unacceptable dispensation where Urhobo governors superintend over resources extracted from Itsekiriland.[xxv]

In this context we see history repeating itself but with a reversal of roles. In the early colonial period, it was the Urhobo who led separatist agitations, refused to pay taxes to Itsekiri dominated Native Administrations and overlaboured to convince the colonial administration that they were 'naturally' different from the Itsekiri. In 2005, it was the Itsekiri that had to convince the post-colonial state that: 'Within the Delta state, the Itsekiri have no ethnic or linguistic affinity with any other people more so with their immediate geographical neighbours.'[xxvi] The changing contexts and fortunes notwithstanding the abiding impact of state policies on ethnic definition are unmistakable. The principles of Native Administration, which emphasized ethnic difference continues to haunt nation-building projects that privilege state and regional identities.

The Niger Delta, the Major Ethnic Groups and the Nigerian State

Since the early 1950s, elites from minority ethnic groups have tried to construct a narrative of politics in which the relevant cleavage is between the major ethnic groups and the minorities. This was the outcome of the creation of regions dominated by the Hausa/Fulani, Igbo and Yoruba. The major ethnic groups whose domination minorities of the Niger Delta resented were the Igbo (Eastern Region) and the Yoruba (Western Region). In the evolving political alliances of the time it was the practice for minorities in each region to align with the dominant party in another region (unmiskably associated with the major ethnic group in that region) in order to achieve their objectives of state creation. Thus, while most of the western minorities aligned with the Igbo dominated NCNC against Yoruba domination, the eastern minorities aligned with the Yoruba led AG against Igbo domination. In addition, both eastern and western minorities valued relations with the Hausa/Fulani, the dorminant group in the Northern Region whose support was crucial for the creation of states. It is therefore not surprising that these minorities did not want to antagonise the Hausa/Fulani led Northern Peoples Congress (NPC). Thus, the NPC is conspicuously missing in the manifesto of the Niger Delta Congress, which was: 'Away! Away! Away! With the NCNC. Away with the Action Group. Vote for the Niger Delta Congress. Vote for the fish in the triangular net or trap.'[xxvii] The preference of southern minorities for alliance with the Hausa/Fulani was also evident in the opposition of the minorities to the Igbo led Biafran secession and the electoral victories of the Hausa/Fulani led National Party of Nigeria (NPN) amongst the eastern minorities in 1979 and all southern minorities states in 1983.

However, these political alliances suffered in the 1980s following the return of military rule in which successive military heads of state were of northern origins. This period was also characterised by the continuous splitting of states which by the last exercise in 1996 had culminated in a situation where the major ethnic groups had more states. The southern minorities of the Niger Delta resented the fact that these states were sustained by oil exploited from their region. Whereas internal revenue effort had sustained the regions, a new revenue allocation formula which deemphaised derivation was adopted after the discovery of oil in the territory of southern minorities under the period of military rule. The southern minorities claim this new regime of allocation was foisted by the unholy alliance of the three major ethnic groups (WAZOBIA) who control the Nigerian state.

The Niger Delta ethnic groups have therefore mobilised against fiscal centralization and advocated for more revenues to be distributed on the basis of derivation instead of the current practice where population and territorial size and other criteria that favour the WAZOBIA is privileged. This mobilization which accentuated in the 1990s was characterised by rising number of anti-state and anti-transnational oil corporation protests in various Niger Delta communities. In response to rising discontent in the region over the diversion of resources to develop WAZOBIA non-oil producing areas- especially the 'majestic' Federal Capital Territory at Abuja-, the military government created the Oil Mineral Producing Areas Development Commission (OMPADEC) with special funds to administer development in oil producing communities. However, to the chagrin of the minorities, OMPADEC was alleged to have been programmed to serve the interests of the WAZOBIA. Not only were persons from non-oil producing areas appointed to the Board, most of the contracts were awarded to cronies and proxies of the military rulers who not surprisingly were not from oil producing areas.

However, the establishment of OMPADEC succeeded in creating new identities. Southern minorities were indiscriminately seen as oil producing communities. It created a context in which minorities East and West of the River Niger were brought together under a common platform. This southern minority identity was further concretised by the division of the country into six geo-political zones by the military regime in 1996 as southern minorities became coterminous with the South South zone. The minorities in this region have resisted the inclusion of members of the WAZOBIA groups in any programme associated with the region. Thus since 1991 there has been a clamour for the creation of the 'real' Delta State because the Babaginda regime included the Ika-Igbo in Delta State. Moreover, the minorities opposed the inclusion of Abia, Imo and Ondo states in the Niger Delta Development Commission (NDDC) established in 1999 to replace the defunct OMPADEC, alleging that the three (Igbo and Yoruba) states are not part of the historical and ecological Niger Delta.

The opposition to the inclusion of oil producing Igbo and Yoruba states in the NDDC and the appointment of an Igbo as the maiden chair of the Commission stemmed from perceptions among southern minorities that the Yoruba and Igbo dominate the oil and gas industry. In addition, the Igbo and Yoruba and the Hausa/Fulani are also perceived as dominating the Nigerian National Petroleum Corporation (NNPC), which represents the interest of the Nigerian state in the oil industry. This dominance is seen as a calculated attempt to deny the minorities of their God-given resources, because in the immortal words of the martyred Ogoni leader, Ken Saro Wiwa, there was no Ogoni man on the Cocoa and Groundnut Marketing Boards respectively established in the Western and Northern Regions.

Such perceptions have generated anti-WAZOBIA mobilizations across generational, gender and class strata in the region. The youths have canvassed more employment opportunities in the industry which is currently dominated by WAZOBIA personnel.[xxviii] The elites have campaigned for the reservation of the portfolio of Petroleum Minister and Managing Director of the NNPC to the South South. These anti-WAZOBIA mobilizations led by both elite and mass social movements as well as militant and non-militant groups have culminated in the demands for resource control and for a South South President. The mobilizations have been accompanied by increased incidents of oil bunkering, killing of Nigerian soldiers deployed to protect oil facilities, destruction of oil pipelines and kidnap of expatriate oil workers with disastrous consequences for Nigeria's oil production capacity and revenue base (see, Omeje, 2006). Paradoxically, these crises are occurring at a time when relatively speaking the 'core' Niger Delta oil producing states are receiving the largest share of funds from the Federation Account due to the implementation of the 13 per cent derivation fund.

Although the derivation formula was increased to 13 per cent by the constitutional conference of 1994, its implementation had to wait until 1999 following the return to civilian rule. The liberalised political environment emboldened both elected officials and elite organizations to join forces with youth organizations to canvass for resource control. This followed the judicial victory recorded by the Conference of South South Governors late in 1999 when the Supreme Court ruled that the payment of the 13 per cent derivation fund should be backdated to May 29, 1999 when the Fourth Republic came into effect. Since then there has been an unprecented unity among southern minorities in their mobilization against the Nigerian state and the hegemony of the three dominant ethnic groups. An indication of the strength of the movement is that the NPRC convened by President Olusegun Obasanjo to brainstorm on ways of strengthening Nigeria's federal democracy ended unceremoniously after a boycott by south-south delegates over disagreements on what percentage of oil revenues should be distributed on the basis of derivation. Moreover, the ruling Peoples Democratic Party (PDP) gave the vice presidential ticket for the 2007 elections to an Ijaw politician (the largest southern minority ethnic group) to assuage the anger of the Niger Delta peoples. President Olusegun Obasanjo who had appointed several southern minorities as service chiefs has also appointed a southern minority to the post of Petroleum Minister in his last cabinet.

It remains to be seen, however, whether these measures are sufficient to assuage aggrieved communities in the region. Hostage taking and demands for ransom, incidents of pipeline vandalization, oil bunkering and killing of Nigerian soliders are yet to abate in the Niger Delta. On the contrary militant groups like the dreaded Movement for the Emanicpation of the Niger Delta (MEND) have dismissed the concessions are palliatives. There are threats of more militant action unless Niger Delta 'heroes' such Diepreye Alameiyeiseigha the impeached Governor of Bayelsa State and Asari Dokubo, leader of the Niger Delta Peoples Volunteer Force who are currently standing trial are released and there is a full implementation of resource control.[xxix]

Moreover, while unity can be taken for granted as far as the principles of resource control and South South presidency are concerned there is disquiet and disunity when it comes to implementation. There are different views of what resource control would entail. For instance, host communities and minority groups have canvassed the idea of sidelining the state and remitting funds directly to communities and local government areas where oil is actually exploited, as evident the position of the Itsekiri highlighted above.

Conclusion and Recommendations

This chapter has traced how the incorporation of communal groups into the world system through trade and the establishment of the colonial state led to the transformation of identities. From a setting where residence was the criteria for citizenship, ethnic identity which was putatively based on descent has been privileged above other identities. As a result of the colonial indirect rule policies and the introduction of racist discourses and categories, coastal and hinterland communties were differentiated and perceived inequalities between the two sets of communities set the context for conflictual relations. The improvements in communications, entrenchment of the colonial state and the introduction of majoritarian electoral systems all contributed to overturning the early advantages of coastal communities who subsequently became political minorities.

The argument advanced in the chapter is that ethnic conflicts were worse in cases where reverse domination occurred, that is, where historically dominant groups are being dominated by groups they had hitherto dominated. This is why of the three cases examined in the chapter the Nembe-Ogbia have experienced the least conflict because both groups became part of the minimum winning coalition in Rivers State. It is also this logic of reverse domination where the Niger Delta communities who were historically at the centre of the country's political economy find themselves at the margins of its contemporary politics that defines the context for the resource control conflicts in the region.

To overcome these intra-Niger Delta conflicts and conflicts between the Niger Delta and the Nigerian state which is perceived as serving the interests of dominant ethnic groups, there is first the need to rethink the basis of state citizenship. The emphasis on ethnicity and statism based on descent is counterproductive. There is need for a constitutional review to recognise residence and not descent per se as the basis of membership of the political community, commonly referred to as indigeneship. People who have lived in a state for a certain period of time and performed civic obligations there should be allowed to claim indigeneship of such a state.

Secondly, the conflict in the Niger Delta as the chapter has shown derives from the political economy of Nigeria where the state depends solely on oil for its reproduction. There is need for restructuring of the country's fiscal federalism to ensure that all tiers of government source locally for a certain percentage of their revenue. The remaining portion can be supplied from the Federation Account. In other words, the objective of the Federation Account should be to subsidise and not underwrite the entire revenue of the federal, states and local government areas. Such requirement would necessarily make taxation an attractive source of revenue and *ipso facto* facilitate the transformation of resident tax-payers into bonafide members of the political community. The present trend of sharing the national cake derivable from the oil and gas extracted from the disempowered and aggrieved Niger Delta communities is no longer sustainable as the crises in the region all point to.

Notes

1. Note that early records referred to Itsekiri as Jekri and the Urhobo as Sobo.

2. Mustapha (1999) makes the same point with other notable pre-colonial kingdoms in Africa.

3. We do not posit that it was all rosy for the slave. The system was oppressive leading revolts as evident in the revolt of 'the Bloodmen' in Old Calabar. See Nair 1972.

4. This might be in reference to the trans-Atlantic slave trade as earlier studies of the Itsekiri document the existence of domestic slavery. See. Granville and Roth (1899).

5. This writers were themselves influenced by the rise of the ideology of race in Europe from the mid nineteeth century. See, Flint 1969.

6. Others were the Sultan of Sokoto, Emir of Kano, Alafin of Oyo, and Mr. Sapara Williams. The second council which was inaugurated in 1919, Dore Numa was replaced by the Shehu of Bornu while Henshaw was retained. See, Tamuno (1966).

7. Cited in Akpan, N. U. (1955) "A Study of Local Government", MSS. Afr. S. 1505 (II), Rhodes House Archives, Oxford, p. 27.

8. E. Falk "Notes on the history of taxation, affecting the Eastern Provinces and more especially Calabar Province". 1933. MSS Afr. S. 1000(1) (our emphasis).

9. For instance, while there were 82 Efik pupils and 31 Ibibio pupils in the premier Hope Waddell Training Institute in 1919, Ibibio enrolment climbed to 86 in 1931 with Efik retaining a slight lead with 119. See. Noah (1978:22-23). By 1936, Urhobos had bridged the educational gap with the Itsekiri. There were 157 Urhobo students in Government School, Warri as against 155 Itsekiri pupils. See, Ikime (1969:243). It should be noted that in ratio to the population the Efik and Itsekiri were still ahead.

10. This was facilitated by improvements in transport and communications as European trading firms established outposts in the hinterland. Hinterland producers could do without coastal middlemen that took their produce to the coasts.

11. Itsekiri kingship institution collapsed in 1848 after the death of King Akegbuwa, the Olu of Itsekiri. The cause of the collapse was the tragic death of two heirs to the throne and the movement of the centre of trade from Ode Itsekiri, the Itsekiri capital to Benin River. (See, Lloyd, 1963).

12. While Wolf (1976) observes the phenomenon of non-reciprocal bilingualism in Nembe-Ogbia relations, it is worthy to note that Itsekiri chieftains like Nana Olomu who traded with the Urhobos learnt how to speak the Urhobo language to facilitate his trading activities as he traversed Urhoboland (Ikime, 1995).

13. This refers to the controversial alleged confiscation and acquisition of property left behind Igbo residents in Port Harcourt who fled to the Eastern Region during the civil war.

14. Interview. Coordinator, Federal Character Commission, Cross River State Office, Calabar. 18/01/2005.

15. Interview with several Efik personalities in Calabar in 2005.

16. "Rivers State Memorandum Address to His Excellency, the Supreme Commander and Head of the Military Government of Nigeria" by Rivers Leaders of Thought, 14/9/1966. Reproduced as appendix 5 in Alagoa ed. (2004:235).

17. This change led to riots in Warri province in which Urhobos clashed with the Itsekiri. See Ikime 1969 and Sagay (n.d.)

18. See, Alfred Rewane 'Why Murtala did not create Delta State in 1976,' *Daily Times.*

19. This is often supplemented by appointments at the Federal level, which according to Urhobo and Ijaw nationalists have favoured the Itsekiri.

20. The Delta State Government asked for revenue allocation on the basis of states but the Itsekiri preferred local governments. Moreover, the State wanted local government to be under the supervision of state governments, the Itsekiri opted for autonomy of LGAs and asked for the scrapping of the Local Government Service Commissions. See, Memoradum of the Government and People of Delta State to the National Political Reform Conference, March 2005.

21. Memorandum of the Itsekiri Ethnic Nationality of Delta State of Nigeria Submitted to the National Political Reform Conference Holden at Abuja. March 2005. P.4-5

22. Ibid, p. 8.

23. It is important to note that this has been the position of advocates of a sovereign national conference. There is a contrary view, which opines that Britain did not colonise ethnic nationalities but created them.

24. Nwajiaku (2005b) observes a similar trend in the Kolo creek of Bayelsa State.

25. 'Memorandum of the Itsekiri Ethnic Nationality…,' *op cit.*, p. 5.

26. Alagoa ed. 2004. Appendix 4, p. 199.

27. Interview. Prof. Onigu Otite. 21/08/2005. Warri.

28. See, A. Agbo 'Voting Against Tokenism', *Tell*, January 22, 2007.

References

Afigbo, A. E. (1965) 'Efik Origin and Migrations Reconsidered', *Nigeria Magazine*, No. 87, p. 267-280.

_____ (1975), 'Anthropology and Colonial Administration in South-Eastern Nigeria, 1891-1939', *Journal of the Historical Society of Nigeria*, Vol. 8, No. 1, pp. 19-35.

_____ (1977) 'Fact and Myth in Nigerian Historiography', *Nigeria Magazine*, No. 122-123, p. 81-99.

Akak, E. O. (1986) *The Palestine Origin of the Efiks*, Calabar: Akak and Sons

Alagoa, E. J. (2004) 'History and Policy in the Niger Delta Crisis,' in E. J. Alagoa ed. *The Uses of Hindsight as Foresight: Reflections on Niger Delta and Nigerian History*, Port Harcourt: Onyoma Research Publications, pp.63-90.

_____ ed. (2004) *Harold Dappa-Biriye: His contributions to Politics in Nigeria*, Port Harcourt: Onyoma Research Publications.

Aye, E. U. (1967) *Old Calabar through the Centuries*, Calabar: HWTI Press

_____. (2000) *The Efik People*, Calabar: APELAC.

_____ (ed.) *The Efik Language and its Future: A Memorandum Produced by APELLAC*, (Calabar: APELLAC, nd.)

Colonial Office (1958) *Nigeria: Report of the Commission appointed to enquire into the fears of Minorities and the Means of Allaying them.* London: Her Majesty's Stationery Office.

Ekeh, P.P. (1996) 'Political Minorities and Historically-Dominant Minorities in Nigerian History' in O. Oyediran ed. *Governance and Development in Nigeria: Essays in Honour of Billy Dudley,* Ibadan: Agbo Areo Publishers.

Dike, K. O. (1956) *Trade and Politics in the Niger Delta,* London: Oxford University Press.

Glassman, J. (2000), 'Sorting out the Tribes: The Creation of Racial Identities in Colonial Zanzibar's Newspaper Wars', *The Journal of African History,* 41, pp.395-428.

Goldie, H. (1890) *Calabar and Its Mission,* Edinburgh: Oliphant Andersen and Ferrier

Granville, R. A. and F. Roth (1899) 'Notes on the Jekris, Sobos and Ijos of the Warri District of the Niger Coast Protectorate', *The Journal of the Anthropological Institute of Great Britain and Ireland,* Vol. 28, No. 1/2, pp. 104-126.

Hackett, R. I. J., (1989) *Religion in Calabar: The Religious Life and History of a Nigerian Town,* Berlin and New York: Mouton De Gruyter.

Hart, A. K. (1964) *Report of the Enquiry into the Dispute over the Obongship of Calabar,* Enugu: Eastern Region Govt. Printer.

Ikime, O. (1963) "The Coming of the C.M.S into the Itsekiri, Urhobo and Isoko country", *Nigeria Magazine,* No. 86, pp. 206-215.

_____ (1969) *Niger Delta Rivalry: Itsekiri-Urhobo Relations and the European Presence 1884-1936,* London: Longman.

_____ (1977) *The Member for Warri Province: The Life and Times of Chief Mukoro Mowoe of Warri 1890-1948,* Ibadan: Institute of African Studies, University of Ibadan.

_____ (1995) *Merchant Prince of the Niger Delta: The Rise and Fall of nana Olomu, Last Governor of the Benin River,* (Special Centenary Edition) Ibadan: By the Author.

Jeffreys, M. D. W. (1935) *Old Calabar and Notes on the Ibibio Language,* Calabar: HWTI Press.

Lentz, C. (2000) 'Colonial Constructions and African Initiatives: The History of Ethnicity in Northwestern Ghana,' *Ethnos,* 65, (1), pp. 107-36.

Lloyd, P. C. (1963) 'The Itsekiri in the nineteenth century; An Outline social History,' *Journal of African History,* IV, 2, pp. 207-231.

Mustapha, A. R. (1999) 'Back to the Future: Multi-ethnicity and the State in Africa' in L. Basta and J. Ibrahim eds. *Federalism and Decentralization in Africa*, Fribourg: Institut du Federalism.

_____ (2000) 'Transformation of Minority Identities in Post Colonial Nigeria' in A. Jega ed. *Identity Transformation and Identity Politics under Structural Adjustment in Nigeria*, Uppsala & Kano: Nordic African Institute and Centre for Research and Documentation, pp. 86-108.

Nair, K. K. (1972) *Politics and Society in South Eastern Nigeria*, London: Frank Cass.

Nnoli, O. (1978) *Ethnic Politics in Nigeria*, Enugu: Fourth Dimension Publishers.

Noah, M. E. (1978) 'Efik Expansion and Influence in the Cross River Basin, 1884-1935', *The Calabar Historical Journal*, Vol. 2, No. 1, p. 1-31.

_____ (1980) *Old Calabar: The City States and the Europeans 1880-1885*, Uyo: Scholars Press.

Nwajiaku, K (2005) 'Oil Politics and Identity Transformation in Nigeria: The Case of the Ijaw of the Niger Delta", *D. Phil Thesis* (University of Oxford)

_____ (2005) "Between Discourse and Reality: The Politics of Oil and Ijaw Ethnic Nationalism in the Niger Delta', *Cashiers d'Etudes africaines*, XLV (2), 178, 2005, pp. 457-496.

Okorobia, A. M (1999) 'The Impact of the Atlantic Trade' in E. J. Alagoa ed. *The Land and People of Bayelsa State: Central Niger Delta*, Port Harcourt: Onyoma Research Publications p. 205-218.

Omeje, K. (2006) *High Stakes and Stakeholders: Oil Conflict in Nigeria*, Aldershot: Ashgate.

Onor, S. O. (1994), *The Ejagham nation in the Cross River Region of Nigeria*, Ibadan: Kraft Books Ltd.

Post, K. W. J. (1963) *The Nigerian Federal Elections of 1959*, London: Oxford University Press.

Pratten, D. (2006) 'The Politics of Vigilance in Southeastern Nigeria", *Development and Change*, Vol. 37, No. 4, 707-734.

Ranger, T. (1983), "The Invention of Tradition in Colonial Africa' in Eric Hobsbawn and Terence Ranger (eds.), *The Invention of Tradition*, Cambridge: Cambridge University Press

_____ (1994) 'The Invention of Tradition Revisited: The Case of Colonial Africa' in Preben Kaarsholm and Jan Hultin (eds.) *Inventions*

and Boundaries: Historical and Anthropological Approaches to the Study of Ethnicity and Nationalism, Rosklide: Rosklide University.

Roschenthaler, U. (2002) 'A New York City of Ibibioland? Local Historiography and Power Conflict in Calabar' in A. Harneit-Sievers ed. *A Place in the World: New Local Historiographies from Africa and South Asia*, Leiden: Brill, pp. 87-109.

Sagay, J.O.E (n.d.) *The Warri Kingdom*, Sapele: Progress Publishers.

Tamuno, T. (1966) *Nigeria and Elective Representation 1929-1947*, London and Ibadan: Heinemann, 1966.

_____ (1972) *The Evolution of the Nigerian State: The Southern Phase*, London: Longman.

Vail, L. ed. (1989) *The Creation of Tribalism in Southern Africa*, London and Berkeley, CA: James Currey and University of California Press.

Vickers, M. (2000) *Ethnicity and Sub-Nationalism in Nigeria: Movement for a Mid-West State*, Oxford: Worldview Publishing.

Wali, O. (1982) 'Rationale for the Demand of Port Harcourt State' in O. Adejuyigbe, L. Dare and A. Adepoju eds. *Creation of States in Nigeria: A Review of Rationale, demands and Problems up to 1980*, Lagos: The Federal Government Printer, pp. 119-123.

Wolf, H. (1976) 'Language, Ethnic Identity and Social Change in Southern Nigeria' in A. O. Sanda ed. *Ethnic Relations in Nigeria: Problems and Prospects*, Ibadan: Department of Sociology, University of Ibadan, pp. 52-60.

Chapter 3

Building Democracy in a Regressive State: The Travails of Electoral Politics in Nigeria

Usman A. Tar

Democracy is a process...Elections are just an important event in that process. Under my leadership, we shall strengthen democracy by deepening and widening the democratisation process through dialogue (Obasanjo, 1999).[1]

Introduction

This chapter examines the challenges and opportunities that confront Nigeria – classified in this chapter as a regressive state, albeit perceived in many international quarters as a fledgling democracy. The chapter argues that in Nigeria the practice of liberal democracy and associated institutional machineries such as election (administration, funding and monitoring), party politics, the constitution etc are held hostage by a number of defective practices, faulty legislation and zero-sum power politics. These problems, it is argued, need to be overcome if democracy is to flourish in Nigeria; otherwise, the country risks autocracy or even military re-intervention.

The chapter is predicated on the contradictory gulf between the *ideal* and *practice* of democracy, state-building and power politics in Nigeria. This dilemma is amply demonstrated in the above 'politically-correct' ambitious statement, pronounced by President Obasanjo at the on-set of his first term in office in May 1999. The pronouncement was received with great expectations by jubilant Nigerians celebrating the end of over two decades of brutal military dictatorship, and the beginning of a new democratic era. Yet, today the lofty ideals set out by President Obasanjo and his colleagues have proved elusive as Nigerians are worse off than they were in 1999. The economy is performing below expectations, even though micro-economic indicators suggest significant improvement in the last 8 years compared to the preceding two decades of military rule; corruption has proved endemic, particularly in 'high places'; Nigeria's human development index leaves much to be desired; Nigeria is one the poorest nations in the world, in spite of the country's endowments of nature. Indeed, Wole Soyinka's (1997) raging description of Nigeria as 'an open sore of a continent [Africa]' – written in the heat of military rule – is very much in evidence, implying that a return to democracy has scarcely transformed Nigeria or reversed the status quo.[2] This situation is not uncommon: Nigerians are used to empty and broken promises; over four decades of misrule has taught them not to trust their leaders and/or their political promises, unless proven to the contrary.

Nigeria has always been embroiled in a constant search for a working political system – a key feature of all political systems. But Nigeria stands out for its paradox. While many societies including some so-called 'third world' countries have achieved significant progress in democracy and development[3], Nigeria remains 'an unfinished state of uncertainty', weighed down by a host of structural anormalies, 'contested aspirations, the dearth of reality and other tragedies' (Agbaje, 2004:203). Udogu (1997) aptly describes these dilemmas as 'the politics of survival as a nation' – a scenario in which Nigeria is evidently regressing, and not progressing. A current 'contested aspiration' in Nigeria, particularly following the dramatic exit of the military rule in 1999 after about two decades of repression untold hardship democratic denial, is concern with the survival of the country's fledgling liberal democracy.[4] Recent events have confirmed widely-held doubts, both within and without Nigeria, about whether the country can sustain and consolidate its hard-earned democracy. An example is the controversy surrounding anti-corruption and politicisation of key governmental agencies by the President – in particular, the Independent Financial Crime Commission (IFCC) – as a means of witch-hunting political enemies, having failed in his attempt to amend the constitution to enable him contest for the presidency under the so-called *third term agenda*. Paradoxically, the President's 'hidden agenda' has generated speculations about his determination to remain in power come what may – with huge implications for Nigeria's fledgling democracy. An astute commentator on Nigerian politics observes:

> ...in spite of the sound defeat of Third Term agenda, public opinion remained sceptical about the president's promise to go. This

scepticism has now been rekindled by rumours of a presidential plan to shift the April elections to October. The plan, as the speculations go, is to be implemented by simply bribing the National Assembly to approve the shift. The carrots to be dangled before the legislators are said to include the usual "Ghana-must-go" in hard currency and a reminder that with most of them defeated or rigged out of contention in their party primaries, the six months or so between May and October is a bonus' (Haruna, 2007, np).

The foregoing domestic speculations are reinforced by a similar opinion held outside Nigeria. For instance, on 27th February 2007, both the Associate Press and CNN reported that the Director of U.S. intelligence, Mr Mike McConnell warned of 'instability in Nigeria amid concern that outgoing President Olusegun Obasanjo is manipulating the political process ahead of April's elections.'[5] Mr McConnell raised doubts about 'democratic [re]transition in a country of 140 million that is infamous for graft and corruption, electoral and otherwise'. At issue, therefore, of appalling report card of the political class (read elected representatives) who are driven by a lust for wealth and power, rather than public good or sustenance of democracy.

A related dilemma is the tendency to perceive *democracy* as synonymous with *elections* – a problem prevalent at all levels of society. Though many have cautioned against the tendency to equate democracy with election, it still pervades public imagination and remains the bane of electoral democracy in Nigeria. This tendency is problematic for a number of reasons. First, though elections constitute the cornerstone of any democracy, it ought to exist complementarily with a host of behavioural and institutional factors: e.g. a functional executive, legislature and executive, capable of checkmating one another; a neutral but fearless judicial system; a competitive party process; a responsible bureaucracy; an enlightened electorate; an autonomous 'civil society'; a selfless elite etc. Secondly, it is important to view democracy beyond election – which, though important, component of a democratic system does not exist in isolation. An election-oriented (or electionistic) view of democracy is quite premature: it creates a situation in which election becomes the only essence of political existence – after election it is 'business as usual'. Thirdly, there is danger in taking election or democracy as a zero-sum game. This is a majoritarian view which is likely to constrain minority rights and encourage abuse of power. Fourthly, and by extension, it is important to appreciate the fact that both democracy and election flourish in an environment of compromise and dialogue, rather than violence, confrontation and tyranny.

Liberal Democracy and Electoral Politics – Conceptual Dilemmas

The debate on the relevance of Western conceptual tools and visions (and concomitant political structures) in non-Western societies is highly sensitive[6], but unavoidable. At issue is the need to deconstruct conventional wisdom beyond their face value and, by extension, to engage the correlation between theory and practice. There is need for a constructive engagement with taken-for-granted intellectual and political constructs to reflect the dynamic connect between vision and reality, theory and practice, concept and context (Mamdani, 1990:374). While many concepts such as the *state, democracy, market,* etc are universal (i.e. they evolved in diverse guises in different societies), dominant gumptions on these concepts are quite novel, even counter-productive, to 'new states' of Africa, Asia and Latin America. That is, they are socially and politically constructed in the dominant moulds of the developed West. This has generated at least two mutually reinforcing dilemmas, with huge implications for knowledge claims and power relations that underlie them: intellectual correctness and political correctness.

The Dilemma of Intellectual Correctness

This is the predicament of having to employ 'Western' theoretic and philosophical models to explain non-Western realities as if the latter lacks any capacity for 'wisdom'. As noted by Ake (1985) Western knowledge claims are not always rational or universally applicable; they could be oblivious of non-western realities and susceptible to grand standing. More recently, Celestine Monga (Monga, 1997, Ch. 2) raised fundamental questions on the intellectual and political correctness of Western theories and its reservation for anything non-western as savage, superstitious and antiquated. Above all, Western theoretical grand standing has huge moral implications for Western political imposition – see below.

The Dilemma of Political Correctness

The tendency to construct realities in Western philosophical moulds has given rise to 'given' visions of modern institutions-building: the state, civil society, democracy, legislature etc. Kabeer notes the obvious relationship between Western intellectual and political correctness: 'there is an intimate relationship between the world-view of powerful development agencies and the kinds of knowledge that they are likely to promote, fund and act upon' (1994:72). For instance, in defining *civil society*, Western theorists and donors see it as an 'open, voluntary, self-generating, at least partially self-supporting, autonomous from state, and bounded by a legal order or set of shared rules' (Diamond, 1994:6). A contrary but marginal definition of civil society includes all hues of associations – ethnic, cultural, voluntary, ascriptive, religious etc – in so far as they are engaged in collective activity and political action (see Tar, 2006, Ch. 2).[7] The latter is argued to be quiet relevant to new states of the global south, even though from European and North American viewpoints it is constructed as quite bizarre and unacceptable.[8] The tendency to consign non-Western conceptualisations and cultural relativity into oblivion, no matter how relevant, is described by Edward Said as *Orientalism* – a 'systematic discipline by which European culture was able to manage –even produce – the Orient [developing world] politically, sociologically, militarily, ideologically, scientifically, and imaginatively' (Said, 1979, p. 3).

In light of the foregoing dilemmas, it is necessary to problematise the conceptual substance and linkages of liberal democracy and election in terms of the sharp contrast that exists between the ideals and realities, as they manifest in fledgling democracies like Nigeria.[9] What are the conceptual and institutional imperatives of liberal democracy? To what extent is democracy and competitive electoral politics, as couched in the liberal vocabulary, applicable to Nigeria? How can they be made to serve the political challenges of plural, unstable polities? We need to understand liberal democracy and election, as they are couched in the liberal idiom, and then examine their problematic relevance in the particular context of Nigeria. The aim is imply the need to evolve necessary evolutionary measures for making democracy and election work in Nigeria. This is not to suggest an alternative to liberal democracy (e.g. social democracy, which, at the moment, is a remote possibility)[10] but to expose its problems and offer a constructive analysis of Nigeria's existing political order, built on the pedestals of political and economic (neo)liberalism.

Liberal democracy is defined as 'a procedural system involving open political competition, with multi-party, civil and political rights guaranteed by law, and accountability operating through an electoral relationship between citizens and their representatives' (Przeworski, 1991:ix). An important challenge facing most liberal democracies is how to conduct free, fair, transparent and orderly elections and, a more important one, perhaps, is the effectiveness and efficiency of the mechanisms for resolving conflicts arising from the conduct of such elections - for instance, court litigations arising from the credibility of elections instituted loosing contenders. Liberal democracy is distinguished by a superficial reverence of election as a crucial instrument for citizens to make rational choices on policy and leadership issues.

The core substance of liberal democracy is competitive electoral politics involving, on the one hand, regular, open and competitive elections whose outcome is 'uncertain [and] indeterminate ex ante' (Przeworski, *ibid*) and, on the other, a periodic machinery for making popular choice with the widest possible provisions for popular participation. These provisions, being the bedrock of the democratic process, are believed to enable citizen hold their representatives to account for their (in)actions and, simultaneously, make impact on the substance and orientation of public policy. Ideally, liberal democracy is predicated on widest participation of citizens in the political process. To achieve this, election is conventionally invoked as the key institutional guarantee for inclusivity and participation.

The ideals of liberal democracy cannot be said to apply to all societies; predicament with the practice of democracy abound even in developed democracies.[11] And in developing plural economies like Nigeria – where power and legitimacy are at the mercy of elite manipulation – elections have often been abused in reproducing dominant forms of power and the concomitant political order turn out to be anything but expedient and stable (Tar *et al*, 1999). On the whole, Nigeria's experience with liberal democracy (1960-66; 1979-83 & 1999-date) has been largely marred with instability, chaos and impermanence (see, Beckett and Young, 1997). First, as a modern political institution, liberal democratic election is alien to Nigeria.[12] Its utility remains limited because the structures and mores that drive them – e.g. guarantee of civil liberty, rule of law, economic stability etc – are in short supply (Jinadu, 1995). Secondly, contrary to liberal democracy's emphasis on a functional link between electorate and representatives (particularly, the capacity of the former to hold the latter to account for their actions and, if necessary, to dispose them of), in Nigeria such relationship has remained absent and erratic or, at best, driven by the sheer realities of survival in which rich politicians and power brokers hold sway over the political choices of poor voters:

> In the history of electoral politics in Nigeria, the vital connection between elected and electors necessary for a liberal democracy has been missing. That is to say, the political responsibility of elected public office holders, their accountability to the electorate, and the sanctity of the electoral process all remain elusive...the level of political will needed to ensure the realisation of this objective has been absent or has yet to take firm root in the country's political culture (International IDEA, 2001:216-217).

Thirdly, contrary to the practice in developed democracies, in Nigeria elections are always characterised by irregularities, violence and abuse of power: the stakes are always high and volatile. The 1964 and 1983 elections were characterised by massive electoral fraud and wanton violence, resulting in military intervention, lasting for more than a decade before democratic restoration (Diamond, 1988). This trend was repeated in the 2003 election and is likely to be repeated in 2007. Key militating factors in Nigerian elections include sectarian/ethnic politics, and faulty constitutional and institutional engineering.

A final dilemma of Nigeria's democratic and electoral politics, by no means exhaustive, is the symbolic value attached to election, as opposed to its utilitarian values:

> ...there appears to be this general tendency to perceive democracy as all about elections. Resources, time and energy are spent on the conduct of elections. The moment politicians are voted into power and inauguration carried out, they are simply left to carry on with the business of politics and democracy until perhaps another election (TMG, 2003:1).

In Nigeria, election and electors come into the political limelight only once in while. This raises serious doubt in the practical relevance of liberal democracy *per se*.[13] As a result, elections become mere façade for political endorsement and power struggle, competed for and sustained by violence and irregularities. The foregoing is not to suggest that liberal democracy and electoral politics are anathema in Nigeria. On the contrary, the evolution of democracy requires genuine political will and endurance from all stakeholders in state and society. In particular, we need to pragmatically rethink ways of turning around the democratic structures and electoral processes.

Nigeria: a Regressive State

The debate on the travails of electoral democracy in Nigeria is influenced heavily by the character and misfortunes of the Nigerian state and its citizens. Nigeria is cast in the ores of controversy, instability, stagnation and retrogression. It is termed as a 'regressive state'. A regressive state is defined as a fragile state that is drifting backwards, in developmental terms, when its contemporaries are moving forward, irrespective of the speed and level of progress. This descriptive terminology is somewhat congruent with previous conceptual expressions used in the past to describe failing states of Africa: 'the hollow giant' (Rimmer, 2003), 'the collapsed state' (Zartman, 1995), 'the soft state' (Rothschild, 1987), 'the failed state' (Helman and Ratner, 1993), 'the shadow state' (Reno, 1995), 'the quasi state' (Jackson, 1990), 'the weak state' (Forrest, 1994), 'the shrinking state' (Kasfir, 1987), 'the lame leviathan' (Callaghy, 1987), 'the prebendal state' (Joseph, 1987), etc. A running current in most of the foregoing descriptions is that an authoritarian, weak, repressive and elite-serving political culture was gradually but steadily built in most of post- colonial Africa and that the state was diverted by the elite class from serving its part of the social contract. It is worthy of note, however, that the term 'regressive state' is used in a comparative sense to denote a state which, in addition to demonstrating the manifest features of a failing state, spirals backwards in spite of having what it takes to develop – e.g. a relatively developed industrial base, abundant natural resources, a highly skilled manpower replenished by numerous educational institutions, a huge reserve of unskilled labour, and market etc. One key feature of a regressive state is a selfish political and bureaucratic class, intent on enriching itself at the expense of a deprived mass of society.

It may sound misleading to declare Nigeria as regressive – particularly given the country's relative improvement in economic performance (following available macro-economic indicators) since 1999. Based on official statistics, Nigeria has recorded considerable economic growth in recent years (see chapter 1 in this volume by K. Omeje). However, official records in Nigeria are oblivious of key determining factors of poverty and underdevelopment: for instance, they do not reflect official corruption, communal and political violence, or real life conditions of peasants and those at the lower echelon of society. Too often, official statistics appear to obscure the harsh realities of a subsistence economy.

> 'The Nigerian Ministry of Finance boasts of impressive 6 per cent economic growth in 2005; *but this is growth without a human face, as it is not reflected in the life of the ordinary citizen*. The world's 6th largest oil exporter continues to languish in the bottom quartile of the Human Development Index, with over 70 percent of its population surviving on less than $1 a day (Adebowale, 2007, np; my emphasis)'.

Nigeria's dilemma is rooted in the country's contemporary heritage as a product colonialism which brought disparate communities and political forms into a forced alliance banded by the interest of imperialism, rather than political expediency. As a result, post-colonial Nigeria commonly seen as 'a mere geographic expression' has been anything but stable – it has been riven with fragile democratic orders, a theatre of civil war (1967-70), several military interventions, prolonged military rule and short spans of democratic order. Associated with these, a number of composite primordial factors – ethnicity, religiosity, sectionalism etc – have combined to shape the behaviour of political actors, including voters who are often cajoled and preyed into fake political tendencies by political elites and power brokers.

For most of its post-independence life, Nigeria has operated a federal structure which ought to ensure tolerance and co-existence amongst the country's 300 or so ethnic communities. But this has not been the case as demonstrated by the highly wavering relationship between its three tiers of the federation – federal, state and local government areas – particularly in terms of resource allocation.

Currently, Nigeria comprises a central authority situated in Abuja, the federal capital; 36 states, including the Federal Capital Territory (FCT) and 774 Local Government Areas (LGAs). Each of the 36 states and their constituent LGAs are demarcated into National Assembly constituencies. Each state elects three senators and an average of 10 House of Representative members to form the bicameral National Assembly. At the federal centre, therefore, elected representatives drawn from the states and LGAs, run the affairs of the nation. Also, at states and LGAs – the middle and lowest levels of the federation – there are elected representatives that run public affairs at those levels. Each of the 36 states has a *Governor* and a *State House of Assembly*. The former is elected for a maximum of two four-year terms and serves as the Chief Executive of the state. The latter elected in the same terms as national assembly members but are drawn from smaller local constituencies that are drawn from LGAs. The total number of assembly members in each state is tangent on the total number of LGAs that a state has, its population, geographic size etc. Each state has between 24 and 40 assembly members who are elected for renewable four-year term. The final tier of federation – judiciary – is non-political and professional in nature and its organisation and conduct is therefore not subject to election.

It is worthy of note, however, that at both national and local levels, politics is murky game influenced largely by primordial factors such as ethnicity, religiosity and sectionalism or crude economic gains – allegations abounds, for instance, that most, if not all, representatives struggle to make the most of economic benefit during their tenure through corrupt practices such as with-holding deliberation on or passage of bills from the executive until they are induced with material reward such as bonuses, increment of salary and allowances and award of contract approved for their constituencies.. As a result, the passage of each legislation or policy is bereft with controversies. Out of this emerges the dominant political interest promoted by a heterogeneous section of the political class who seems to dominate the game by uniting across individual generational, cultural and political difference, all of which are the dividing force of other sections of the society.

A key contested question, with huge implications for politics at all levels of the federation and in all arms and tiers of government, relates to fiscal federalism. It is singled out here because of pivotal significance. The Nigerian state 'receives between 70-80 per cent of its resources from oil industry' (Zalik, 2004:404). Given the centrality of Nigeria's petroleum wealth, the struggle to control central power and, with it, the structures of resource distribution, has defined the nature of national resource politics. Oil wealth has contributed to layers of contradictions. First is the contradiction between foreign capital, which almost wholly controls Nigeria's extractive economy, and the local state – the latter struggling to maintains its materialist link with foreign capital and sustain its 'cut' through patronage.

Secondly, Nigeria is bedevilled by conflict over access to and distribution of power between fractions of the dominant political classes, in particular, between those in control of state power and those vying to penetrate the corridors of power and political relevance. A third factor inducing conflict in Nigeria is conflict over scarce resource and the means to control it. For many years, Nigeria has witnessed sectarian and resource clashes between the agents of the state – those perceived to be tapping the gains of petroleum wealth – and those who feel economically deprived, politically marginalised, or whose environment and livelihood are affected by oil extraction and environmental pollution. 'Because the Nigerian state controls access to the nation's disposable wealth in the form of revenue from petroleum production, [this] has provoked intense resentment [by marginalised communities] in southern Nigeria towards a system of governance widely viewed as biased, exploitative and repressive' (Joseph, 1999, p. 361).

Nigerian oil wealth derives mainly from the Niger Delta region – its proceeds are then 'shared' across the whole country. The contested nature of the revenue sharing formula from Nigeria's federation account has led to long-standing feuds between the federal state and regions/states with disproportionate natural endowments, in particular, 'oil-bearing communities' whose environment and livelihood are devastated by oil exploitation with no attempt, from the part of the state, to address the destruction caused by exploitation through environmental conservation, reconstruction and social welfare provisioning. A key example of resource conflict in the Niger Delta is the one being staged by the Ijaws and Itsekiris demanding 'fair share' from the federation reserves (see Omeje, 2004; Ikelegbe, 2001 for details). Here too, the state has been involved in repressing, on behalf of domestic and foreign capital, popular protests and dissent emerging from civil society groups (see Naanen, 1995). Where the productive activities of oil multinationals are threatened by worker militancy or mass protests, the coercive instruments of the state are often applied in containing them. In doing so, blanket repressive measures adopted by the state have blurred the boundaries between different forms of protest – oil and non-oil related; minority rights and ethnic rights; workers' and mass protests etc.[14]

The state and, in particular, ruling fractions of the petty-bourgeoisie, are often blamed for this failure. Omeje argues that millions of dollars channelled, often through corrupt biddings, into turn-around maintenance of Nigeria's local refineries have not yielded any positive outcome. He blames the Nigerian ruling class for promoting oil importation and sabotaging subsidised domestic refining: 'the importation of refined petrol on behalf of the state is a highly rewarding business for some of the influential members…of the political regime, just one of the numerous contradictions of Nigeria's highly dependent mono[cultural] economy' (Omeje, 2004:427).[15] The failure of the state to cater for peoples' needs has generated popular protests for economic and political change and such protests coalesce into struggles for democratic reform.

The Travails of Electoral Democracy in Nigeria: Critical Diagnosis; Constructive Prescriptions

> Nigeria has a long history of electoral rigging and fraud that have been frustrating the wishes of the people to choose who exercise power. Precisely because of this history, elections in the country have often been associated with political tensions and indeed violence and crises. The outcome of many elections in Nigeria have been so contested that the conditions for the survival of democratic order have been compromised (Ibrahim, 2006:5).

Nigeria offers a complex testing ground for the practice of liberal democracy and electoral politics. It provides no less controversial ground for other political projects such as federalism and secularism. Yet, history has revealed that in Nigeria political and developmental projects are better planned than executed – they are often couched in flowery utopian rhetoric but hideously executed. Key examples of projects that have plummeted, stagnated or remained uncertain include the expensive transition-to-civil-rule programmes initiated by military regimes, various development plans (1st, 2nd, 3rd, etc) and visions

(Vision 2010) whose lifespan are contingent on the political regimes than initiated them. The point is that most political projects seem to have failed because of the lack of political will and transparency – particularly of the ruling class who are motivated by their material and communal inclinations rather than any sense of nationalism.[16]

Nigeria has undergone several democratic renewals – often following prolonged military rule. Almost always, democracy has not been consolidated.

Table 3.1: Democratic Renewals in Nigeria: An Endless Game

Democratic Regime	Period	Democracy Consolidated?	Remark
Balewa	1960-1966	No	**Key Symptoms:** Political elites were unable to agree on rules of the game and politics was bedevilled by ethnicity, political victimisation, violence, and zero-sum approach to power. **Repercussions:** In 1966, young 'southern' military officers led by Major Chukwuma Nzegu Kaduna violently toppled the democratic regime assassinating many notable political figures, particularly from the 'north'. The coup was foiled and General Johnson Thomas Umunakwe Aguyi Ironsi, the highest ranking military officer took over power. Successive military regimes took over power until 1979 when Nigeria returned to democracy led by President Shehu Usman Aliyu Shagari.
Shagari	1979-1983	No	**Key Symptoms:** Democracy was hampered by elite bickering, election irregularities, corruption, ethnicity, favouritism, and nepotism and an abhorrent culture of zero-sum politics amongst political elites. **Repercussions:** Following a spiralling economic crisis and hotly contested violent elections in 1983, the military led by General Muhammadu Buhari toppled the Government of Shagari. A succession of military remained in power till 1999.
Obasanjo	1999-date	No	**Key Symptoms:** Separation of power remains erratic; a number of institutions e.g. constitution, electoral law, etc, remain faulty and contested; corruption, violence, ethnicity, and religious intolerance thrive at a monumental scale. The rise of political Islam and Shari'a law in many northern states has endangered rhetorical secularism enshrined in the 1999 constitution. **Repercussions:** The future is highly unpredictable. Military 'hangovers' beset the country's fledgling democracy – particularly the inheritance of military's

			violent and autocratic style of governance.
Yar'Adua	2007-Date	Remains to be seen	**Key Symptoms:** Most of the anomalies that character Obasanjo era are 'inherited' by this government – itself widely seen as midwifed by the outgoing President **Repercussion:** Democracy has been seemingly 'saved' but remains at the mercy of identified prevailing factors. Controversies surrounding the conduct of the 2007 Elections are likely to undermine this government. The future is highly unpredictable.

In the following sections, I examine the key factors bedevilling Nigeria's current democratic era. These factors have remained recurrent in past democratic experiences and constitute the bottom line

Popular Imaginations of Democracy

As noted above, in Nigeria, perhaps more than elsewhere, there is a flawed perception of democracy: it is closely linked to, indeed equalled with, the concept of election. For instance, consider the following statements by two Nigerian citizens regarding their perception of the link between democracy and election in Nigeria:

> Everywhere in Nigeria, there is a craze for election as if it is the only political tool needed for achieving Nigeria's democracy. Much as election is important to sustaining democracy, it is not the only institutions required for democracy. This perception [election equals democracy] has set a dangerous precedent: democracy [election] comes once in four years! (Mr Nadaba, a civil activist, Interview held in Abuja 15th August 2003).
> As far as I am concerned, election is the key thing in our democracy. Win election, you are sure to play role in our democracy. Loose election, you are an outcast. If you want to influence public policy or get power, go to the polls. Otherwise, forget it (Mr Jide, an elected representative and former military personnel, Interview held in Lagos, 13th January, 2003).

The first statement cautions against the tendency to equate democracy with election. However, it is a rare imagination amongst majority of Nigerians. On the other hand, the second statement which is common amongst Nigerians sees no fault in equating democracy with election. Both statements draw attention to the need to recast popular imagination on both democracy and elections: election is an important component of democracy, but democracy is much more than periodic election.

Popular perception of democracy is wrongly-pitted and influenced by the state, its agencies of mass media and political socialisation, as well as by Nigeria's power-obsessed political class. Nevertheless, Nigeria's vibrant civil society and independent media have been struggling to counter wrong impressions of political concepts and educating Nigerians to a proactive viewpoint of democratic institution. For instance, in the run-up to the 2007 elections, many civil society organisations – Transition Monitoring Group, Electoral Reform Network, Citizens Forum for Constitutional Reform, the Nigeria Labour Congress, the Civil Liberties Organisation etc – have been deeply involved in voter education projects that target Nigerians at the grassroots levels. However, civil society's voter education and mass mobilisation drive is often limited because they are periodic, selective (not able to reach all and sundry), and far less effective than the influence of 'money', 'primordialism' and 'prebendalism' on the psyche of the ordinary Nigerian: 'money talks', as the popular statement goes, and with money politicians and incumbents have a licence to toy around with how Nigerians perceive and practice their democratic rights.

The Party System

The Nigerian party system is perhaps the most is dynamic and fast changing of all democratic institutions in the country. It is a volatile theatre and breeding ground for Nigeria's crisis of governance and democracy, a product of Nigeria's amorphous and crises-ridden political history (see Sklar, 1963; Diamond, 1988; Agbaje, 1997 for a historical overview). In the context of Nigeria's party system since 1999, its density grew from three political parties[17], who participated in the 1998/99 elections, to thirty in the 2003 elections. Several factors were responsible for this phenomenal growth. First, having being influenced, if not imposed, by the military in 1998, the then existing triadic party system was generally seen as unconventional and lacked the sufficient space for representing the diverse political interests of Nigerians. Secondly, in the context of real multi-party system admonished by liberal democratic tradition, the triadic party framework appeared to be insufficient to accommodate the aspirations marginalized political elites and pressure groups who became unhappy with the system and sought to form political platforms to facilitate direct participation in the democratic process.

Thirdly, and subsequent upon the foregoing factors, concerted pressures from several political actors, including civil society groups such as the Electoral Reform Network (ERN), Citizens Forum for Constitutional Reform, (CFCR), and Transition Monitoring Group (TMG) and others, impacted in prevailing on the political establishment and INEC to accept the idea of registering more parties as a reinforcement of the country's multi-party system. Subsequently, the existing ban on the registration of more parties was formally lifted by INEC in 2001, albeit with strict, even insurmountable, conditions. On 23rd June 2002, out of the 34 political associations that applied for registration, INEC used its constitutional powers to register only three.[18] This sparked a court action spearheaded by Chief Gani Fawehinmi, a veteran lawyer, human rights activist and the leader of one of the unregistered parties – Nigeria Conscience Party (NCP). On November 8, five of the un-registered parties, including NCP, eventually succeeded in getting a favourable court verdict, which compelled INEC to repeat the party registration exercise. This led to the registration of 24 more parties[19] on December 3. This development was described by one civil society organisation as a triumph of the freedom of association and multi-party system in Nigeria (CRP, 2003, p. 15). In the run up to the 2007 general elections, more parties have emerged, often following skirmishes between ambitious politicians within existing parties. A key example is the Action Congress floated by the Vice President Atiku Abubakar following his fall-out with the ruling PDP or, more precisely, the President.

As opposed to the existing dominant parties (AD, ANPP & PDP), most 'new' parties[20] registered represent marginalised segments of the political class (including some political ambitious civil society activists) intent on delving into the competitive power struggles. With the probable exception of AD whose support base was decimated by nascent political tendencies emerging from the expansion of the party space, the existing dominant parties are known to have upper hand (compared to weaker new ones) in the 2003 elections – having participated and fielded representatives into elective posts in previous elections and consolidated their support since the return of democracy in 1999. This perhaps explains why 10 of the 27 'new' parties did not field any candidate for the presidential elections in 2003 (EU-EOM, 2003, p. 8). In terms of membership, 'some [of the 30 new parties] have fewer than 30 members. The [so-called] "memberless" parties are hard pressed in the struggle to field candidates everywhere' (Iloegbunam, 2003:7). This vindicates the claims that that these new parties emerged primarily to provide opportunity for their founders to reinvent their political profile and to negotiate favourable grounds for self-centred political bargain and trade-offs, rather than providing a genuine basis for productive political engagement and/or genuine participation in competitive elections.

A trend that is most visible in the emergence and existence of all political parties in Nigeria post-1999, and a recurrent bane of Nigerian political system, is that their membership and leadership reflect ethnic and regional tendencies. To overcome this, most constitutions (notably the 1979, 1989 and 1999) mandated parties to cross local primordial boundaries and reflect the federal character in membership and fielding candidates for elective posts. However, the fact remains that parties reflect the sectarian coloration of dominant figures within them. As noted by Ikhenemho Okomilo,

> Parties have set agenda for ethnic politics, with the Alliance for Democracy (AD) promoting the interest of Yoruba South West and All Nigeria Peoples Party (ANPP) rooting for the Hausa/Fulani north while the All Progressive Grand Alliance (APGA) is carrying the Igbo banner (2003:8)

Though Okomilo notes that the ruling Peoples Democratic Party (PDP) 'has a strong national character, drawing membership from all sections of the coutry' (*ibid*), this observation is oblivious of PDP's character as a party of choice for dominant political elites who temporarily shed their sectarian tendencies in the interest of power struggle and sustenance of status quo. Okomilo is also seemingly unmindful of the fact that the power brokers in PDP strategically evoke primordial appeals (for instance, Obasanjo's Yoruba, Christian status in the South West; Atiku's Hausa Muslim status in the north), far more than the so-called 'ethnic parties', in maximising PDP's political loots. Needless to say, no party in Nigeria has yet overcome sectarian and primordial divisions.

It is thus reasonable to argue that contrary to conventional wisdom party politics in Nigeria is essentially divisive, and at the mercy of ethnic politics. Similarly, parties are floated for power, rather than democratic engagement *per se*. This contrasts sharply with the reality in advanced liberal democracies where parties exist for a host of reasons – some of which are quite marginal to mainstream politics. This irony was exposed by Chuks Iloegbunam in the context of Nigerian elections, when the stakes for political posts were highest and parties provide the only route of accessing power:

> In other countries [of Europe and America], you would find political parties uninterested in attaining a governorship position, let alone presidency. Sometimes the Green Politicians are solely interested in campaigning on environmental issues, fielding *no* candidates for any election...Of course, people everywhere are aware of political parties interested in no other matter than the strengthening of gay rights.
>
> In Nigeria, however, the establishment of a political party is synonymous with the gunning for presidency and gunning for every seat in contention right down to the local council level (Iloegbunam, 2003:7; emphasis added)

Distribution and Separation of Power

A healthy democracy is predicated on a functional separation of power between 'tiers', 'levels' and 'arms' of government. Nigeria offers an extreme antithesis of this idealism. The country operates a presidential system of government with seemingly functional provisions for check and balance between the three arms of government – the Presidency, National Assembly and Judiciary – as enshrined in the 1999 Constitution. At the apex is the office of the president, with the constitutional power of the Head of State, Chief Executive and Commander-in-Chief of the armed forces of the Federal Republic, albeit by no means absolute in exercise of power (FRN, 2000). Constitutionally, both the legislature and judiciary exist not only to complement the executive in the exercise of power and pubic service, but also to checkmate each other against tempting abuse of power. For instance, subject to the scrutiny and approval of the national Assembly (NA), the President is empowered by the constitution to appoint members of cabinet and other high level political posts.[21] However, there are allegations that this provision is often abused by the President as a means of political reward and/or punishment, in line Nigeria's prebendal politics. Reminiscent of Nigeria's age-long political impasse, separation of power and inter-governmental relations have remained dysfunctional. Consequently, none of the arm has functioned efficiently and, overall, the turnover of policies and legislations has been erratic and politically contested.

In several respects, power in Nigeria is disproportionately distributed and exercised. First, at the governmental level, the executive (in both state and federal tiers), have arrogated more power to themselves to the detriment of the legislature and even judiciary. This has too often resulted in bitter rivalry between the Presidency/state executives and respective legislative houses – as for instance, regarding the passage of key bills on appropriation, executive power of expenditure, security and corruption. Secondly, the federal government reserves more power than state and local government levels, with implications for the stability of Nigeria's federal formula and, by extension, democratic stability. This is argued to be a key defect of the Constitution (1999): 'although it is normally a federal constitution, it gives too much power to the federal government in relation to state governments while leaving the third tier of government (i.e. local government) literally at the mercy of state governments' (Agbaje, 2004:209). In addition to faulty provisions in relations to separation of power, the 1999 Constitution has several other defects – see below.

The State of the Constitution

In Nigeria, constitutions have always been a subject of controversy. This is perhaps because most Nigerian constitutions emerged from the vestiges of undemocratic structures and dictatorships. The processes leading to the writing of most constitutions were arbitrary. In the case of the 1999 Constitution, for instance, it was written at the behest of an outgoing military regime (the Abubakar Junta) that was intent of bequeathing a 'constitution' in the absence of one. The defect of the

1999 Constitution was obvious even at the on-set of the current democratic order in 1999. Since then, both the Presidency and National Assembly have set numerous machineries to review the Constitution – albeit to no avail. In 2001, the President inaugurated the Presidential Committee on the Review of the 1999 Constitution. A draft report of the Committee submitted to President Obasanjo in 2002 was immediately condemned by the Nigerian opposition and civil society – particularly, the Citizens Forum for Constitutional Reform (CFCR) and the Centre for Democracy and Democracy (CDD) – who observed that the committee set up to review constitution did not reflect the aspirations of critical segments of Nigeria. Hence, they argued, the proposed review document did not address fundamental issues that beset the 1999 Constitution. Amongst the key criticism of the 1999 constitution, advanced by Nigerian civil society, include (a) disproportionate arrogation of power to the executive at the expense of other arms of government; (b) provision of higher authority to the federal government at the expense of other tiers of Nigeria's federation; (c) a controversial provision on Nigeria's secularism allowing states and political actors to politicise religion; (d) faulty preamble ('we the people of Nigeria') when in reality the constitution was written by an outgoing military regime; (e) Lack of affirmative provision, particularly on gender-sensitive language and incentives that ought to allow equal participation of women and men in appointive and elective posts; (f) Poor provision on fiscal federalism; (g) control of natural endowment, particularly land, by the federal government; (h) excessive control by the federal government of key democratic processes such as party formation, elections, and authority over electoral agencies etc.

In view of the foregoing, both the CFCR and CDD have carried out numerous popular surveys and conferences aimed at democratising the constitution and making it worthy legal reinforcement for Nigeria's search for a viable democratic order. The CFCR and its affiliates noted that a new constitution for Nigeria should be sensitive to the following principles:

- *Inclusivity* – All segments of the Nigerian society should be represented and their views reflected in the design, drafting and enforcement of a new constitution. This includes minority groups, sub-nationalist movements, students, the armed and security forces, the illiterate, the disabled, the poor, the rural dwellers, the youth, professionals, trade unions, religious groups, traditional rulers, community organisations, prisoners, human rights organisations, pro-democracy groups, political parties, cultural organisations etc. The need for an inclusive constitution derives from the fact that it enshrines the legitimate aspirations of entire society, rather than a section of it. Needless to say, an exclusive constitution is a recipe for domination and anarchy.

• *Diversity* – This entails the challenge of crafting a constitution that is responsive to a plethora of interests and identities – ethnic, culture, linguistic, religion, gender etc – which constitute Nigeria. 'It is the responsibility of the country's leadership and those leading the process to ensure that this diversity is reflected. If this diversity is not reflected, the final document cannot claim to be democratic, legitimate and reflective of popular view' (Igbuzor, 2002:11).

• *Participation* – This entails the provision of diverse and sufficient mechanisms for involving wide-ranging sections of society at all levels of constitution-making. 'Those leading the process must ensure that they put mechanisms in place such as accepting oral memoranda; organising debate and discussion in local languages and aggressive publicity to make sure that people participate in the process' (Igbuzor, 2002:11). Participation by all fractions of society is essential, it is argued, to take on board a broad range of interests and, by extension, avoid tyrannical tendencies from groups who are likely to corner the constitution-making process. A participatory approach, it is argued, provides the best means of avoiding marginalisation, alienation, domination and apathy.

• *Transparency and Openness* – The process of constitution-making – as well as the constitution – 'must be transparent and open and must be seen by all to be so'. Pervasive practices, such as 'hidden agenda' or 'no go areas' which have plagued previous constitutions should be avoided. Instead, every issue of constitutional importance should be open for discussion and dialogue to allow for tolerance and consensus-building.

• *Autonomy* – It is argued that there should be an independent body responsible for reviewing or drafting the constitution. Ideally, this body should be free from undue influence, particularly from those who are in charge of power. Ideally, such a body should be established by an act of the National Assembly; its structure and activities should be transparent and open, and its output must be free from any improper influence.

• *Accountability* – An autonomous institution charged with the responsibility of reviewing the constitution must have leverage to report to parliament and the people. That is, it must not work at the behest of a specific individual or governmental body – such as the president or a ministry. To achieve this, it is argued, the body must be managed by reputable and merited individuals who are willing and able to defend the constitutional process. The body must be sufficiently funded by statutory grant from public revenue, free from bureaucratic limitations and accountable to the people, or their delegation.

• *Legitimacy* – This entails a popular acceptance of a constitution by the entire society, as representing their wishes and aspiration for building a sustainable democratic society. To achieve this, it is argued that a national plebiscite should be conducted to gauge the popularity of a draft constitution. The document passes the test of popular acceptance if voted favourably by at least 51% or more of voters. 'The referendum will further popularise the contents of the constitution and give the people the opportunity to review the draft constitution and be sure that politicians have not eliminated their collective views' (Igbuzor, 2002:13).

The foregoing principles constitute ideal propositions which, if followed to the letter, will enable Nigerians to emerge with an acceptable constitution. In spite of the disagreement between the Nigerian civil society and government on the nature of the constitution and strategies for reviewing it, there is a relative consensus on several fundamental issues. For instance, it is agreed that the 1999 constitution is unsuitable, in its current form, and needs to be re-written to make it sensitive to the expansion and consolidation of democracy. Nevertheless, the 1999 Constitution, which remains unchanged – in spite of numerous reviews – is likely to remain so with huge implication for democracy. In sum, it could be argued that the state of the constitution in Nigeria is terrible and not conducive for the growth of democracy (see also Egwu, 2002).

Militarism and Civil-Military Relations

It is perhaps paradoxical that all attempts at democratic transition in Nigeria since its independence in 1960, have been determined and implemented by the ruling faction of the military, the very managers of institutionalised violence (Obi, 2004:4).

The Nigerian state has seemingly been emancipated from the strangulating grip of military dictatorships of yesteryears. The 'dark years' of military dictatorship is reminisced for all the wrong reasons.

With the restoration of democracy in 1999, the foundation has seemingly been laid for an enduring democracy, in particular, the inviolable supremacy of civil democratic order over the military and security institution. No doubt, the Constitution enshrines, if literally, strict provisions on the subservience of the military and security institutions to civil democratic order. In addition, the Obasanjo administration has since its inception been bent on security sector reform by setting mechanism for ensuring their submission to, and respect for, Nigeria's civil democracy. Two key steps taken by the civilian government are worth noting. First, democratic and human rights education have been aggressively pursued amongst the rank and file of the military and security agencies, with a view to indoctrinating them to the ethos of human rights and rule of law. Secondly, the government is reported to have 'flushed-out' (compulsorily retired) 'high-risk' officers in the Nigerian armed and security forces. High risk officers are those who have held political positions in the past military regimes and are therefore perceived to be prone to consider a military coup given the slightest opportunity.

It is arguable, even doubtful, if the foregoing steps are sufficient to forestall future military coups or tame ambitious elements within the Nigerian military. It is premature to predict that the Nigerian military will not carry out a coup in future. Nevertheless, in the meantime Nigeria and the international system are probably in no mood for military dictatorship of the 1960s and 1990s. Therefore, it is reasonable to assume that military coup is a remote possibility, but cannot be ruled-out if the necessary excuses are created for staging one.

If coups are a remote possibility in Nigeria, the country still suffers from the debilitating impacts of militarism with implications for democracy. Nigeria's unstable democracy has been, and still is, held captive by 'military hangover' in at least two key respects: (a) the impact of military's 'barrack culture' on society-in-general and (b) the repercussions of the military institution on political society, particularly the political class. In terms of the impact of military hang-over on society, Ojo (1999) has documented that military norms, attitudes and language are pervasively prevalent in the streets of Nigeria. This is very much the case even after the military men have retreated to their barracks, mostly located within the vicinity of local neighbourhoods. Similarly, in study commissioned by the Centre for Democracy and Development to examine the impact of the military in

Nigerian polity, its authors Agozino and Idem reported that the average Nigerian citizens behave likes a military person – a zombie in civilian attire: s/he is violent, might-driven, chaotic and brutish. They conclude:

> It is clear [from the study] that the dominance of military rule for much of Nigeria's post-colonial era has resulted in the creeping militarisation of society and a systematic erosion of viable institutions, which should ordinarily from the back borne of any democratic process" (Agozino and Idem, 2001:5).

The CDD study confirms an earlier observation of Ibrahim (1997) writing in the peak of military dictatorship – suggesting that even after leaving power the military tends to have a virulent effect on Nigerians and their institutions:

> Military rule has strongly impacted on the country's cultures and institutions…[it] impacts negatively in society by generalising its authoritarian values which are in essence anti-social and destructive of politics…military regimes have succeeded in permeating civil society with their values – both the formal and military values of centralisation and authoritarianism and the informal lumpen values associated with 'barrack culture' and brutality that were derived from the colonial army (1997:160-161).

A second impact of militarism is on the Nigerian political class. Apparently, some elements of the Nigerian politicians and elected representatives are ex-military personnel, former appointees of military regimes, power brokers and/or staunch military loyalists. A sizeable number of these political actors demonstrate military bias and 'barrack culture' in their political activities. Key actors with military connection include the President, ministers, members of the Senate and House of Representatives, as well as state Governors. Their approach to politics is quite militaristic and dictatorial. For instance, President Obasanjo was heavily criticised and his military background blamed for his approach to the Odi Massacre in 1999 when federal soldiers invaded the town on the orders of the President in response to 'breach of security' by clandestine civil militia forces who were alleged to have taken cover in the town.[22]

Institution Building and Reform

Building and reforming state institutions, to make them responsive to the nascent challenges of democracy, is a key to democratic transformation and consolidation. In Nigeria, democratic institution-building is closely associated with military regimes and the state. Paradoxically, some of Nigeria's enduring state institutions are built by the military, even though they too are always characterised by controversies. Key examples include the creation of new states and local governments areas; party system; the constitution and its concomitant structural provisions; electoral commissions etc. At issue are: (a) the dominance of the military – an hierarchical, autocratic, and command-driven institution – in the building and reform of democratic institutions (b) the carry over of military culture and orientation to a new democratic dispensation and (c) the seeming incapacity of succeeding 'democrats' to fundamentally restructure and rebuild institutions which are bequeathed by the military, to make them responsive to the challenges of democratic expansion.

A key example is the Independent National Electoral Commission (INEC). INEC is the central institution that is directly responsible for the administration of elections and all related functions. It came into existence, in its current form, following the promulgation of Decree No 17 of 5th August 1998. The decree, which reinforces other enabling laws, specifically Section 153(f) of the 1999 Constitution, empowers INEC to organise, undertake and supervise all national and state-level elections – Presidential, National Assembly, Gubernatorial, State Assemblies.[23] It is also empowered to conduct related functions such as registration of voters, political parties and candidates; monitoring and regulation of the activities of parties; and the enactment of bye-laws and the provision of guidelines to regulate the conduct of elections.

However, as a public institution formed and controlled by the state, the neutrality of INEC as an electoral umpire has always been a subject of controversy. Nigeria's civil society and opposition parties have questioned INEC's ability to conduct free and fair elections, indicting it of serving dominant political interests. An independent enquiry after the 1998/99 Elections justified such reservation:

> The Nigerian state has a responsibility to provide adequate logistics [and other provisions] for the INEC to successfully discharge its

statutory duties of organizing and conducting elections. This responsibility does not mean that the state authorities should exert undue influence on the election process; their's should be only a supporting role, with INEC making all the policy decisions, and state authorities assisting in carrying them out. However, this relationship can easily become inverted...In consultation with INEC, it became clear that its independence status is not properly safeguarded. In the series of transitional elections culminating in the handover of the Government to civilian control...INEC feels that its performance was compromised ...[and] therefore unable to safeguard the integrity of the election process" (International IDEA, 2000:222).

INEC's plethora of problems is manifest in its performance during elections (see chapters 1, 4, and 9 in this volume).

The Electoral Process

The Nigerian electoral process is a dynamic, evolving and controversial one and subject of constant calls for reform (Abubakar, 2003; Cook, 2003; Okosun, 2003). Apparently, the electoral process is robust, albeit in principle, but operates at the behest of INEC allegedly controlled by the President. INEC serves as the ultimate umpire of the electoral process; it engages in several activities aimed at regulating the overall conduct of all stages of the election – release of guidelines governing party primaries, conventions and campaigns; procurement of logistics necessary for the elections; recruitment and training of *ad hoc* election staff to reinforce it existing manpower; voter education, voter registration; registration of political parties, accreditation of election monitors and so on. In practice, INEC has proved to be quite ineffective, particularly in regulation the expansion of party political space; party funding; internal democratic practices within parties etc. Key reasons cited for INEC's incapacity include:

- Its dependence on the government, particularly the Presidency, who appoints Electoral Commissioners and control funding of the commission. There is a need to reform INEC to make it more independent and financially autonomous.
- Its inefficient and selective stance on the regulation of political parties and politicians. There are allegations that INEC favour the ruling national party in it policies and activities;

- Its rigid bureaucratic orientation particularly towards civil society, the media and pressure groups.
- Recently, its unwillingness to allow international observers to monitor Nigerian elections.

A key indicator of Nigeria's faulty electoral process is electoral legislation. The Electoral Act has been a subject of controversy since 1999. Dissatisfaction with document has been consensual; however attempts to review it have generated disagreements, including legal battles. The first Electoral Act was enacted by the Obasanjo government in 2001 but soon became a source of concern particularly from civil society, marginalised politicians and international observers. It is argued that the Electoral Acts 2001 and amended versions of 2002 and 2003 did not address fundamental issues affecting Nigerian election – such as executive abuse of power, citizenship, party funding, election campaign, election violence etc. Of particular importance is allegation about abuse of legislation as a means of political control: 'it does seem that the easiest means of achieving control of the proverbial political space is through the Electoral Act or indeed any other law dealing with the organization and conduct of elections be it national or local.' [24]

Conclusion: Challenges and Opportunities for Building Democracy

This chapter reveals that building democracy in a regressive state like Nigeria appears to be depressing and disappointing. Nigeria has always performed below expectations in terms of democracy and nation-building. The fault with Nigeria is manifested in the chaotic nature of its nascent electoral democracy. Two symptomatic phenomena are worth considering here. First is the third 'term agenda' – 'a creeping sign of dictatorship' in a democratic era! (Ibrahim, 2006:2). As the second tenure of the current democratic regime came to a close, there emerged a movement for *incumbency continuum* – a move allegedly perpetrated by representatives in power – aimed at amending the 1999 Constitution to allow for a fresh five year single-tenure for executive representatives who have exhausted their constitutional chances. Thanks to counter-third terms moves, particularly from civil society organisations, the 'creeping dictatorship' was crushed as the Nigerian Senate voted against the move. This is an indication of triumph for Nigeria's fledgling democracy: at least, in extreme circumstances, the Nigerian National Assembly can use its power to check the excesses of the executive arm.

The second symptomatic issue is the intensification of power politics in the run-up to 'Election 2007.' According to news reports, failure to secure a 'third term' has led to a determination by the President to influence the up-coming elections, including the arbitrary suspension of perceived and potential enemies from the ruling party, the Peoples Democratic Party (PDP), as well as the imposition of candidates favourable to the president:

> The retired General [Obasanjo] has imposed candidates at the local and state levels, causing widespread disaffection among the losers. Critics accuse him of using the government's anti-corruption squad to intimidate opponents.[25]

The foregoing development should not be a cause for alarm. Democracy and nation-building are evolutionary (sometimes revolutionary) processes that require patience, endurance and selfless commitment and sense of nationalism, not only from the ruling class, but also from the masses. Building democracy requires proactive participation of all citizens and progressive forces. Almost always, the route to democracy is dotted with dangers and opportunities. At issue are the challenges overcoming dangers and patronising opportunities in strengthening Nigeria's fledgling democracy.

The challenges of building democracy are presently explored by Nigerians at all levels of society – from floors of national and state assemblies, conferences, to public rallies. For instance, in February 2007, less than two months to the Nigerian general elections, the newly established American University in Nigeria convened a panel comprising of prominent Nigerian scholars, to explore the up-coming elections and the challenges of democratic sustenance and consolidation. At the meeting, Rotimi Suberu, a professor at the University of Ibadan, advanced key reasons for optimism and pessimism with Nigerian democracy. The reasons for optimism, according to Suberu, are (a) the proactive nature of Nigerian civil society, in particularly it capacity to influence public opinion notwithstanding state control; (b) the presence of a strong political opposition, in the face of strong ruling party (PDP); (c) the relative peacefulness of the military, nourishing hopes of perpetual end to military intervention and (d) the relative success of the new democracy in withstanding crises. On the other hand, Suberu notes the following reasons for pessimism: (i) the incompetence of the institutions charged with carrying out the elections, particularly INEC; (ii), the country's poor record of civilian managed elections; (ii) lack of internal democracy within the political parties; (iv) pervasive doubts about the integrity and sincerity of the incumbent government, and (v) embarrassing profile of Nigeria in relations to the impending insurgency and instability in the Niger Delta.[26] Suberu's points are valid indications of the challenges and opportunities that often trail the road to 'democracy'. To build and consolidate Nigeria's fledgling democracy, all challenges should be frontally confronted – not avoided, obscured or deferred – and every opportunity should be embraced creatively and patriotically. This requires a rebirth of 'a new democracy from below, rooted in the people and a developmental state, representing and reflecting their quest for dignity, equity, welfare and freedom' (Obi, 2004:14).

Notes

1. Cited in International IDEA, 2000:4.

2. Many influential democratic representatives and power-brokers in Nigeria as closely linked to the military institution, whether as former officers or regime loyalists. Soyinka notes that: 'Nowhere in... most other West African countries are the spoils of power thus routinely handed down from villain to villain and extended retroactively to shield past villains' (1997, ibid).

3. Key examples in Africa include Botswana, Comoros and Seychelles who have developed relatively stable democratic systems with a established structures for rule law, personal liberties and civil rule. In the context of Botswana, Gloria Somolekae argues that 'Botswana is a unique case in Sub-Saharan Africa. It is perhaps one of the few countries that upheld a multi-party democratic system at a time when many countries in the region were either under military or one party regime (1998:4). Outside Africa, Papua New Guinea offers a good example of a functional democracy. Indeed, Benjamin Reilly, writing on the success of democracy in Papua New Guinea, describes it as 'an unusual example of an economically underdeveloped 'Third

World' Country which has nonetheless been able to maintain democratic government and meaningful elections (Reily, 2001:60). Unlike Papua New Guinea and other countries, Nigeria seems to have failed in sustaining democracy.

4.   This dilemma forms the theme of a series of meetings and roundtables organised by the Centre for Democracy and Development, a West African civil society Organisation. CDD has been involved in Nigeria's democracy since late 1990s and provided a much needed space to discuss relevant issues on democracy and development in Nigeria and other West African countries. On 21st April 2006, CDD organised a Nigeria Roundtable to discuss the state of democracy in Nigeria as the nation prepares for the 2007 elections. Similarly, on 6th June 2007, it organised a meeting themed *Nigeria at Crossroad* featuring the Assistant Secretary-General of the Nigeria Labour Congress, a key Nigerian civil society organisations and pioneer of its democratic struggles.

5.   Available: http://edition.cnn.com/2007/WORLD/africa/02/27/us.nigeria.ap/index.html accessed 28th February 2007.

6.   For instance, Mamdani has observed that 'to talk of a "western tradition" is necessarily to indulge in a degree of ideological mystification because this was neither homogeneous nor consistent. It varied not only from one geographical location and/or historical period to another, but also from one social class/group to another, and its contradictory character reflected internal struggles' (1990, p.360-361).

7.   Similar discrepancies abound on definitions and practice of the state, market, election etc.

8.   For Instance, Simone Chambers and Jeffrey Kopstein, writing on sectarian associations, describe them as 'Bad civil society' (2001, p. 837-865) arguing that they are counterproductive and cannot be expected to play any useful role in a democracy.

9.   This conceptual choice is informed by the fact that since independence, the substance and orientation of democratic systems adopted in Nigeria, seem to be fundamentally influenced by western-type liberal democratic theory and philosophy. Being a former British colony and its political elites ever closely allied to the metropolitan bourgeoisie, it is not a coincidence that Nigeria's democratic transitional processes - national conferences, constitutional drafting,

institution-building and so on –always produce outcomes that are heavily leaned towards liberal democratic tradition.

10. To be sure, Nigeria possesses the necessary conditions for building a functional social democracy – e.g. a fledgling civil society, a vibrant trade union movement reinforced by an independent media and a rebellious intellectual culture). But the political class and its international guarantors are in no mood to allow the triumph of any political system or policy that carries a hint of the word 'social'. Given this, it is worthwhile to offer a constructive critique of Nigeria's political-system-of-the-day – liberal democracy – rather than propose a radical alternative.

11. Consider, for instance, the controversy following the US Presidential election in Florida in 2001 (see: http://news.bbc.co.uk/1/hi/world/americas/1372065.stm) and alleged scandals in UK local elections in Birmingham in 2005 (see: http://news.bbc.co.uk/1/hi/uk/4410743.stm). These instances suggest that even in developed democracies, election irregularities cannot be ruled out.

12. A more ideal option (and an historically relevant practice) would perhaps be direct 'big tree' election/democracy where communities come together to make public/communal choices. This is rather utopian.

13. Indeed, Joseph Schumpetter, a highly influential liberal theorist admits, to the relief of the critics of liberal democracy that 'democracy does not mean and cannot mean that the people actually rule in any obvious sense of the terms the 'people' and the 'rule' (1943:283). He notes that democracy is an institutionally-mediated system involving a process of competition and compromise between contending elites (see also Luckham and White, 1996:3). Implicit in this is the tendency to obscure the determinative relevance of the people as the essence of democracy.

14. Omeje (2004) describes this strategy as 'oilification' which he defines as a state policy aimed at confusing – or 'oilifying' – the different forms of struggle as a means of illegitimising them and necessitating violent state intervention to 'restore order'.

15. For a further analysis of the contradictions of Nigeria's oil economy see the volume *Oil and Class* edited by Petter Nore and Terisa Turner (1980). In particular, Chapter 10 (by Turner) lays bare the

saboteur role of the "comprador bourgeoisie". For a recent re-look at the subject matter see also Forrest (1995).

16. See, for instance, Egwu 2002 & Igbuzor 2002 for accounts of failure in fiscal federalism and resource control; Paden 2002 for dilemmas of secularism in federal Nigeria; and Olukoshi 1995 for an account of failure in structural adjustment. The list is by no means exhaustive.

17. Old parties include Alliance for Democracy (AD), All Peoples Party (APP, later transformed to All Nigeria Peoples Party [ANPP]) and Peoples Democratic Party (PDP that produced the president and dominate the national legislature and, on average, most lower level elective institutions in the Nigerian federation).

18. The three parties registered in June 2002 are National Democratic Party (NDP), United Nigeria Peoples Party (UNPP) and All Progressive Grand Alliance (APGA). The Chairman of the Commission, Chief Abel Guobadia, stated in a press briefing that other associations failed to satisfy INEC's criteria such as meeting a specified number of registered members, evidence of funding, and national spread among others (see CRP, 2003:14).

19. The 24 parties are National Conscience Party (NCP), Nigeria Advance Party (NAP), Justice Party (JP), Nigeria Peoples Congress (NPC), Democratic Alternative (DA), Progressive Action Party (PAP), Movment for Democracy and Justice (MDJ), Party for Social Democracy (PSD), Peoples Mandate Party (PMP), the Green Party of Nigeria (GPN), Peoples Redemption Party (PRP), Peoples Salvation Party (PSP), National Reformation Party (NRP), Better Nigeria Progressive Party (BNPP), Mass Movement of Nigeria (MMN), Liberal Democratic Party (LDP), African Renaissance Party (ARP), New Nigeria Peoples Party (NNPP), New Democraats (ND), United Democratic Party (UDP), All Peoples Liberation Party (APLP), Community Party of Nigeria (CPN), National Action Council (NAC) and National Mass Movement of Nigeria (NMMN).

20. Genealogically, the terms 'old parties' and 'new parties' may sound rather confusing considering the fact that some of the new parties – such as PRP and NAP – have their progenitors in the first and second republics. Indeed, in the current dispensation the founders and flag bearers of both parties (Alhaji Abdulkadir Balarabe Musa and Dr Tunji Braithwaithe respectively) have been the leaders of these parties and contested elections in the second republic. In this sense, the parties

we now consider as 'old' are far younger than PRP and NAP. Therefore, it is safer to claim that the current classification of parties only makes sense in the context of Nigeria's democratic experience since 1998.

21. Apart from the appointment of ministers, other key political appointments that require the seal of the presidency include Special Advicers/Assistant to the president on diverse issues – some with brief to advice the president on traditional ministerial matters – defence, agriculture, education, legal affairs and so on – but others to advice/assist him on special matters – privatisation, civil society relations, special duties and so on. Cabinet members function as head government ministries and agencies and are responsible to the president but may often be invited to appear before the National Assembly to clarify on specific issues.

22. Text of a Press Conference by Leaders of Human Rights and Civil Society Groups Who Visited Odi, Bayelsa State on Wednesday December 8th 1999 available: http://www.nigerdeltacongress.com/oarticles/Odi%20massacre.htm accessed 4th March 2007.

23. At the state government levels, the Constitution provides for a concurrent electoral body known as State Independent Electoral Commissions (SIECs) to conduct local government elections. SIECs are bedevilled by a greater measure of problem – particularly they are alleged of freely promoting the interest of state governors and their dominant parties.

24. The Vanguard (Lagos) available: http://www.vanguardngr.com/articles/2002/features/law/law230062006.html accessed 3rd March 2007.

25. Reported by in Al-Jazeera available: http://english.aljazeera.net/NR/exeres/8C23E716-EDFF-40CE-B3B2-1BB66E717638.htm accessed 5th March 2007.

26. Unger, Mike 'Panel analyses upcoming Nigerian elections', available: http://veracity.univpubs.american.edu/weekly/021307/021307_nigeriaelections.html accessed 19th March 2007.

References

Abubakar M. A. 'Voting process, collation and results declaration: the need for review' Presentation at the National Conference on *the 2003 General Elections: The Lessons and the Way Forward,* Conference Hall, International Trade Fair Complex, Kaduna, July 28-30, 2003.

Adebowale, Akande, 'Millennium Development Goals' available: http://uk.oneworld.net/guides/nigeria/development?gclid=CNWRvYK 2g4sCFRizEAod4FixGA accessed 10th March 2007.

Agbaje, Adigun. A. 'Nigeria: the prospects for the Fourth Republic' in Gyimah-Boadi, E. (Ed.) *Democratic Reforms in Africa: the Quality of Progress,* Boulder, Col., Lynne Rienner, 2004.

Agbaje, Adigun A. 'Party system and civil society' in Beckett, P. A. and Young, C. (Eds.) *Dilemmas of Democracy in Nigeria* Rochester, NY; Suffolk: University of Rochester Press, 1997.

Agozino, Biko and Unyierie Idem 'Nigeria: Democratising a Militarised Civil Society' *Occasional Paper Series No 5,* London: Centre for Democracy and Development, 2001.

Ake, Claude *Social Science as Imperialism – the Theory of Political Development* Ibadan: University of Ibadan Press, 1979.

Akinola, A. A., 'Issues in Nigerian democracy' *West Africa* 9-15 June, 2003.

Beckett, P and Young, C., (Eds.) *Dilemmas of Democracy in Nigeria,* Rochester: Rochester University Press, 1997.

Callaghy, T. 'The State as Lame Leviathan: The Patrimonial Administrative State in Africa', in Ergas, Z. (Ed.), *The African State in Transition* London: Macmillan, 1987.

Cook, Margie 'Voting process, collation and results declaration: the need for review' Presentation at the National Conference on *the 2003 General Elections: The Lessons and the Way Forward* o Conference Hall, International Trade Fair Complex, Kaduna, July 28-30, 2003.

CRP (Constitutional Rights Project) *Transiting to Democracy: Report on Political Party Primaries for 2003 General Elections in Nigeria* Lagos: Constitutional Rights Project, 2003.

Diamond, L. 'Rethinking civil society: towards democratic consolidation' *Journal of Democracy* Vol. 5(3): 4-17, 1994.

Diamond, L. 'Nigeria: pluralism, statism and the struggle for democracy' In Diamond, L., Linz, J. J. and Lipset, S. M. (Eds.) *Democray in Developing Countries: Africa* Boulder: Lynne Rienner, 1988.

Egwu, Sam 'Contending positions and issues in debating the future of federalism in Nigeria' in Igbuzor, O. and Bamidele, O. (Eds.) *Contentious Issues in the Review of the 1999 Constitution*, Lagos: Citizens Forum for Constitutional Reform, 2002.

EU-OM (European Union Election Observation Mission, Nigeria) *National Assembly Elections 12 April; Presidential and Gubernatorial election, 19 April 2003; State Houses of Assembly elections 03 April 2003 - Final Report* available www.eueom.com accessed 28th January 2007.

Forrest, Jashua B. 'Asynchronic Comparisons: Weak States in Post-colonial Africa and Medieval Europe' in Dogan, M. and Kazancigil, A. (Eds.) *Comparing Nations: Concepts, Strategies and Substance* Cambridge Mass, Blackwell, 1998.

Forrest, Tom *Politics and Economic Development in Nigeria* Boulder: Westview Press, 1995.

FRN (Federal Republic of Nigeria) *The 1999 Constitution* Abuja: Federal Republic of Nigeria, 2000.

Hann, C. and Dunn, E. (Eds.) *Civil Society: Challenging Western Models* London: Routledge, 1996.

Haruna, Mohammed 'People and politics: the president and his credibility problem' available: http://www.gamji.com/ accessed 28th February, 2007.

Helman, Gerald B. and Ratner Steven R. 'Saving Failed States' *Foreign Policy* 89, 1993.

Ibrahim, Jibrin 'Obstacles to democratisation in Nigeria' In Beckett, P. A. and Young, C. *Dilemmas of Democracy in Nigeria* Rochester: University of Rochester Press, 1997.

Ibrahim, J., *Legislation and the Electoral Process: the Third Term Agenda and the Future of Nigerian Democracy* Paper for the Centre for Democracy and Development (CDD) *Nigeria Roundtable*, London, April 2006.

Igbuzor, O., 'Introduction' in Igbuzor, O. and Bamidele, O. (Eds.) *Contentious Issues in the Review of the 1999 Constitution*, Lagos: Citizens Forum for Constitutional Reform, 2002.

Ikelegbe, Augustine 'Civil society, oil and conflict in the Niger Delta region of Nigeria: ramifications of civil society for a regional resource struggle' *Journal of modern African Studies* Vol. 39 (3): 1-24, 2001.

Iloegbunam, C., 'Eye on Nigeria: posters and candidates' *West Africa*, 10 -16 February, 2003.

International IDEA (Institute for Democracy and Electoral Assistance), *Democracy in Nigeria: Continuing Dialogue(s) for Nation-Building*, Stockholm: International IDEA, 2000.

Jackson, Robert, H. *Quasi State: Sovereignty, International Relations and the Third World* New York: Cambridge University Press, 1990.

Joseph, Richard, 'Autocracy, violence and ethnomilitary rule in Nigeria' in Joseph, R. (Ed.) *State, Conflict and Democracy in Africa* Boulder, Col: Lynne Rienner, 1999.

Joseph, Richard *Democracy and Prebendal Politics in Nigeria: The Rise and Fall of the Second Republic* Cambridge: University Press, 1987.

Junadu, L. A. 'Electoral administration in Africa: a Nigeria case-study under the transition to civil-rule process' in Adejumobi, S. and Momoh, A. (Eds.) *A Political Economy of Nigeria under Military Rule: 1984-1993*, Harare: SAPES Books, 1995.

Kabeer, N., *Reversed Realities: Gender Hierarchies in Development Thought*, London: Verso, 1994.

Kasfir, Nelson 'Class, Political Domination and the African State' in Ergas, Z. (Ed.) *The African State in Transition* London: Macmillan Press, 1987.

Kawonise, S. "Normative impediments to democratic transition in Africa" in Caron, B. Gboyega A.and Osaghae E. (Eds.) *Democratic Transition in Africa* Ibadan, Nigeria: CREDU, 1992.

Keane, J. *Civil Society and the State: New European Perspectives* London: Verso, 1993.

Luckham, R. and White, G., 'Introduction: democratising the South' in Luckham, R. and White, G. (Eds.) *Democratisation in the South: the Jagged Wave* Manchester: Manchester University Press, 1996.

Madunagu, E., 'Non-governmental organisations and political parties in the transition to popular democracy in Nigeria: a critique of the new imperialism" In Uya O. E. (Ed.) *Civil Society and the Consolidation of Democracy in Nigeria* Calabar: Institute of Public Policy and Administration, 2000.

Mamdani, M., 'The social basis of constitutionalism in Africa' *Journal of Modern African Studies* Vol. 28(3): 359-374, 1990.

Monga, C., *The Anthropology of Anger: Civil Society and Democracy in Africa* Boulder Col., Lynne Rienner, 1996.

Naanen, Ben 'Oil producing minorities and the restructuring of Nigerian federalism: The case of Ogoni people' *Journal of Commonwealth and Comparative Politics* Vol. 33 No 1: 46-78, 1995.

Nore, Petter and Turner, Terisa (Eds.) *Oil and Class Struggle* London: Zed Press, 1980.

Obi, Cyril 'Nigeria: Democracy on trial' *Occasional Electronic Paper 1*, Uppsala, Nordic Africa Institute, 2004

Ojo, Oluwaseyi 'Military Language and Democratisation in Nigeria' In Olowu, D., Williams A. and Soremekun, K. (Eds.) *Governance and Democratisation in West Africa* Dakar: CODESRIA, 1999.

Okomilo, I., 'Obasanjo, his records and his prospects' *West Africa* 10th-16th March, 2003.

Okosun, Mary Omoye 'Voting process, collation and results declaration: the need for review' Presentation at the National Conference on *the 2003 General Elections: The Lessons and the Way Forward*, Conference Hall, International Trade Fair Complex, Kaduna, July 28-30, 2003.

Olukoshi, A., 'The political economy of structural adjustment programme' in Adejumobi, S. and Momoh, A. (Eds.) *The Political Economy of Nigeria under Military Rule: 1984-1993,* Harare: SAPES Books, 1995.

Omeje, Kenneth 'The state, conflict and evolving politics in the Niger Delta, Nigeria' *Review of African Political Economy* No.101:425-440, 2004.

O'oghorie, I. B., 'Now that elections are over' *West Africa* 2-8 June, 2003.

Paden, J., 'Islam and democratic federalism in Nigeria' *Africa Notes* No. 8, Centre for Strategic and International Studies, Washington DC, March 2002.

Prezeworski, A. *Democracy and the Market: Political and Economic Reform in Europe and Latin America* New York: Cambridge University Press, 1991.

Reilly, Benjamin, *Democracy in Divided Societies: Electoral Engineering for Conflict Management*, Cambridge, Cambridge University Press, 2001.

Reno, William *Corruption and State Politics in Sierra Leone* New York: Cambridge University Press, 1995.

Rimmer, D. 'a hollow giant?' *West Africa* 23rd-29h June 2003.

Rothschild, Donald 'Hegemony and State Softness' in Ergas, Zaki (Ed.) *The African State in Transition* London: Macmillan Press, 1987.

Said, Edward *Orientalism* New York: Vintage, 1979.

Schumpetter, J. A., *Capitalism, Socialism and Democracy,* London: Unwin, 1943.

104

Sklar, R., *Nigerian Political Parties: Power in an Emergent African Nation* Princeton: Princeton: University Press, 1963.

Somolekae, Gloria, *Democracy, Civil Society and Governance in Africa: the Case of Botswana,* Government of Botswana available:http://unpan1.un.org/intradoc/groups/public/documents/CAF RAD/UNPAN009287.pdf accessed 20th March 2007.

Soyinka, Wale, *The Open Sore of a Continent: A Personal Account of the Nigerian Crisis,* Oxford, Oxford University Press, 1997.

Tar, Usman A., Oumar, Saidou B. and Gazali, Kalli A.Y. 'Understanding Democracy: Towards a definition' *J. Soc & Mgt Sci* Vol. 6 (1 & 2) 59-70, 1999.

Tar, U. A. 'Contested Spaces in Democratic Expansion: the State, Civil Society and Voting Public in Neo-liberalising Nigeria' Doctoral thesis, University of Bradford, 2006.

TMG (Transition Monitoring Group) (2003) 'Beyond the elections' *Democracy Watch* Issue No. 15, May 1-May 15.

Udogu, E. Ike, *Nigeria and the Politics of Survival as a Nation State* Lampeter: Edwin Mellen Press, 1997.

White, G., 'Civil society, democratisation and development' in Luckham, R. and White, G. (Eds.) *Democratisation in the South: the Jagged Wave* Manchester: Manchester University Press, 1996.

Zalik, Anna 'The Niger Delta: 'petro-violence' and 'partnership development'" *Review of African Political Economy* No.101: 401-424, 2004.

Zartman, William I. (Ed.) *Collapsed States: The Disintegration and Restoration of Legitimate Authority* Boulder: Lynne Rienner, 1995.

Chapter 4

Elections and Election Rigging in Nigeria: Implications for Democratic Growth

Gani Yoroms

Introduction

Elections have become one of the most important cardinals for instituting modern democracy. It provides the basis for determining who governs, and who ever governs determines the authoritative allocation of values. This therefore, makes election competitive, controversial and conflictual. As a result election in Nigeria is a matter of life and death. Hence a foremost politician in the first Republic Fani Kayode said 'Whether you vote for us or not we will remain in power' (Dudley, 1973:42). This means that election is only a camouflage as it does not actually determine the choice made by the electorates. As a result of this, political contestants take to unconstitutional means to win in election. This has implications for constructing a sustainable democracy in deeply divided societies like Nigeria. In the light of this, this chapter attempts to analyze the linkage between election and democratic growth. On the basis of this, it explains what constitute election and election rigging. This is clearly understood by the sketchy history of election rigging in Nigeria. It further assessed the recent elections and how rigging has become sophisticated to undermine the growth of democracy in Nigeria. The chapter brought out the implications of all these and further made some recommendations.

Elections, Election Riggings and Democratic Growth

Election supposedly is the method by which political leaders are conferred with power and responsibility to govern constitutionally by the citizens as part of the exercise of their political rights. It is a means by which *citizen-electorates* express their political responsibility.[1] There are several methods of conducting election, depending on the nature of the political system. Some elections are conducted through secret balloting while others are done through open ballot system. In other instances it could be by selection, appointment or consensus. Whichever way it takes what matters is whether the process and procedures are duly constitutional, transparent and fairly accepted by the citizen-electorates and the society.

On the whole, election provides the confidence for the citizens to express their political rights in popular political participation by deciding or contributing to the direction of policy. It symbolises popular sovereignty and the expression of social pact between the state and the citizens, which defines the basis of political authority, legitimacy and citizens (Adejumobi, 2000)· Because of the significance of election political parties, sponsors and contestants spend a lot of resources to win. Though resource spending during elections is constitutionally allowed but what makes it worrisome is when resources are used to undermine the constitution by means of rigging in election. Attention is diverted to resources rather the election which should be the precursor for authoritative allocation of values and resource. Ideally the voting behaviour of the electorates should determine the voting pattern (Ofondu, 1994). However, because the system does not create confidence and trust, the political behaviour of the voters and the political contestants are at variance on how to achieve their interest in the course of the conduct of election. Election rigging takes different patterns .It involves electoral manipulations which include among others recruiting juvenile to vote, stealing or vandalizing voting materials, losing of ballot booklets, duplicating of ballot papers, tampering with the materials and voting by impersonation among others.

Rigging is the manipulation of electoral processes in favour of candidates in elections. There are two levels of rigging. These are the rigging process and rigging events. Rigging process is the sequence of steps taken over a period of time planning and scheming to rig elections in favour of a particular candidate. While rigging event is the actual manifestation of rigging on the day voting takes place. The two are mutually reinforcing. Rigging cannot be successful without the support of the Electoral Officers in the Polling stations. The causes of election rigging stem from four main factors. First, there is lack of faith in the system. Many of the political candidates and their sponsors believe the political system cannot last. This fear results from the long period of military intervention in politics. It is believed that there might not be another election for fear of military re-entry into the political arena. Second, loopholes in the conduct of the election necessitated by lack of resources for the electoral officers to effectively cover electoral wards in some impenetrable areas do create room for free-rigging. Third, politics is seen as a business. And as a business it must yield profit. Therefore, winning in an election is like making profit in business. The fear of losing in election after much resources have been invested is appalling. Thus many politicians look for political god-fathers not only to win in elections but also to enhance their chances in the rigging process without being identified. Lastly, the fear of post-election tyranny that might be perpetrated by those who win against opponents make election look like war rather than a political contest. Those who win celebrate their success with intimidating arrogance that make the opponent regrets participating in politics. Thus, the zero-sum politics, which makes the winner to even encircle the constituency of the opponent, makes it difficult for any one to think of failures in politics. This indeed is the bane of the politics of bitterness in Nigeria (Omoruyi, 1992). A further insight by Olurode (1999) noted that:

> ...rigging and manipulation of figures arise from what an individual regard as what constitutes his interest. To win in an elective office in Nigeria is like wining a life-long fortune...most politicians are prepared to buy votes. Purchasing of votes are worthwhile investment. When votes could not be bought outright, rigging results.

It is in the context of the outcome of election that Marxist scholarship does not see election in liberal democracy as sufficient measure for the oppressed to gain political power. Though election could be used as a means to orchestrate the struggle for popular democracy it is seen as a deceptive device by the ruling elite to keep the oppressed from taking their destiny into their own hands. Earlier in his seminal work Miliband noted that democratic claims and the actual political interplay are not coterminous in Britain (Miliband, 1969). Therefore, democracy does not, according to him, exist in Britain as the system prevents rather than facilitates the exercise of popular democratic rule. However, whatever it takes that prevent democratic rule in Britain is different from what occurs in Africa. In the case of Nigeria elite behaviour is antithetical to mass democratic rule and what sustains them is the art of election rigging. This is manifested through the assumption that first, politics is a zero sum game. Secondly, there is lack of normative rule of the game that governs the electoral behaviour or rather there is a low level of institutionalised electoral norms of behaviour. Thirdly, in line with the above, rigging therefore, become a norm and a culture in itself. Thus accordingly, Dudley tries to explain that success of election rigging is part of elite efforts to carve out for themselves an image that appears that their leadership mandate draws its constitutional power from the electorate to the disadvantage of those in opposition. The African state is powerful. As noted: "the state....appropriates the sovereignty of the people ostensibly in the name of the people but with the aim of using the more in service of capital and capitalists and less in the interest of labour and labourers (Amuwo, 2003:4).

Those who occupy the state ensure that personal interests are taken as state policy. Leaders try to maintain themselves and their interests by ensuring that elections are conducted in their favour. Thus, the personalisation of leadership ensures 'status permanence' as a way of officialising the rigging process (Dudley, 1973:42). To achieve this, various electoral malpractices are undertaken. These include the violation of the rules governing the secret voting, the destruction of the ballot boxes of opposing candidates, the introduction of illegal ballot papers, or the prevention of opposing candidates from filling their nomination papers to ensure that one's candidates were 'returned unopposed'. In the second place, support could be bought, either directly through the offer of such inducements as jobs and money, or indirectly through the selective distribution of welfare as epitomized in the statement by Dr. Okpara when addressing the electorate in the dissident areas of the Eastern Region; 'if you want light and water, you will first have to vote for me (Dudley, 1973:42)

In view of this, it is also important to note that electoral rigging has become too sophisticated that various aspects of anti-democratic activities have been concretely built into it. These include, among others:

i) Providing counterfeits ballot box, ballot papers and voting cards,
ii) Giving money to voters to vote for particular party and/or candidate.

iii) Buying off the electoral officers and party agents to manipulate the results for a particular political party or candidate(s)

iv) Changing of the figures of results counted at the polls or collation centres in favour of political parties or candidates.

v) Replacing genuine ballot boxes with fake ballot boxes containing illegal voters' cards.

vi) Stealing or mutilation of electoral materials to avoid the conduct of the election.

vii) Inciting or causing violence at the polling units and/or in the course of election so as to threaten voters from voting or for the elections or the results of the elections to be cancelled.

viii) Attempts by electoral officers, party agents and security operatives to share votes cast in elections among the political parties.

ix) Giving wrong information to the voters on the dates of the elections or voting procedures as to misguide them to vote for a party which is not of their choice, and

x) Creating fear, intimidation and threatening the voting atmosphere.

In summary there exists a rigging triangle which begins with a rigging process leading up to rigging event. Both levels may involve promises of such substance as monetary entreaties, job offers and the use of official facilities to influence one's chances for winning in elections. The third aspect of the triangle is outcome of the rigging process and rigging event which often leads to skimming, political assassination, MOD actions, protest violence and final resolution of the differences by electoral tribunals weather party is favoured by the electoral tribunal or not it works the being process of the next election. Hence an effective rigging on the Election Day is determined on how much is put in the process. Thus the introduction of electronic voting machine is likely to lead to digital rigging. This means that the process of planning for digital rigging in the 2007 election might have started.

Historical Context of Election Rigging

The history of election in Nigeria is generally tied up to election rigging, even in the mundane form of it. The first election, which was direct election in Nigeria, took place in 1923 under the 1922 Clifford constitution. Though there were no evidence of rigging it was clear that the mortgaging of the political rights of the colonised by the colonialists gave a psychological predisposition that access to power was narrow and restricted. Therefore the inability of the nationalists in their

110

struggle to enforce their rights to political participation presents a scenario of what they foresaw from the colonial administrations which requires political brinkmanship. This was because more increasingly the colonialists brought in the concept of divide and rule, which made the nationalities to see the struggle for liberation from different perspectives, especially primordial cleavages. Gradually this began to create the mentality that attaining political power would require sharp competition between ethnic groups rather than between nationalists and the colonialists.

For instance, indirect election was later introduced in 1946 under the Richard's constitution to take care of northern interest where education was low, and indirect rule had taken firm roots. The gap in education was a colonial determination to separate development of regions. This was intended to serve as model of conflict among nationalities which the colonialist would in turn become arbiter. With time, the north and the south began to have different systems of elections. Political parties were regionally formed and had the inbuilt of how to relate with each other and the colonial administration differently. Therefore political parties became active in winning elections, not only to occupy power but also to defend their regional interests. This led to acrimony, riots and violence following the 1953 crisis in Kano between the major political parties-the Northern People Congress (NPC) the Action Group (AG) and the National Council of Nigerian Citizens (NCNC) to control the Federal government. 7 As noted by Anifowose 'the 1959 Federal elections marked the beginning of political competition in Nigerian politics (Remi Anifowose, 1982). Subsequent elections, especially the 1964 and 1965, became engrossed in electoral violence as a result of rigging and malpractices. The 1963 population census figure, which gave the north more constituencies than the other parts of the federation, was one of the kernels for the immediate post independence elections malpractices. However, the 1979 election took place after a long period of military interregnum. So the rigging content of the 1979 elections was insignificant but what was disturbing to the contestants was the way the government of the day handled the elections results.

According to the four Presidential candidates; Dr. Nnamdi Azikiwe, Chief Obafemi Awolowo, Mallam Aminu Kano and Alhaji Ibrahim Waziri; the announcement of Alhaji Shehu Shagari of the NPN as the winner of the controversial presidential election contradicted

Electoral laws because none of the parties or candidates met the requirements of securing 'not less than one-quarter of the votes cast at the election in each of at least two-thirds of all the states in the Federation' (Ofonagoro, 1979:292). The protesting parties wanted an electoral college to decide the finality of the election. The failure to rescind the result led to a legal action in the Supreme Court that resolved the case in favour of Shehu Shagari. It was believed that even if the Electoral College had been inaugurated it would have certainly still favour Shagari because:

> Since the NPN was seen to be full of rich men who had greater access to wealth, it was feared that a resort to an electoral college could be an automatic walkover for the NPN (Adam and Ogunsawo, 1982).

The presidential candidates of the political parties expressed their bitterness over the elections and were given assurances by the outgoing military president, General Olusegun Obasanjo in a meeting, August 20th 1979 that the ruling NPN would create a government of national unity and ensure even development that should work against any act of violence. As a result of this, NPP went into coalition with NPN to form a government of national unity while other political parties decline. Short of this, the NPN government became rascally in ruining the economy and causing social disaffection among the citizenry. It was expected that in subsequent elections the ruling NPN would ensure integrity in electoral organizations. Unfortunately the 1983 elections were nationally devastating that NPN won a landslide victory. The malpractices were so much that criticism of it led to military intervention in late 1983. According to Major General Muhammadu Buhari:

> The shameless rigging and wide spread perversion of the electoral process could not, in all honesty, have been said to have produced a government of the people by the people. What we had, through the manipulated results both at federal and state levels, were governments imposed on the people by the scandalous use of mixture of political thuggery and wide scale bribery... However, it was clear to [our people] that the political leadership that emerged in 1979 showed that it had learnt nothing and forgotten nothing in the years between the first and second Republics...The intervention of the

armed forces, was to arrest the imminent catastrophe which would have been the inevitable result of the course being charted by the politicians (Olagunju *et al*, 1993:64)

The interplay within the military threw up other elections that culminated in the annulment of June 12 1993 election. The 1993 elections remains or it seems to be, the freest and fairest elections Nigeria ever had. The aftermath of the annulment led to the most critical period in Nigerian political history until the death of the architects of the scenario, General Sanni Abacha and Chief M.K.O Abiola. The death of Abacha opened another opportunity offered by the new military junta of General Abdulsalami Abubakar to set up the Independent National Electoral Commission (INEC) which the 1999 constitution empowered to handle the process of elections in Nigeria. INEC has conducted two elections that of 1999 and 2003. The litmus test of INEC performance is the 2007 elections where the transfer of power from one dominant civilian president and party to another. This is important because the scarce of the 1999 and 2003 elections where allegations of rigging was pronounced is still hunting INEC .What really happened in the 1999 and 2003 elections?

The 1999 and 2003 Elections: The Rigging Dynamics

The year 1999 was a period for sober reflection, after a long period of military rule characterised by deceit, corruption and manipulation, which was peaked by the violence that followed the post- June 12 1993 election. The writing on the wall had shown that the transition process was laying the autocratic foundation of Nigeria's forthcoming third republic (Agbese, 1992). Indeed, as the republic was still-birth the country was further plunged into the darkest moment of its political history, which recorded the most gruesome human rights abuses, from 1985 to 1998. The regimes that ruled at that time were similar in their orientations and manifestations; only that one was too overzealous that its track records were easily painted more demonic than the other. Never the less at the death of General Sanni Abacha in June 1998 the political floodgate was opened, according to some religiously inclined scholars, by divine intervention. General Abdulsalami Abubakar became the head of the military junta saddled with the responsibility of redeeming the image of the military by returning the country back to civil rule. The major task was organizing a credible election.

However, General Abdulsalami was faced with the task of managing hanging issues" of the June 12 election when the presumed winner chief MKO Abiola, was locked up in detention. The first step was for him to convince Chief MKO Abiola's immediate constituency, the western part of the country, about his sincerity to return to civil rule. But the problem was how to deal with Abiola, which a section of the North would not like to see as the symbol of the new democratic dispensation. Thus the rigging process that took place under General Abdulsalami's regime was the mysterious elimination or rather death of Chief MKO Abiola from detention. To balance up the death of General Sani Abacha. This paved way for the search of a candidate that was from the South West, Abiola's immediate constituency who could not be rejected by his people, being 'scion of the soil,' and could as well find acceptability by the other sections of the society, especially the North. This was how Chief Olusegun Obasanjo, from the southwest, was thrown up as an alternative candidate in the 1999 elections. Though Obasanjo was not accepted by the south west because he was a northern delight, it however helped to ease out political tension in the country. Hence, though a northern candidate, by affinity the south west cannot disown its own however bad he may be. As the saying goes blood is thicker than water. It would be a serious political miscalculation to do so.

It was expected that after a long period of military rule the electoral process would provide final exit strategy for the military from the body politics though this depended on the political behaviour of the political class, however and unfortunately too, both the military and the political class were interested parties on the transition process. This, therefore, gave room for free rigging at both federal and state as well as in local governments. This was a mutual rigging as the oppositions had the opportunity to retain their constituencies. But because the nation was emerging from the trauma of a long period of military interregnum it was felt that the rigging not withstanding, the elections should be accepted as given; so that the political transition would not suffer set backs. One of the international team of Observers that was skeptical about the election was President Jimmy Carter who was enraged and refused to endorse the 1999 elections results (Kew, 2003). However, for fear of not scuttling the democratic process as done by General Babangida in the June 12 1993 election, most observers decided to make less critical remarks about the 1999 elections, hoping that lapses could be taken care of in future elections (Kew, 2003).

Meanwhile, the election that would remain a case study for the rest of this century in Nigerian political history, by political Scientists and keen observers of Nigerian politics, was the 2003 General elections. This chapter may not be able to critically assess what happened, as there were much to meet the eyes. It is recommended that the Nigerian Political Science Association or any Department of political science in the country should commission a study of this election for the purpose of understanding the changing political behaviour of the Nigerian electorate, if actually normal election took place; and if it did what pattern of voting took place.

Indeed the conduct and outcome of the 12 and 19 April 2003 National Assembly and Governorship/ Presidential elections have become contentious in all the elections in Nigeria. The sophistications of the rigging and the mastery of the manipulations surpassed any attempt in the history of elections in Nigeria. The elections were criticised as ineptitude of the INEC. The election drew the widest attention across the world as several international observers and local monitors were credited to assess the election condemned widespread rigging.

The preparation for the 2003 elections started with the voters registration exercise. The exercise had the largest turnout of voters who spent hours in the harsh weather to register their names. The expectation was that the election would be free and at least fairer because of the seriousness the international community was interested in it .So, it was not necessary the recommendation that praetorian guard is required in checking rigging: 'In future elections, it may be necessary to deploy soldiers and university students and senior staff to administer the elections nation wide, or deploy civil service and military personnel to carry out' (Ofonagoro, 1979:262).

The use of the security personnel in election is intended to give credence to the exercise. But unfortunately, most of the accusations for electoral rigging have been directed at the security personnel and the officers of the INEC, government and party officials of most of the ruling parties, especially the People Democratic Party, PDP. The 2003 election was fraught with rigging because the contestants had no issues to raise to solicit for the support of the electorates. Most of the parties, especially the old ones had no concrete ideological manifestoes. And between the period of the lifting of the ban on electioneering campaign and the election period there was insufficient time for campaign and political polemics, which the electorates expected from the political class.

Therefore, political elites and contestants depended on their money, power of incumbency and the support of INEC to perpetrate the rigging process. First, both INEC and the Presidency attempted to tamper with the electoral law in 2001 and 2002, in order to scuttle the registration of new parties to the advantage of incumbency authority. The Supreme Court overturned this action by granting the new parties the legal rights to register. This led to the over-bloated political parties, numbering up to 50 as at December 2006. The second attempt was the refusal of the presidency to release funds on time to INEC for the registration of voter exercise. At the time the money was released INEC had no enough time than to proceed, as Darren Kew noted, on a 'Hollywood train wreck. Many registration centres were opened days later than scheduled, if they opened at all, often forcing confused citizens to give up the endeavour' (Kew, 2003: p.8). Thirdly, INEC staff were even accused by the INEC, the then chairman Dr. Abel Gubadia for hoarding electoral material, presumably to sell to the highest bidder (Kew, 2003:8). Lastly, according to the petition made against INEC it failed, neglected or omitted, as it was expected of her, to subject the electoral officers in the conduct of elections to an oath or affirmation of loyalty to the Federal Republic of Nigeria, and neutrality in the conduct of election contrary to section 18 of the Electoral Act 2002.This robbed the electoral officers the competence reposed in them to conduct a free and fair election (*The Guardian*, 2003:1-2) There were also reported cases of electoral misconduct by the police, which the Chairman of the Police Service Commission Chief Simon Okeke, promised to investigate (*Daily Trust*, April 23, 2003:1). Meanwhile, most of the incumbents contravened the electoral law by using official facilities to enhance their campaign strategies through rigging process. For instance the 2002 electoral law forbad those seeking electoral offices like the president, vice president, Governors among others, from using the paraphernalia of the state for campaign. However, Most of them would plan state functions to coincide with their political campaign .It was neatly planned in such a way that after state functions the occasion would be turned to campaign arena. As a rigging process it contravened the electoral law.

The alleged governorship rigging in Plateau state remains one of the puzzles of the elections. The ANPP Gubernatorial candidate in the state, Air Cdr. Jonah Jang (retired) had proved that by Governor Joshua Dariye paid N18 million as gratification to Jacob Nwakpa the Plateau state Electoral Commissioner from state government fund. The money was alleged to have been paid into his Bank Account in Abakaliki, Ebonyi state. He made effort to tender the teller of the back account .However, the Electoral Tribunal refused to accept the exhibit on technical grounds. Surprisingly the Independent Corrupt Practices Commission (ICPC) did not also take it as a serious security and corruption issue. In the same vein, how Adolphus Wabara got to the Senate and rose to the post of Senate President without winning in an election remains also a mystery of Nigerian electoral politics. It seems that in view of the contradiction that the ruling PDP had with the National Assembly which almost led to the impeachment of the President during his first tenure, made the party to resolve, that it must have a firm control of the legislature by crook or by hook. The possible way to achieve this was what led to the over bloated rigging process. This was also the pattern that most parties controlling the states adopted to retain their seats except a few that could not withstand the weight of parties that overturned them, especially Ogun, Oyo, Ondo and Ekiti The most gruesome case of rigging was clearly demonstrated in Anambra state. Peter Obi, a gubernatorial candidate of APGA had taken the purported PDP winner of the 2003 governorship election ;Dr Chris Ngige to the Electoral Tribunal over the issue of serious electoral fraud perpetrated by the party and individuals. INEC defended the election of Dr.Ngige as credible and the defence was upheld by the tribunal .However, Peter Obi took the case to the High Court at the time Ngige felled out with his political god-father and his party, PDP; INEC turned against Ngige and produced evidence to the effect that Ngige's election as a governor was fraud ridden. As a result Ngige was removed from office and Peter Obi of APGA was sworn in as Governor. The double-speak by INEC has made the electorate to lose confidence in INEC as an independent electoral umpire.

Unlike in the pre-independence era when soldiers were used in the conduct of elections the military is no longer trusted. In a legal issue raised by General Buhari and others who challenged the April 12 and

19 elections in court, the military was accused for being used to thumb print thousands of ballot papers, allegedly on the instructions of the PDP. Soldiers posted to the local government areas for the elections were said to have been instructed to report to the PDP secretariat. According to General Buhari, for instance in Akwa Ibom state the sum of N200, 000 were given by the PDP to military men on duty on Election Day to help rig the election in its favour (*The Guardian*, 2003:1-2). In various states the incumbent governors ordered their commissioners, permanent secretaries and senior civil servants to go to their local areas and to ensure the delivery of their areas to the party. In some areas the electorate reacted and attacked those agents. The available example was the death of a female commissioner who was sent by Alhaji Abdullahi Adamu, the incumbent Governor of Nasarawa state, to Toto Local government area for a similar exercise.

In a non-PDP state like Gombe the ANPP never expected the magnitude of the rigging that led to the exit of Alhaji Abubakar Hashidu. In Yobe state when the ANPP governor, Alhaji Bukar Abba Ibrahim saw the signs at hands, he allegedly gave out Thuraya handsets to his agents' stationed in strategic collating centres to monitor the results. This was how Alhaji Ibrahim was saved from losing his seat. In Enugu state, a Police officer allegedly told his men on guard for the 19th April 2003 elections that any policeman that arrested anyone rigging in the election should be prepared to take the person to his house, and not to the police station. The rigging brinkmanship, which the PDP demonstrated in the states controlled by the Alliance for Democracy, AD, was also amazing. The outcome of the results released from most states of the federation placed Chief Olusegun Obasanjo ahead of other contestants, with General Buhari taking the second position. Some results of the National Assembly in some states were haphazardly announced with changes that hardly defined the confidence and trust expected of INEC by the public. In Anambra state like some states in the Eastern part of the country candidates who contested elections and won had their candidature supplanted by different persons who were not accredited by INEC to contest the election. It remains a surprise that INEC never question the party, PDP for anti- electoral activities. As Munzali Jibril noted:

> The Peoples Democratic Party, which is a national coalition of the rich and the powerful, bulldozed its way into its second term at the centre

118

and in all but one of the states it controlled before the elections while making in-roads into eight new ones. Through an aggressive manipulation of the security forces, the media and electoral officials the party and electoral officials the party has established itself as the dominant political force on the Nigeria landscape (*This Day*, 17th May 2003:20).

The international Observer groups were more vociferous than the local Transition Monitoring Group (TMG) in condemning the elections results generously. Like the Commonwealth the European Union Elections Observation Mission (EU EOM) deployed 118 observers in 31 states. The report received showed there was widespread electoral fraud. According to Mr. Max Van Den Berg, the Chief Observer 'many instances of ballot stuffing, changing of results and other serious irregularities were observed in Cross River, Delta, Enugu, Kaduna, Imo and Rivers'(*Daily Trust*, April 23, 2003:1). Patriot, an organization of some senior citizens doubted the result of the elections and called for the formation of Interim Government. Professor Wole Soyinka also admitted that the elections suffered some fraud but it was wrong for General Buhari to call for the assassination of Chief Olusegun Obasanjo (*The Guardian*, 2003:1-2). In the same vein the leaders of the Arewa Consultative Forum faulted the elections and called for fresh elections.

Fortunately for the political class, the Nigerian press was did not as usual scathing about previous elections especially as it were in the 1983 elections and the vehement support given to the June 12 1993 elections. The Nigerian press received commendation from Professor Jerry Gana the information minister, as he severely criticised the international observers. According to Gana:

As far as I know, we have not politically intervened in the editorial positions, never manipulated, and never obstructed them. They were all guided by professionalism. This is the first time it has happened in the history of this country... Let me commend the Nigerian Media for a job well done. They did not announce premature results, they waited for INEC, and they play according to the rules. I want to salute the integrity of the media for doing their job (*The Guardian*, 2003:1-2).

However, he was very scathing with the foreign observers as well as the foreign media. On the foreign media he noted that:

... most of the correspondents made premeditated idea of what the election should look like .They came to just find faults; they did not come to cover the elections. That is why they just close their eyes and pray that nothing should happen. They even announced fictitious results for the elections when the results have not been collated (*The Guardian*, 2003:1-2).

Gana, under the 2003 Election dispensation expressed his displeasure with the EU for giving contradictory results from the polls and also castigated the EU observers for indicting the Nigerian press on the grounds of bias coverage before the polls as it was not possible for them to be in all over the 120,000 polling units in the country. Gana's position raised some critical issues concerning the elections. First, it is clear that as a Minister of a government involved in the electoral contest he was not expected to defend the electoral behaviour at the polls. The INEC has a whole department on information management .It was left for INEC to defend and launder its credibility in the conduct of the elections, because in the period of the election INEC was the umpire and not the government. Secondly, some of the results that were announced or recorded by the international Media and the international observers were actually released by INEC but were later withdrawn and replaced with different contestants from parties emerging as the winners. And thirdly, the Nigerian media may not have been bought over or had their editorial/news items interfered with by the government but their attitudes which received commendation from the government is a demonstration that they were interested parties in the elections. By their actions it is possible to believe a popular proposition that because the concentration of the press is in the south west of the country and because Obasanjo is from that geo-political zone, the tendency for the press to play the primordial card cannot be ruled out Hence this same section of press condemned the 1983 election which relieved Alhaji Shehu Shagari to power it went further to call for military intervention. Indeed the military intervened in December 1983.

Furthermore, the 1999 Constitution and the 2002 Electoral Law made provisions for those aggrieved with the conduct of the elections to seek legal redress. However, it sounded insulting to the intellect of Nigerian electorate when the INEC Secretary, Dr. Hakeem Baba Ahmed said that if no body appreciated what INEC has done they should go to court or the tribunal. The approach, which Dr Hakeem

Baba Ahmed told those aggrieved with the conduct of the 12 April National Assembly elections smacked on the arrogance and the partiality of INEC. In a manner of patting INEC in self-congratulatory remark, Baba-Ahmed said that 'we have done what we can (wanted to) do; anybody who does not like it should go to the tribunal; I stand corrected' (NTA News, 15 April 2003, 11 p.m).

Though the ruling party also accused other parties for malpractices in states where PDP was ineffective in winning or rigging elections however, the president Chief Olusegun Obasanjo as the symbol of democratic expression has acknowledged the wide spread rigging, which he drew the attention of INEC to the report of the Commonwealth Observers Team for the 2003 elections .In his written remarks on the rigging to INEC Obasanjo noted that 'I am of the opinion that where the report raises issues on which administrative and legal actions are possible , such remedial actions should be promptly taken. By this note to INEC it is clear that the presidency was not comfortable with the rigging brinkmanship demonstrated by the parties. De spites these criticisms; the INEC and government officials believed that the 2003 elections had broken the jinx of civilian-to-civilian transition. Therefore, for the sake of peace and democratic stability Nigerians should accept the results and those not satisfied should go to the Electoral Tribunal. Two issues are worth raising. Firstly, the 2003 elections were not the first civilian-to civilian elections in Nigeria. We had the first post independent elections in 1964/65 until 1966 when the military intervened to truncate the democratic process. The second time was in 1983 when the Shagari's government had elections that were truncated again in 1984. So civilian regimes have been having successful elections but the problem is the lack of confidence and trust in the system. It has often led to electoral malpractices and the election of 2003 is a striking example. Secondly, it is unfair for institutions of democracy to create scenarios for electoral frauds and later turn to those who lost in the elections to go court. There is no way that the aggrieved would find justice in the Tribunal. Therefore, except in few cases that the results have been successful, several of these petitions have been dismissed for lacking evidence.

Furthermore, indications of rigging were brought out in a face-off between President Obasanjo and Audu Ogbe, the former chairman of PDP. Accordingly, Audu Ogbe was worried by the shocking news of the devastating attack on Anambra state by hoodlums who used dynamite in the full glare of the police which had led to scathing criticism against the party, the President and Government. He added that: "I am afraid we are drifting in the same direction again. In life, perception is reality and today we are persuaded in the worst light by an angry, scornful Nigerian public for reasons which are absolutely unnecessary. I call on you to act now and bring any, and all criminal even treasonable, activities to a halt .we do not have too much time to waste (*The Guardian*, December 13 2004, p. 8).

The president reacted sharply and accused Audu Ogbe of making so many unnecessary and unwarranted insinuations which he has taken judicial note of. However President Olusegun Obasanjo confirmed the issue when he noted that: '… I got the real shock of my life when Chris Uba looked Ngige straight in the face and said "you know you did not win the election" and Ngige answered "yes, I know I did not win" Chris Uba went further to say to Ngige "you do not know in details how it was done." I was horrified and told both of them to leave my residence' (*The Guardian*, December 13 2004:8).

Implications of Election Rigging for Democratic Growth and Governance

Election riggings have serious implications for democratic growth in Nigeria. First, it creates fear rather than confidence and faith in the system. Thus, to overcome this fear every one would like to be associated with the government of the day. Those who want to seek eye service now engage in rigging as their contribution towards keeping the government in power. Persistent and consistent rigging prepares grounds work for dictatorial tendency as opposition is frozen. When the system tolerates this political adventurism it has the tendency for architecturing dictatorial tendencies than democratic ethos. This is more destructive when the press is swallowed up and cannot defend the rule of law. More so, when those who should constitute opposition are decamping to the ruling party in order to belong to the centre of power. In this process the Nigerian state becomes a one party state.

Secondly, because there is a narrow space or none at all for the opposition the likelihood of praetorianism to take roots becomes a possibility. The over-securitisation of election and electoral process has turned out to enhance rigging to the detriment of institutionalising democracy. When the security sector becomes partisan it is difficult for the political system to be stable. Thirdly, which is linked to the second point, is the tendency for the system to be sustained by perpetual violence. Where there is electoral violence the results of the elections are held in suspect which put to question the legitimacy of the governing authority .As Ochoche among others pointed out, election periods are periods of great promises by politicians and raise a lot of expectations in the mind of the electorate (Ochoche, 1997). Therefore, any thing to the contrary would certainly be met with violence or unconstitutional pressure by the people. In order words, opposition can become stronger in places where it has been weakened. Currently, for the first time the northern part of Nigeria is taking on the position of the opposition after several years of being in corridor of power. This is encouraging as they would understand what it means to be in opposition, having been in government for the larger part of Nigeria's political history. The governing style of Obasanjo's leadership has skewed most of the north out of the pleasure of power. As a result the north has taken all measures to oppose his government, including the demand for power to shift back to the north.

Fourthly, electoral rigging does not only create circumstance for violence but the threat it poses to the security of the nation makes it possible for a democratic state to turn to a police state. And when the state becomes a police state the citizens lose interest and trends in the democratic culture as they are brought up in the culture of dictatorship. A democratic regime that fades into a police state is likely to face the overwhelming wrath of the Africa Union, which has become aghast with military rule and dictatorship on the continent. But as whether the international community will be capable of resisting a successful military coup is another issue of discourse. However, if Mauritania could get away with it the feasibility of Nigeria being confronted again by a military regime is possibly zero.

In the light of the above, it is important to make some recommendations. First, democracy cannot be earned on platter of gold. Therefore, it is important that the success of a democratic growth in Nigeria, in the light of emerging civilian autocracy is dependent on the Conference of Political Parties to inaugurate itself into political relevance by challenging the derailing process of Nigeria's democratic ethos. Secondly, it is important too that the National Assembly should give attention to the establishment of the constitutional court to take care of some of the deep seated electoral issues which tribunals cannot handle in a fiat immediately after elections. In short, the process towards constitutional amendment should take the issue of constitutional court into consideration. Tribunals are time-specific and lack the wherewithal in addressing serious electoral issues. Thirdly, rigging thrive because of fear .In order to create confidence in the minds of the people to avoid being used for rigging or the zero-sum tolerance of rigging, INEC should create enabling environment for electoral confidence-building. The task is for the leadership of INEC to exert its status as the umpire. The government of president Obasanjo also has the constitutional mandate to create credibility in the system.

Fourthly, INEC and especially the security operatives must prove their worth in prosecuting any electoral offenders. There is no where this has been done. If this remains so it goes to support the assumption that electoral rigging is tolerated and permitted by the authority because it is done by incumbents who use their offices as means to perpetuate themselves in power. Lastly, to make INEC truly independent and legitimate umpire a provision should be made in the law to allow political parties to be represented in policy echelon of INEC to understand the processes and technicalities involved in conducting elections. This will help them to appreciate the effort of INEC and also enable them to have confidence in the system. This is important, as the government will be finally exonerated from blames whenever there are electoral misunderstandings. Finally it is important to note that because elected offices are lucrative, the political class sees election into political offices as means for amassing wealth. People seek political offices not because they want to serve but get a part of the national cake. It is therefore, advisable that political offices should be made less attractive and be more of service oriented than to be wealth – enticing. Therefore anyone who aspires to any elective office, from the office of the President to that of Local Government Chairman, should be paid working allowance rather than salary. The National Revenue Mobilisation and Fiscal Allocation should be empowered to fixed allowances rather than salary for elected officers. Nigeria is developing country, it needs resources for development than paying the lots of a few. In this way politics will be less lucrative and only few and committed political class will show interests to serve the nation.

Conclusion

This chapter does not claim to have established the criteria for stopping rigging in Nigerian politics. However, what it has done so far is to demonstrate the manifestations of election rigging and how they undermine democratic growth in Nigeria. What is clear and worrisome is that rigging is becoming too sophisticated as it can be done without violence and be seen to be credible. With the introduction of electronic voting the fear now is that Nigeria might begin to experience digital rigging. Indeed, the April 2007 elections have clearly proved to be the worst elections ever held in Nigeria. People resort to violence when the state apparatus is not capable to provide redress to the aggrieved. In other words, the overwhelming weight of the repressive apparatus of the state can contain opposition, yet it fails to provide enabling environment for redress in the event of election rigging and irregularities. This paves way for 'imperial democracy'. Imperial democracy is the type that tends towards consensus or where joint decisions are taken by compulsion as no one questions the why and how of the decision making process, as tradition demands in a functional democracy. This is what the Germans called *politikverflechtung*, democracy of the graveyard consensus. Because the consensus process is solo it is itself imperial as it denies the people the right to their legitimate claims to opposition, political participation and rules out the application of rule of law.

It is important to note that Obasanjo's recent handover of power to Alhaji Umaru Yar'Adua, who is of the same ruling PDP, signifies that Nigeria has overcome one minor hurdle that has kept its democracy unstable. This is the hurdle of transferring power from one civilian regime to another. However, the most difficult hurdle that Nigeria faces is inter-party transfer of power .This might prove difficult and might provide a leeway for palace coup if there emerges a chaotic situation, such as clearly stolen electoral victory at the level of presidency. Even in the present circumstance, many would see a palace coup as an option because of the flawed general election of April 2007 coupled with the fact that the 8 years of Obasanjo's regime has squeezed life out of the majority of the people. Only the political elites and their clients can boast of benefiting from the regime. That is why some section of the ruling PDP, and the public to a lesser extent, tended to prefer either General Ibrahim Babangida or Alhaji Atiku Abubakar, who they perceive to be more liberal in financial spending, to succeed Obasanjo. Comparatively, both Yar'Adua and the main opposition leader, Mohammadu Buhari, are seen to be highly inflexible, even among the northerners.

Lastly, whatever the case, it is important to encourage the political class to work on issue based-politics rather than on mundane politics of personalities. Therefore, INEC or relevant government bodies should insist that political parties and individual politicians should establish an elaborate ideological or issue-based policy plan for the electorates rather than 'money laundering brand of political campaign'. A lot of campaign activities are predicated on spreading money rather than issue based. This is also because most of the candidates lack acceptable social credentials. The system does not give room for independent candidates and because of this the imposed candidates often lack credible credentials that would require the electorates to decide whom to cast their votes. The alternative left is for the contestants to take to rigging knowing that not many would vote for them. One fact that needs to be mentioned is that Obasanjo is a leader whose government has recorded a number of well-meaning achievements. However one mistake Obasanjo made during his first spell in the office as a military head of state (1976-79) was that he organized a shoddy election and handed power to an unwilling and weak leadership. The outcome of that plot was that Nigeria was denied a credible leadership, resulting in the extensive damage done to the national economy and politics. We may not be too far from a re-enactment of the dismal history in the present conjuncture of the 4th civilian republic. Only time will tell.

Notes

1. The concept of citizen-electorate is used here to distinguish the voters from those other citizens who are not politically conscious and apathetic .Citizen- electorates are those citizens that register for elections and have electoral identification marks or cards to vote in elections. They are apprehensive, conscious and political, and not just voters.

2. Most countries have placed limit a financing election campaigns. This is common in the US .Nigeria is learning to cope with this in spite of effort by INEC to ensure its compliance.

References

Adamu, H & A. Ogunsawo 1982, *Nigeria: The making of the Presidential System: The 1979 General Elections*, Kano: Triumph Publishers.

Agbese, P. 1992, 'The Autocratic Foundations of Nigeria's forthcoming Third Republic,' *The Journal of International Studies*, No.28, January.

Anifowose, R. 1982, *Violence and Politics in Nigeria: The Tiv and Yoruba Experience*, NY: Nok Publishers.

Adejumobi, S. 2000, 'Elections in Africa: A Fading Shadow of Democracy' in Okwudiba Nnoli, 2000, *Government and Politics in Africa: A Reader*, Harare: AAPS Books.

Dudley, B. J. 1973, *Instability and Political Order*, Ibadan: University Press.

Campbell, A. *et al* 1966, *Elections and the Political order*, NY: John Wilie & Sons.

Miliband, Ralph 1968, *State in Capitalist Society*, London.

Ofondu, N. C. 1994, 'The History of Elections: A perspective study of political Behaviour in Nigeria', *Nigerian Journal of Democracy*, vol.1, number 1, October.

Omoruyi, Omo 1992, *Challenges of Democratisation in Nigeria*, Lagos state University Inaugural Lecture, Lagos.

Olurode, L. 1990, *A Political Economy of Nigeria's 1983 Elections*, Lagos: John West Publishers.

Olagunju, T. *et al* 1993, *Transition to Democracy in Nigeria 1985-1993*, Ibadan: Safari/Spectrum Publishers, p. 64.

Ofonagoro, Walter 1979, *The Story of Nigerian General Elections 1979*, Lagos: Federal Ministry of Information.

Chapter 5

The State, Civil Society and Curtailing the Proliferation of Small Arms in Nigeria

Oshita O. Oshita

Introduction

This chapter discusses the problem of small arms proliferation in Nigeria. It argues that the Nigerian state can explore a number of opportunities for government and civil society to partner in curtailing the hazardous proliferation of illicit small arms and light weapons in the country. The focus is on the role that state actors (government) and non-state actors (civil society organisations) in Nigeria can play in reducing the proliferation of illegal small arms and light weapons (SALWs) in the country. The study also outlines some of the steps through which collaboration between government and civil society organisations can achieve a reduction in the quantum of dangerous weapons in unauthorised hands in Nigeria. From a peace research perspective, the analysis identifies a connection between the preponderance of illegal weapons in the society and the palpable threat to peace, order and security of life and property in Nigeria. The objective of this chapter, therefore, is to explore government - civil society interface and how this could become a constructive framework for reducing the preponderance of small arms and light weapons in Nigeria, *ipso facto* curbing the spate of gun-related violent crimes in the country.

The new global security discourse recognises the nexus of peace and development as one of the complex issues that must inform policy planning and implementation. Thus, as peace practitioners and other development actors intensify their search for viable strategies for peace and sustainable development, a number of African nations remain painfully burdened by the spectre of violence, insecurity, poverty and underdevelopment, due to the unrestricted availability of mainly automatic hand guns from conflict zones. Coupled with the introduction of convoluted macro-economic programmes that fuel unemployment and job losses, this scenario no doubt exacerbates the tendency towards state failure since the regular state security agencies are incapable of dealing with the situation. As a key player in the socio-economic and political landscape of Africa, Nigeria is constantly confronted with vertical and horizontal conflicts among segments of her population arising from the challenges of managing development. This makes the notion of 'securitized' development applicable in describing recent trends in the socio-economic, political and development history of Nigeria.[xxx] In a bid to grapple with the fallouts from the ensuing volatile and contested development environment, the Federal Government of Nigeria established the Institute for Peace and Conflict Resolution (IPCR) in February, 2000.

Background to the Present Scenario

No doubt, one of the hangovers of Nigeria's military rule is the construal of the issue of proliferation in illegal small arms and light weapons as a 'restricted subject' of national security that is not to be engaged in the public domain. Against this backdrop, the approach of commentators on this subject has been one of a mixture of optimism and caution in the diagnosis, analysis and prognosis. However, with democratisation and the feeling that security and defence issues are meaningful only in relation to the citizens of the state, the label of sacredness on these critical domains is beginning to fade.

A significant upward movement in the number of violent intra and inter community conflicts in Nigeria was recorded from 1999 when the civilian regime was inaugurated.[xxxi] While the rate of urban and rural criminality fluctuated from year to year, the socio-economic and political indicators continue to show that the tendency towards violent criminal behaviour is likely to rise sharply in the short term. The system reform agenda of the government, though might be beneficial in the long run, appear at present to exacerbate unemployment, under-employment, and job losses, thus accentuating poverty, disempowerment and the propensity for crime. The value of labour as a factor of production is on the decline and an increasing army of youthful persons is waiting and willing to be hired by anyone to do anything, from the not so dignifying, the bad and the outright ugly! For example, there have been evidences of young men being hired as mercenaries in inter community conflicts and as assassins to settle political and business scores for a (promise of) very little financial reward.[xxxii] The availability of guns makes all these a lot easier. Given the above picture, one of the avenues open to government for a meaningful engagement with the myriad of social problems in Nigeria is a multi-track diplomacy involving civil society, religious, business, non-governmental groups, multilateral development partners, etc.

Only a few years ago in Nigeria state actors, including policy makers, wondered with curious indignation what they had in common with non-state actors, the latter construed as intruders in the business of ensuring a peaceful and secure society. Until recently, state actors in Nigeria had a monopoly of the driving seat in all governance, security and development issues. This was indicative of the prevailing global state-centric development paradigm, which shut out people-driven institutions and prevented non-state actors from engaging with issues pertaining to defence and security 'in the national interest'.

Obviously, the prolonged period of military rule in Nigeria negatively impacted on the evolution of a versatile civil society culture. Where state and non-state actors interfaced, the inherent gale of distrust between them saw the former unwilling to concede any role to the latter. Indeed, non-state actors were perceived as interlopers merely complicating the 'normal processes' of government control and manipulation of the public space. Thus, under the military regimes civil society as a constituency was detested for what was considered its nuisance value of prying into the business of governance.

As noted above, the exclusion of non-state actors as constructive allies of the government was consistent with the prevailing traditional Westphalia paradigm according to which state security was the primary unit of concern in strategy. From the traditional security perspective, realists and their intellectual allies argued that nation-states retained their central position in the affairs of society; that civil society activism was very much an unsolicited and pedestrian engagement with the politics of delivery of social goods. However, in the early 21st century, with the changing strategic parameters in the global governance architecture, the unprecedented demand for transparency and accountability, the United Nations was compelled to rethink its state-centric strategy of over fifty five years. National governments were also compelled to have a rethink in favour of strategic partnerships with non-state actors. On their part, state actors in different African countries are gradually yielding grounds to civil society participation in domains previously thought to be the exclusive preserve of the government.

One outcome of the emergent global governance and critical security debates was the United Nations acknowledgement of the serious limitations that existing intergovernmental machineries have for enhancing human security. In other words, protecting human rights and promoting international peace and security became 'deregulated' to accommodate civil society groups as social vehicles for people participation and empowerment. It had also become obvious that the world could no longer ignore the significant roles that the civil society groups could play in the promotion and strengthening of governance at the sub-national, national and international levels. Thus, coalitions of non-state actors at different levels began to intensify their rights-based claims to partnership with government in security and development administration.

Understandably, the Military regimes that dominated the Nigerian political scene for a good part of the post-independent history were unrepentantly anti-CSOs. The few CSOs that existed lacked the institutional capacity to impact significantly on the political space. However, in the 1990s as military rule was running out of fashion in Africa, activist groups of various shades began to emerge. Today, under the present civil (democratic) dispensation that became operational from May, 1999, CSOs have not only flourished, but have increased their capacity to play important roles in the search for and the sustenance of peace, security and good governance in Nigeria. This is not to minimise the suggestion that the absence of a strategic vision and a positive orientation could see pan/sub-ethnic CSOs in Nigeria thwarting the peace agenda and derailing the development processes in the country.

Definition of Concepts

Before we further contextualise the discussion it is important that we define what we mean by the 'state', 'civil society organisations' (CSOs), and 'small arms and light weapons'. The State refers to the entire apparatuses of governance – the legislature, executive and judiciary, including the institutions and agencies of government, and the public service structures. While government is transient, the state is a permanent institution with a stamp of sovereignty and territorial independence. Based on the principles of the Peace of Westphalia espoused in 1648, Nigeria became an independent and sovereign state on the 1st day of October, 1960, although the structures of the ethnic nationalities are rooted in pre-colonial history.

The term 'civil society organisation' means different things to different people. Scholte (2005:324) speaks of 'civil society' as "a political space where voluntary associations deliberately seek to shape the rules that govern one or the other aspect of social life. 'Rules' in this conception encompass specific policies, more general norms, and deeper social structures." Generally, civil society comprise a variety of actors – business forums, academic institutions, clan and kinship circles, consumer advocates, community development initiatives, environmental movements, ethnic lobbies, faith-based associations, human rights groups, labour unions, community-based organisations, peace movements, philanthropic foundations, professional groups, relief organisations, women's organisations, think tanks, youth associations, etc.

Scholte's definition presents us with a number of conceptual and practical difficulties. First is the challenge arising from the sheer number and complexity of actors involved and the diverse agenda that each of these promote. Second, in practice many of the actors in the civil society sector pursue goals that are not only contradictory to one another, but may be inconsistent with the fundamental objectives of illicit arms state policy as enunciated in the 1999 constitution of Nigeria. Third, there is some evidence that problematises the role of identity and pan/sub-ethnic CSOs in the proliferation of small arms and light weapons in Nigeria. This is particularly so when we profile the role of pan- and sub-ethnic organisations like the O'dua Peoples Congress (OPC), Movement for the actualisation of the Sovereign State of Biafra (MASSOB), Movement for the Survival of Ogoni People (MOSOP) and other comparatively less visible sub-ethnic organisations. Along with their diaspora hoses for funding and ideological guardianship this category of CSOs has sometimes impacted negatively on the efforts towards peace and reconciliation in the country. The subject matter of Diaspora involvement in the prosecution of dysfunctional conflicts in Nigeria is one that would require a closer and dedicated analysis by students of society for practical purposes.

Fourth, civil society in Nigeria can also be problematised within the context of the socio-political realities that marked the colonial strategy of divide-and-rule. Following independence the Nigerian state has conducted the business of governance with a conquest mentality devoid of a vision for social inclusiveness. The issues of marginalisation, fiscal federalism, resource control, among others, were merely padded along with no patterned mode of resolution. With a population of 140 million people[xxxiii] spread across 400 ethnic and linguistic nationalities, contemporary Nigeria is an organised hurly-burly of civil society groups seeking to attain highly diverse goals.

The conception of civil society organisation therefore, stretches beyond the formally organised, officially registered, and professionally administered non-governmental organisations (NGOs). Thus, NGOs represent only part of the story of the broad terrain covered by civil society organisations. Civil society actions may target formal and informal processes and activities in the public domain – legislation, social constructs (e.g. gender roles), conflict management, crime prevention, etc. The aims and advocacy campaign strategies of civil society organisations fall broadly within the conformist, reformist and transformationist agendas. Our concern here is to explore how the cooperative efforts of CSOs and government could lead to the curtailment of the proliferation in dangerous weapons that have continued to fuel criminal behaviour and violent community conflicts. This will complement ongoing efforts at reducing the number of SALWs and support Nigeria's transition from a nation on the precipice of violence, insecurity and predictable chaos to the one on the threshold of peace and sustainable development.

It can be argued that the failure of the Nigerian state to strengthen the opportunities for promoting centripetal energies from the abundant material and human resources of the constitutive groups worked against social integration in the country. In other words, the absence of equitable development of infrastructure and the disempowerment of the mass of the people is responsible for the present volatile socio-political environment in the country. Thus, the social forces which were to coalesce into vibrant civil society platforms were clamped upon and forced to manifest negatively in response to the unjust social structures. Worse still, successive regimes were unsuccessful in addressing the appalling state of public infrastructure/utilities and the pervasive material and mental poverty in the land. These cumulative developments fuelled pockets of social discontent and turned the energies of many civil society groups into centrifugal pressures, leaving the state without effective mechanisms for absorbing the emergent tension. In the ensuing process, agents of the state resort to defending themselves by fanning and deploying enemy images of one group against another.

The present scenario in Nigeria is that of an obfuscating social tension which often compelled aggrieved groups to adopt self-help strategies in the pursuit of their goals. As the use of self-help is not addressed by government, it translates into widespread 'uncivil' methods for realising personal and group agenda. What this means is that the weakness or incapacity of the Nigerian state to provide security (physical, human and social) is the launch pad for the liberalisation of violence further ignited by the easy access to automatic weapons. Against this backdrop, the proliferation of illicit small arms and light weapons is fuelled by the feeling of insecurity among individuals and communities. In fact, the maintenance of public order has remained a major challenge for the police and other internal security institutions. This security gap is conveniently exploited by criminal gangs who have access to hand guns that are often more sophisticated than those possessed by the police and other state security agencies.

The literature on SALWs defines this class of weapons as hand weapons that are easily moved and manipulated by a single individual. These range from (poisoned) bow and arrow to the automatic and highly sophisticated hand-held guns. Apart from the locally fabricated pistols and short guns, the arms in circulation among unauthorised persons in Nigeria include Mark 4, Aviomat Kalashnikova – 47, popularly known as AK-47, Beretta AR-70/90, FMK-3/5 Sub-Machine Gun (SMG), etc.

Issues Concerning the Proliferation of SALWs in Nigeria

The scenario of the proliferation of small arms and light weapons (SALWs) in Nigeria has rapidly assumed the dimension of a 'complex political emergency', the aftermath of the post-Cold War global (dis)order. As a 'complex political emergency' the proliferation in SALWs impacts negatively on the national economy, destroys food security, dislocates civilian populations, sustains negative peace, and

134

compromises law and order, including the criminal justice and public safety functions of the government. Stakeholders of peace in Nigeria are unequivocal in asserting the view that Nigeria is experiencing a pervasive public security challenge, next only to what prevailed during the civil war of 1967 to 1970.[xxxiv]   Various studies and conjectures attribute the influx of small arms into Nigeria to different sources.

The Strategic Conflict Assessment (SCA) traces some of the arms in unauthorised hands to politicians who engaged private political thugs in the pursuit of their desire for power.[xxxv]   Indications from the ongoing updating of the 2002 SCA by the IPCR point to an increasing number of illegal arms made their way into Nigerian communities each time intra or inter-party political activities intensify. What this shows is that the economic stakes in Nigerian politics have continued to rise, thus fuelling the spectre of desperation for positions among contending politicians. This is due to the fact that the appropriation of political office [by (s)election or appointment] has come to be regarded by many Nigerians as the surest way to economic security. Equally implicated is the failure of the government to prosecute political office seekers who had in the past been indicted for fraudulent/violent electoral practices. Political office aspirants seeking re-(s)election are propelled by the reality that political patronage comes with expansive advantages and pecuniary trappings that would otherwise take a lifetime to muster.[xxxvi] This social reality (politics as gateway to wealth) in Nigeria tends to promote the 'god father' or 'strongman' politics syndrome.[xxxvii]

Lewis and Davis (2006; 85) quoted Asari Dokubo, leader of the Niger Delta Peoples Volunteer Force (NDPVF) as saying "We are very close to the international waters and it's very easy to get weapons". Nigeria international waterways constitute the channels through which arms dealers bring weapons into Nigeria, a view that was also corroborated by Dokubo. Further referring to a 2004 interview by Dokubo, the authors (Lewis and Davis, 2006:85) write: 'He also confirmed the presence of illegal arms dealers along the coast, saying he was able to obtain enough weapons through the arms dealers (AK-47s, general purpose machine guns and rocket-propelled grenades) to equip 2,000 men.'

Nigeria's sea and land borders have remained poorly managed and continue to serve as unrestricted routes for the movement of illegal arms and other trans-border criminal activities. Perhaps one of the most potentially destabilising phenomena for the Nigerian state is the volume of sophisticated weapons in the hands of aggrieved persons, including the militants in the Niger Delta region. Although the origin of some of the arms in the hands of the militia groups could be traced to politicians and 'oil thieves' (AAPW, 2006)[xxxviii] but the overall strength of armed criminality across the country seems to derive from the economic injustice perpetuated by years of what Galtung refers to as structural violence[xxxix] in Nigeria. More militant groups are emerging on the space once dominated by the Movement for the Emancipation of the Niger Delta (MEND) and Asari Dokubo's Niger Delta Peoples Volunteer Force (NDPVF). Hostage-taking, in which expatriate oil workers are the key target, appear to be the unifying bargaining strategy of the different groups for engaging with state and non-state economic actors in the region.

Other sources implicated in the proliferation of small arms in Nigeria include, weapons seized in confrontations with security agencies, break-ins into police stations, weapons sold by the police/army personnel, weapons bought from ex-militia or cult members, weapons stockpiled in community armouries in areas prone to intra and inter-community conflicts, weapons smuggle in by security personnel involved in peacekeeping operations, weapons fabricated by local blacksmiths, and weapons supplied by Diaspora associations of communities in conflict or facing the threat of conflict.

One of the major interventions by the Nigerian government was the establishment of the National Committee on Small Arms and Light Weapons (NATCOM). NATCOM is a multi-agency committee with membership from government and non-governmental groups and it was charged with devising a mechanism for dealing with the problem of small arms in Nigeria. In establishing NATCOM the federal government assumed that the committee would enhance government partnership with civil society organisations and improve the operational capability of both actors in specific areas. Series of capacity building workshops have been held under the auspices of NATCOM.

Government needs to build the capacity of her social engineering institutions and increase the law enforcement capabilities of the security agencies, while civil society organisations require training in specialised skills to engage with the delicate issue of the control of the proliferation of SALWs. Training in the identification and weapons registration process, including basic safety precautions in the handling of firearms and ammunitions would be necessary for CSO partners.

The weapons destruction or retooling process must be environment-friendly in order not to jeopardise human security.

Towards Government - CSOs Partnership

In the light of the enormity of the problem of small arms, an effective framework for Government - CSOs partnership should be evolved to redress the situation. The following six key areas are hereby proposed as possible entry-points for government - civil society partnership for reducing the availability of fire arms in Nigeria.

(i)   Draw up the framework for institutional intervention in dealing with the problem of proliferation in SALWs (preceded by an in-depth study on causative factors, etc).

(ii)   Build the capacity of (relevant) stakeholders for proactive action in reducing SALWs.

(iii)   Provide public education and awareness on the dangers of proliferation in SALWs.

(iv)   Monitor and improve strategies for stockpile management and handling.

(v)   Partner with the National Committee on SALWs (NATCOM) in creating a national policy on firearms consistent with revised local firearms laws and the relevant international protocols.

(vi)   Work out a need-based weapons exchange/retooling programme for individuals and communities.

(vii)   Engage in continued Monitoring and Evaluation of the process.

(i) To determine the strategic parameters for responding to (i) above, we must deal with the channels through which the hand weapons come into Nigeria. As indicated above, one of the major sources of SALWs in the country today is through the illegal bunkering business in the Niger Delta. Oil thieves bring in sophisticated weapons in order to supply those who 'protect' their economies, to secure favourable political bases in the creeks of the Niger Delta, and for sell to other militia and local arms dealers. This is however, not to minimise the role of security personnel who smuggle in weapons from the various peacekeeping operations at the sub-regional, regional and international levels. To be effective, the framework for intervention must take these into account.

(ii) Building the capacity of stakeholders for proactive action in curtailing the proliferation in SALWs involves inter-agency collaboration in training in such critical areas as disarmament, demobilisation and reintegration (DDR). The membership of CSOs requires specialised training in the specific skills of detection, retrieval/mopping and management of SALWs. The ECOWAS early warning structure took into account the potential of CSOs to provide useful early information on conflict trends (which includes data on SALWs) in providing a place for CSOs in its system. Despite the fragility and fragmented nature CSOs, ECOWATCH still depends on the involvement of local civil society groups for its effectiveness within the ECOWAS sub-region. Apart from developing the human resource base of these organisations, training helps to promote the preservation of institutional memory for addressing specific challenges in the future.

(iii) Public education and awareness creation are indispensable tools in any effort to curtail the proliferation of SALWs. For the public to invest in measures that lead to the control of small arms proliferation the people must be made to appreciate the dangers of proliferating hand guns. Because information is power, it must be available to the people timely and in the right doses. Such awareness is necessary for people to realise the collateral risk that stares us all in the face if we remained complacent about the preponderance of SALWs in the community. The Ministries of Education and Information and National Orientation and their line agencies will need to network with other state and non-state institutions to provide widespread public education and awareness in various local languages, well beyond the 'Wazobia' triangle. The media can also be mobilised to play a constructive role in projecting the agenda for reduction of illegal arms.

(iv) The agencies charged with stockpile management need to be equipped with modern accessories for monitoring and handling dangerous weapons retrieved from the open society. Citizens at the community level are more likely to know where illegal weapons are kept and what could be done to retrieve them using a transparent process. Government-CSOs partnership can regulate the mopping up and stockpiling processes by strengthening supervision to eliminate possible leakages in the handling system. This requires inter-agency commitment to the key objective of achieving efficiency in arms stockpile management. Information on best practices can be assembled as guide to make for sustainable outcomes.

(v) The national committee on SALWs (NATCOM) needs to broaden its base, and therefore its reach, by identifying and engaging with CSOs that can take its message to the grassroots. Surely, people-based organisations are more likely to provide us with viable information on the sources and movement of arms in the different localities. Partnering with such organisations will help NATCOM configure a database for tracking and retrieving hand weapons from unauthorised people in the country consistent with national firearms legislations and international protocols. This would require a lot of confidence-building measures to be put in place.

(vi) Government and CSOs can work together in conducting a participatory needs assessment in the project environment to determine what exactly those who surrender illegal weapons would prefer in exchange for them. As community-based groups the CSOs would be in a better position to brief government on the occupational environment and some of the salient value-based issues that may not be apparent to 'an outsider'.

(vii) The role of monitoring and evaluation is very critical in all these to forestall any derailment of the process. Institutional capacity is to be sustained through training/retraining and the monitoring of process outcomes and objectives.

In summary, government-civil society partnership for the reduction of the proliferation of SALWs in Nigeria must be configured within the context of the realities of widespread youth unemployment, under-employment (low morale), moral disintegration, porous borders, corruption, institutional incapacity, absence of a social contract, and political manipulation. These factors are to be taken into account for a programme for the reduction of the proliferation of small arms and light weapons to have any chance of success in Nigeria. Without a multi-sectoral approach towards arms reduction, taking the economy and politics into account, Nigeria cannot realistically begin the journey towards meeting the benchmarks for the attainment of the millennium development goals.

Conclusion

In most developing countries, the state and civil society live in mutual suspicion and distrust. While the civil society seeks consultation and partnership with the state on issues that affect the larger society, the state often favours unilateralism. During the last fifteen years, we have seen a vast range of literature in Nigeria that inveigh as wrongly-headed the state's unilateralism and tendency to by-pass the civil society on important social issues such as arms control.[xl] It suffices to note that the rise 'civic activism' globally is a boom rather than a deficit for the growth of democratic institutions in developing countries such as Nigeria. The government alone cannot sustain peace and security without the contribution of non-state actors in fighting against the proliferation of SALWs in the society. Apart from the other forms of criminality precipitated by the availability of SALWs, the phenomenon diminishes the willingness for conflict parties to embrace a peaceful settlement of conflicts. Thus, no conflict resolution process can be successful without an integrated plan for the withdrawal of the weapons used in prosecuting violent conflict disorders.

It can therefore be argued that government incapacity in curbing the ready access to guns and other automatic light weapons (together with the availability of idle / unemployed people who can use them), are the unquestionable enemies of Nigeria's open society today. The weak law enforcement regime exacerbates armed criminality. Worse still, in any society where the majority is poor and hungry, the discovery that opportunities exist for grabbing resources using easily accessible weapons becomes very alluring. The negative multiplier effect of this scenario, in the long term, is that more people (individuals, groups, and communities) become predisposed to the use of weapons for self-help in response to perceived or real threat from the environment.

Successive governments in Nigeria ignored the community approach to development and alienated the people through years of culpable abandonment and neglect. Reaching back to these communities through their CSOs, NGOs and Community based organisations (CBOs) to seek the solution to the problem of proliferation of SALWs may just be what government needs to do. One way to do this is to engage these groups in ways that will creatively engender mutual confidence and dispel the enemy images that have long characterised and promoted violent conflicts across the country. It is in the interest of both government and CSOs cooperative relationships are sought in all fronts to 'prevent this house from falling.'[xli]

Given that CSOs are people-based organisations with in-country rich that span across all sectors and corners of the Nigerian nation, the government stands to benefit from the diversity and huge resource repertoire of these groups. To complement this relationship, government has a duty to promote "structures and processes to strengthen democracy, the observance of human rights, the rule of law and good governance, as well as economic recovery and growth" (Bamako Declaration, 2000, p.3). For the government-CSOs initiatives in reducing small arms to succeed, government must lead the process with promiscuous enthusiasm not only because the danger posed by illicit small arms is grave, but because this ultimately seems to be from where the solution to this problem would emerge.

The processes discussed in this chapter involve multifunctional cooperation and collaboration to succeed. They must be institutionalised by the collaborating agencies to enable the stakeholders see reasons for supporting the activities to achieve the desired goals. Advocacy and sensitisation is required to purge the stakeholders of incipient distrust by being transparent through out the process. For example, enlightenment messages should aim to dispel the pessimism with which the public servants often viewed CSOs; that they were busy bodies prying on domains that legitimate belonged to government. A strategic and effective partnership between government and CSOs will indirectly contribute to strengthening physical security and thus curtail and defuse the competition for power by militia and other armed gangs who exploit the absence of ('an over-awing') state authority to perpetuate violence.

The absence of a social contract that compels the leadership to deliver, corruption, youth unemployment, political manoeuvres, and moral disintegration serve as fertile grounds upon which gun-related violence and conflicts thrive in Nigeria. As the activities of criminal networks threaten investment and worsen the unemployment situation in the country, the cumulative negative effects of the impact of excessive illegal arms and light weapons are felt in the open society far beyond the point of origin of the crime or conflict.

The emergence of government-CSOs collaboration in the elimination of proliferation in SALWs in Nigeria would offer all stakeholders significant possibilities for the reduction of the present deficits in Nigeria's democracy (human rights abuses, culture of impunity, electoral fraud, corruption, etc.), that have characterised the chequered political history of Nigeria to date.

Notes

1. The idea of securitized development has come to be associated with the application of a security stamp on development issues to draw more critical attention to the urgency in the development challenges, rationalise increased allocation of resources or legitimise some drastic course of action. See Weaver (1995) and (Omeje, 2006:14).

2. This was proven by a number of studies, notably the Strategic Conflict Assessment of Nigeria (SCA) led by the Institute for Peace and Conflict Resolution (IPCR). Some analysts attribute the sudden upsurge in the number of violent community conflicts to the desire by various groups to ventilate the long bottled up anger, which they could not project under military rule.

3. In 2006, during one of IPCR's interventions in the community conflicts in Plateau State, North Central Nigeria, a truck load of men, armed with guns and charms was intercepted by guard soldiers. Many of the men came from communities other than those involved in the violent conflict and confessed to being hired as mercenaries to fight in that conflict.

4. Nigeria conducted a national population census in 2006. The official population figure, which a number of states in Nigeria, notably Lagos and the Federal Capital Territory are contesting is 140 million people.

5. The Institute for Peace and Conflict Resolution (IPCR) is at present facilitating a stakeholder-led process of formulating a draft national peace policy for Nigeria. The peace policy is intended to address the conflict-generating issues in Nigeria for the purpose of creating a harmonious environment for peacefully engaging with potentially violent social phenomena.

6. The Institute for Peace and Conflict Resolution (IPCR) in collaboration with development partners (DFID, USAID, UNDP, World Bank) and civil society organisations carried out a Strategic Conflict Assessment (SCA) in 2002. The SCA was published in 2003 and it serves as a baseline study for Nigeria's conflict profile; it outlines the causes of conflict, dynamics, stakeholders, actors, etc.

7. This is what Richards Joseph refers to as the Politics of Prebendalism. See Joseph, R. (1987) Democracy and Prebendal Politics in Nigeria: The Rise and Fall of the Second Republic, Cambridge: Cambridge University Press.

8. The 'god father' or 'strongman' syndrome in Nigerian politics has been the source of overheat for the political system. This is a situation where politicians and public officers are sponsored to their positions ([s]elective or appointive) on the understanding that continued material loyalty will accrue to the benefactor through out the tenure of office of the occupant. The instructive cases are those of former Governor Chris Ngige versus Chris Uba in Anambra State and Governor Rashidi Ladoja of Oyo State versus Alhaji Lamidi Adedibu. This is the typical political master-servant relationships that inundate the Nigerian political landscape today, and it amplifies the role of 'money bags' in politics. The public gets glimpses of the under-hand political agreements between 'political master and servant' only when things have gone badly wrong between the parties.

9. In 2006 the Academic Associates PeaceWorks (AAPW), a non-governmental organization engaged in peacebuilding and conflict management in Nigeria organized a Working Group that conducted background studies on the Niger Delta Peace and Security situation. Part of the Peace and Security (PaS) report identified the flow of arms into the Niger Delta, including the channel of illegal oil outfits owned and controlled by 'oil thieves'.

10. Johann Galtung (1990) characterized structural violence as the form of violation according to which injustice and inequity are built into the institutions of governance and perpetuated as a matter of course.

11. See Scholte, J. A., in Wilkinson, Rorden ed. (2005), The Global Governance Reader, London: Routledge. Also, Woodhouse, T. and Ramsbotham, O. eds. (2000), Peacekeeping and Conflict Resolution, London: Frank Cass.

12. This House Has Fallen is the title of one of the apocalyptic literatures written by a foreign journalist about Nigeria as a nation on the precipice. It projected the author saw a fragile peace in Nigeria.

References

Academic Associates PeaceWorks (2006), *Background Papers for Peace and Security (PaS)*, Niger Delta Peace and Security Secretariat, Working Group, Port Harcourt.

Bamako Declaration on an African Common Position on the Illicit Proliferation, Circulation and trafficking of Small Arms and Light Weapons (2000), quoted in SaferAfrica, 2001, Practitioners Guide to SALW Initiatives relevant to Africa, Reference Materials for Regional task force training: Tanzania.

Galtung, J. (1990), 'Violence and Peace', Smoker, P. *et al* (eds.) *A Reader in Social Studies*, New York: Pergamon Press.

IPCR (2003), *Strategic Conflict Assessment of Nigeria: Consolidated Report*, Abuja: Institute for Peace and Conflict Resolution.

Joseph, R. (1987) *Democracy and Prebendal Politics in Nigeria: The Rise and Fall of the Second Republic*, Cambridge: Cambridge University Press.

Lewis, S. and Davis, S. (2006), 'Disarmament in the Niger Delta', Niger Delta Peace and Security Working Group Background Paper, Peace and Security Secretariat, Port Harcourt: Academic Associates PeaceWorks.

Obasi, N. (2000), *Small Arms Proliferation and Disarmament in West Africa: Progress and Prospects of the ECOWAS Moratorium*, Abuja: Aprophyl Productions.

Omeje, K. (2006), *High Stakes and Stakeholders: Oil Conflict and Security in Nigeria*, Hampshire: Ashgate Publishing Limited.

Oshita, O. O. (2005), 'Conflict Dynamics in a Multi-ethnic State: Revivalism and Brinkmanship in Contemporary Nigeria', in Isaac O. Albert (ed.) *Perspectives on Peace and Conflict in Africa*, Ibadan: John Archers.

SaferAfrica, (2001), *Practitioners Guide to SALW Initiatives Relevant to Africa, Reference Materials for Regional Task Force Training*. Tanzania, Pretoria: SaferAfrica.

Wilkinson, Rorden (ed.) (2005), *The Global Governance Reader*, London: Routledge.

Woodhouse, Tom and Ramsbotham, Oliver eds. (2000), *Peacekeeping and Conflict Resolution*, London: Frank Cass.

Weaver, O. (1995) 'Securitization and Desecuritization' in Lipschutz, R. D. (ed.) *On Security*, New York: Colombia University Press.

Chapter 6

Unending Generational Curse?
Youths, Conflicts and Instability in Nigeria

Kenneth Omeje

Introduction

The oil boom is paradoxically associated with a conflict boom in contemporary Nigeria. The youths are at the heart of most violent conflicts in the country, not necessarily as instigators but most often as drivers, prosecutors, accelerators, and prime cannon fodders and casualties of the conflicts. The structures and faultlines of violent conflicts in Nigeria are widespread, deep-rooted and, in most cases, complex. The agencies for activating or transforming structural faultlines and contradictions into violent conflicts, and for catalyzing and recycling the conflicts are preponderant, straddling the state and society. In all of these adverse structural features and manifestations, the youth populations are most vulnerable. Starved of purposeful human capital investment from the rentier state, robbed of access to life chances by the harsh economic realities associated with the World Bank/IMF neo-liberal reform policies, and confronted by a hopeless future, many Nigerian youths are helplessly trapped in what tends to be an unending generational curse: deprivation, crime and violent conflicts. This chapter explores the evolution and changing dynamics of youths' involvement in conflicts in Nigeria. What has, for instance, shifted in the evolution, nature and pattern of youths' involvement in conflicts in Nigeria's political history and why?

The study adopts a reasonably flexible conception of the term youth – a conception that, being mindful of the pitfalls in the conventional fixed-age definition, will not necessarily prescribe or append a fixed age to the term for the understandable reason that it is a concept that has no universal connotation. Youths are broadly sub-adults and young adults for the most part distinguished from the rest of the population by their shared sense of generational identity, burden

145

and aspirations. According to the *United Nations Division for Social Policy and Development (2005)*, the operational definition and nuances of the term 'youth' often vary from country to country, depending on the specific socio-cultural, institutional, economic and political factors. Consequently, even within a particular country or region, the concept is not static, but varies longitudinally in accordance with historical, economic, political and socio-cultural evolution. In the late colonial and early post-independent Nigeria, for instance, when many young people under the age of 30 were privileged to play major roles in the decolonization struggle and subsequently in government, the age of maturity and initiation into responsible adult life tended to be functionally early compared to the present trend. Similarly, in the typical traditional agricultural societies of both the precolonial and, to a lesser extent, post-colonial era where in late adolescent age, one has virtually completed the functional cycles of socialisation, as well as induction into the traditional economy as an independent producer and livelihood provider, the age of maturity and initiation into responsible adult life also tended to be relatively earlier in comparison to the present 'modern' alienatory and deprivationist context. With life expectancy at birth at 43.7 years, Nigeria, like most countries of sub-Saharan Africa, has a predominantly young population (cf. USAID, 2004, 2005; The World Bank, 2006). But relative to their disproportionately large population and generational needs, the youths do not seem to have the measure of security (in terms of livelihood, protection from violence and access to life chances) that most dependent children and independent older adults experience. Placed in a trans-historical perspective, youths in contemporary Nigeria tend to have far less opportunities, security and hope when compared to youths of previous generations of the country's history or youths in modern Western societies. The vast majority of Nigerian youths were raised amidst overwhelming structures of prebendal corruption, anomie, deprivation, hopelessness and violence - factors that have, to a large extent, contributed to shaping their worldviews, including their perceptions and orientations to the state, society and politics.

Placing Youth Involvement in Conflicts in Nigeria in Perspective

Traditional and Modern Patterns

Youths' involvement in conflicts in Nigeria has both traditional and modern dimensions and patterns. The traditional dimension dates back to precolonial history while the modern patterns date back to the anti-colonial struggle. In the various precolonial communities, chiefdoms, and empires that pre-dated the 1914 amalgamation of the northern and southern British protectorates to form the colony of Nigeria, the youths were the bastion and vanguard of inter-group warfare. Depending on the political interests, motives and aspirations of the hegemonic traditional elites in a society, youths were mobilised and armed for offensive, defensive, resistance, retaliatory, imperial and expansionist warfares, including the initial resistance against European colonial expedition. These political community-based fighting forces in pre-colonial and early colonial history, were rarely constituted into professional standing armies – to use conventional phraseology – but were predominantly socialized and inducted into the ethos of military service to their community on account of their generational prowess. In many communities among the Ibo, Edo, Ibibio, Ijaw and a number of other ethnic groups of southern Nigeria that had age grade and secret cult traditions, military service obligations were expected of or conferred on age grades / secret cults of youth populations. For obvious reasons of gender construction, military service obligations were almost exclusively a male affair. Women were not essentially mobilized as combatants in war but were mobilized for supportive ancillary functions such as supply of food and refreshment, nursing the wounded, and mobilising occult and supernatural powers to reinforce the fighting forces and community protection (Omeje, 2005a).

The issue of harnessing of supernatural power to aid combatants' prosecution of warfare through processes like oracular divination and sorcery, etching of cicatrices in remote parts of the body and wearing amulets and talisman believed to provide inoculation against attacks with lethal weapons, and bewitchment and charming of adversaries to weaken, confuse and ultimately defeat them was regarded as highly crucial for the outcome of inter-group warfare. Many traditional communities mobilised their most dreaded 'medicine men and women' alongside the fighting forces in preparing for and prosecuting wars as it was widely believed that ultimate victory in warfare belonged to communities with superior supernatural means (cf. Ellis & Haar, 2004; Kastfelt, 2005). It is significant that the rhetoric of talismanic or occult protection against lethal weapons which was a major feature of warfare in many precolonial societies have become extensively revived as a crucial instrument of combat by a large number of ethnic militia and insurgency groups in contemporary Nigeria, including militants of the Egbesu Boys[xlii] among the ethnic Ijaw, Oodua Peoples' Congress of the ethnic Yoruba and Bakassi Boys of the ethnic Ibo. These ethnic militias are famous for the use of armed violence and occult power to fight their adversaries, notably the state security forces, rival groups and, armed robbers - in the case of the Bakassi Boys that fight the scourge of violent crime in different Ibo commercial cities. It is widely held belief among members of the public that the militia cult members have powerful charms that inoculate them against being hurt or killed by gunfire. This belief that ethnic militias use 'bullet proof charms' is reinforced by claims of the militia cult members and some officers of the state security forces - the militias' principal combat opponents, albeit the state security officers further claim that acquisition of this occult power is not limited to the militia fighters as some of their colleagues use similar supernatural reinforcement (Omeje, 2005a; 2006:144). With the proliferation of incidents of political violence in Nigeria and Africa, especially since the 1990s, acquisition and use of the so-called bullet proof charm has been significantly reported among all categories of combatants (militias, insurgents, mercenaries, government forces), as well as some top politicians, public office holders, and opposition leaders (cf. Ellis, 1999; Harnischfeger, 2003; Alie, 2005).

With regard to the modern dimension of youth engagement in political conflict, the origin could be traced to the students' struggle against colonial dictatorship and its diverse obnoxious policies. As the most enlightened and better organised segment of the youth populations, students have been in the vanguard of the struggle against authoritarian and corrupt regimes in Nigeria dating from colonial history (Dibua, 2006:281). The formation of the Nigerian Union of Students (NUS) in 1940, the first umbrella students body in Nigeria was partly necessitated by the need to create a political forum for students to contribute to the anti-colonial struggle as their African and 'negro' counterparts were doing in the then Gold Coast (Ghana), Sierra

Leone, West Indies, Europe and North America. Through their various meetings and strategic coalition with diverse civil society organisations (labour, ethno-cultural unions, independent press, and professional associations), NUS was instrumental to the formation in 1944 of the first nationalist political party in Nigeria, the National Council of Nigeria and Cameroun (NCNC), later renamed National Convention of Nigerian Citizens (see Dibua, 2006:282). Upon graduation from the leading higher educational institutions in colonial Nigeria, notably, the Yaba College of Technology and University College Ibadan, NUS activists gravitated like King's College, Lagos; Barewa College, Zaria; Hope Wadell Training Institute, Calabar and Dennis Memorial Grammar School, Onitsha (to name a few) also played active roles in the anti-colonial struggle through the various political and communal towards some of the major political parties in Nigeria in furtherance of the anti-colonial struggle. Many young high school leavers, especially products of such leading schools associations they either formed or joined. These activists were radically determined and defiant of the repeated persecution of the brutal colonial regime. Without doubt, the constructive political activism of the Nigerian youths, especially students and young school leavers, played a major part in the success of the anti-colonial campaign. Hence, at independence in 1960 and during the early stage of self-rule, a significant number of youths occupied prominent positions in government such as regional and federal parliamentarians, ministers, ambassadors, and heads of different government agencies. The sheer dearth of educated and skilled manpower at that conjuncture of national history was also an important advantage to the youths.

Students' constructive political activism continued after independence through the years of military dictatorships. During the first civilian republic, students protested against disturbing national issues such as the infamous Anglo-Nigerian Defence Pact that undermined national sovereignty (but thankfully abrogated in 1962 following students protests), the massive rigging of the 1964 election, and the perceived repeated subversion of parliamentary democracy in the opposition party (Action Group) stronghold of Western region by the Northern People's Congress (NPC)-controlled federal government.

In the build-up to, and during the Nigerian civil war, students bodies across the various regions of the federation were, to a large extent, correspondingly divided along the contending ethno-political issues that divided Nigeria and Biafra. Many students joined and supported their governments and political leaders on both sides of the divide. Students' support seemed more intense on the separatist Biafian side ostensibly because of the unifying strength from the collective sense of persecution and loss precipitated by the 1966 pogrom in which over 50,000 easterners (mostly Ibos) were killed in the northern and, to a lesser extent, western regions (Forsyth, 1969).

Cold War Climate and Leftist Influence

Throughout the 1970s and 1980s, organised youth involvement in political conflicts in Nigeria continued mostly through students' movements. National Union of Nigerian Students (NUNS), National Association of Nigerian Students (NANS) and various local chapters of students' unions in universities, polytechnics and other higher colleges were the platforms for most of the students' political activities. Students' campaign and protests were predominantly focused on government educational policies relating to tuition fees, student bursary and federal government subventions to federal universities (majority of the universities were then federally owned), government economic policies such as the devastating World Bank/IMF Structural Adjustment Programme (SAP), as well as peculiar issues of governance relating to study and living conditions in various tertiary education campuses. Given the dominant authoritarian political culture in the country associated with the realism of military dictatorships, a considerable number of non-violent students' protests over some legitimate concerns were challenged with military force, resulting in avoidable violent standoff, destruction of properties and human casualties. Because of the Cold War climate, there tended to be an extensive leftist influence in most Nigerian universities and higher educational institutions with the result that radical leftists dominated students' union leadership in the country. The leftist rhetoric that pervaded students' union discourses tended to aggravate relations between students' leadership on the one hand, and the government and university authorities, on the other hand. Hence, from time to time, university authorities and/or government took drastic measures such as proscription of leading students' association and invitation or deployment of the state security forces to arrest and incarcerate key students' leaders and activists. To a large extent, up until the late 1980s, organized youth involvement in political conflicts in Nigeria tended to be focused on key national issues and legitimate concerns of students. An exception to this, however, was the largescale mobilization of jobless youths by various political parties for political violence (thuggery, election rigging, etc) during the second civilian republic, especially in the run-up to the ill-fated 1983 elections.

Military Dictatorship, Neo-Patrimonial Extremism and Historical Shift

From the 1990s, there has been a marked shift in the character of youths' involvement in conflicts. Two contradictory dimensions are discernible. The first is the largely constructive and proactive pro-democracy, civil society-led struggle against perpetuation of military dictatorship, corruption and gross insensitivity to the plight and aspirations of the populace in the 1990s; and unaccountable rule, abuse of the constitution, disregard for popular aspirations and corruption in the 2000s. The institutional and functional failures of the state to provide economic and political development has been palpable, especially since the introduction of the World Bank/IMF SAP by the General Ibrahim Babangida's regime in the mid-1980s, a phenomenon that has aggravated the discontent of the masses and the legitimacy crisis of the state. Further, it has aggravated state-society relations and the influx of unemployed youths into the civil society to oppose the misrule of the neo-patrimonial hegemonic elites. Consequently, the relationship between the civil society and the state has become intensely antagonistic, with the state resorting to intermittent coercion, repression and restriction of rights (cf. Ake, 1996; Ikelegbe, 2001). It is significant to note that the civil society-led campaign for democracy, the expansion of the democratic space, respect for the rule of law, transparency and good governance is a trans-generational struggle that has in most cases helped to build bridges and robust networks between the youths, organised labour, women's organisations, professional associations and sometimes disaffected sections of the political elites. It is campaign that has been essentially inspired by revulsion for the collective tribulation and set-back inflicted on the federation by the montage of neo-patrimonial, corrupt, divisive and lawless regimes the country has had for a greater part of the post-independent history.

The second dimension has to do with 'the perverse manifestations of the civil society' as it affects the youths, epitomized by 'the role that [un]civil groups play in undermining democracy and national stability' (Ikelegbe, 2001). One of the most pernicious consequences of the nexus of political instability, coups, and prolonged military dictatorship in Nigeria is the institutionalization of lawlessness and idiotization of the national accumulation and political cultures. Regarding accumulation, the social structures of neo-patrimonialism interacting with the regime of impunity entrenched by military misrule have engendered a culture of predatory accumulation that virulently pervades and transcend the state and society. The result is that the state is not only used to promote prebendal accumulation by public office holders and those that have privileged access to the office holders, but also, a semblance of prebendal or primitive accumulation is extensively propagated by other social agents within the society (the youths inclusive) that lack access to the state system. There has been a massive influx of Nigerians - in particular, those alienated from or unable to connect to the mainstream of the state's prebendal largesse - into diverse shadow economies. The influx into shadow economies is marked by an unprecedentedly intense desperation for predatory and disingenuous accumulation. This accounts for the preponderant boom in fake drugs / pharmaceuticals and other counterfeit or adulterated products, hard drugs, money spinning by fetishism and jujuism, internet fraud and counterfeiting of all categories of official documents otherwise called the 'Oluwole syndrome' (a name derived from the notorious Oluwole business district in Lagos known for trade in forged documents, cheques, identity cards, etc), especially since the 1990s. Predation of the oil industry (e.g. kidnapping of oil workers for a ransom, extortion of delivery trucks and contractors working for different oil companies, sabotage of pipelines to spill oil as a means to put up compensation claims to oil companies, etc) by diverse militant youth groups, not withstanding the legitimate anti-oil grievances of the Niger Delta oil communities, is, to a large extent, an extension of the pervasive tendency towards perverse accumulation (Omeje, 2004; 2005b). Similarly, the phenomenon of advance fee fraud (code-named 419 scam – see chapter 1) championed by Nigerian young school leavers and university graduates (the so-called 'the Yahoo Boys') is an externality of this tendency by those unable to penetrate the state's prebendal spoils to accumulate by predatory internationalization of scam. An outrageous consequence of the entrenched culture and industry of perverse accumulation in Nigeria is that accumulation by predation, kleptomania, thievery, scam and other processes of dispossession is widely applauded, celebrated and glamorized in society (see Omeje, 2006:5-11). For obvious reasons, large sections of the youth populations are vulnerable protagonists of predatory accumulation, especially but not exclusively, outside of the state system.

Concerning the idiotization of the political culture, the dominant attitudes and orientations to politics in Nigeria tend to be regressively characterised by primordial considerations, violence and fraud. Following the devastations wrought through decades of political instability, coups, and military dictatorship, Nigeria's political culture more or less interfaces and synthesizes the Laswellian notion that 'politics' is about 'who gets what, when and how,' and the Machiavellian dictum that 'the end justifies the means'. In the face of their generational vulnerability within the rentier political economy, large segments of disadvantaged youths are hired or sponsored by the hegemonic elites as pawns, poodles, pimps, thugs, assassins and fronts in the ghastly political chessboard. In mobilizing the youths for self-serving political violence, the elites often advance rhetorics of common ethno-religious interests and deceptions of ultimate messianism. This explains the high prevalence of thuggery, electoral violence and demagoguery involving the youths in Nigerian politics. One of the most hysterical deployments of youth demagoguery in Nigerian political history was the Abuja two million match spearheaded by the notorious Youths Earnestly Ask for Abacha (YEAA) led by Daniel Kanu to endorse General Sanni Abacha's plan for self-succession as president in the 1998 transition to civil rule programme implemented by the late dictator (Omeje,2000:28). Scores of other groups (mostly non-youth and [sub]elite groups) paraded the political scene in support of Abacha's self-succession plot. It was ultimately providence that stopped General Abacha from a continued exploitation of the idiotized political culture in the country to mesmerize the populace and perpetuate his dictatorship. A semblance of the YEAA parade was more recently in 2006 organized by diverse obsequious groups (youths, women and elites) in support of the ill-fated attempt of President Obasanjo to change the constitution to enable him run for third term as civilian president. Nigerian politics is hardly short of charades of this nature given the potential of demagoguery and scoundrelism as instruments of prebendal gratification and accumulation.

Contemporary Dimensions and Dynamics of Youth Violence

Every geo-political region of Nigeria is characterized by entrenched structures of violent conflicts, with the youths as the principal driving force. In the oil-producing region of the south-south, resource control and environmental conflicts waged by ethnic militias of the Niger Delta have become an endemic stigma on the oil-rich region and Nigeria in general. In the south-west, the youths are principal protagonists of the majority of ethnic and communal violence that tend to be on the increase in the region in recent years. Leading ethnic Yoruba militia groups such as the rival factions of Oodua People's Congress (OPC) and the rag-tag urban hoodlums, the Lagos Area Boys, have been repeatedly involved in anti-establishment violence and intra- and inter-ethnic feud (e.g. factional implosion of OPC, reprisals against minority Hausa and Ijaw communities in Lagos and environs in reaction to perceived attacks on Yoruba minorities in the homelands of these rival ethnic groups, etc). In the three geo-political zones of the old northern region, the enormous damage inflicted on different communities and peoples by the incessant outbreak of ethno-religious conflicts and disputes related to land rights and the indigeneity *problematique* (community squabbles between 'indigenes' and 'settlers') is common-knowledge. The introduction of the radical and high-handed Sharia Penal Codes by 12 of the 19 states of the old northern region since the 4th civilian republic has accorded unprecedented impetus to the revival of Islamist fundamentalism and the mobilization of young Wahhabists, such as the Taliban Nigeria Movement, as vanguards for defending fundamentalist Islam against any contrary aspirations of 'infidels' and moderate Muslims. In the south-east, organised crime and political turbulence have compounded the problem of societal fragmentation and descent into what Kaplan (1994) calls 'criminal anarchy'. Youth militias and community vigilantes, such as the famous Bakassi Boys have cashed in on the vacuum created by the dysfunctioning and legitimacy crisis of government's law enforcement institutions and agencies to ostensibly substitute for the state's function of law enforcement and crime control in a crude and jungle fashion. The separatist campaign of the

154

Movement for the Actualization of the Sovereign State of Biafra (MASSOB), which revives the vision of the defunct Biafian statehood that precipitated the civil war of 1997-1970, tends to compound the *status quo* of political disorder and criminal violence in the southeast.

On top of all these, there is the macro or nationwide problem of political violence, linked to electoral fraud, sponsorship and use of thuggery by many politicians and political parties, as well as the politicization of primordial identities, in particular, ethnic and religious identities.

Many recent studies tend to associate most of the macro- and micro-level conflicts in Nigeria with the problem of deprivation and poverty. This may seem an over-simplification. However, the observation may not be entirely surprising when placed against the backdrop of the fact that the level of extreme poverty in Nigerian defined by the proportion of people that subsist on less than one US Dollar per day is about 70 per cent, estimated to comprise more than 91 million Nigerians (Dike, 2005). Researchers argue that deprivation and poverty translate into conflict in Nigeria through a number of causal and aggravating factors or processes discussed below. Other non-poverty linked factors are also discussed.

1. Staggering level of youth unemployment, leading to hopelessness, restiveness and feelings of frustration, which often precipitates or fuels violent conflicts. Authoritative statistics on current youth unemployment rate in Nigeria does not seem to be available but independent local sources' estimates suggest that 14.7 per cent of primary school leavers, 53.6 per cent of secondary school leavers, and 12.4 per cent tertiary school graduates contribute to the national unemployment rate (see Dike, 2005). Majority of the unemployed primary and secondary school leavers are those that apparently lack the socio-economic and financial opportunities to continue their education, which creates palpable feelings of frustration among victims. With an average GDP growth rate of about 2.6 per cent in the 1990s and 5.7 per cent in the 2000s, expansion of the economy to create employment opportunities for young school leavers and graduates has been rather sluggish (FGN, 2002; World Bank, 2006). This heightens the risk and incidents of anti-establishment protests and frustration-related violence. The frustration and vulnerability of the youths make it possibly for them to be mobilized, instigated or hired for violence with relative ease.

2. The second fact is the problem of dysfunctional structural divide and discrimination at various levels of state and society, which impacts adversely on issues such as employment, promotion, public appointments, as well as group and community relations and land rights, often linked to the problem of indigeneity. Poverty creates resource scarcity and negative competition, thereby predisposing actors to the desperation of hiding under convenient structures and opportunism to out-compete and liquidate potential rivals. A large number of episodic conflicts often described or disguised as ethnic, religious or protracted historical animosities come under this rubric (cf. Suberu & Osaghae, 2005; Ukiwo, 2005).

3. Promotion of violence as an economic opportunity. Under circumstances of massive deprivation and impoverishment of underprivileged classes and social groups visibly contradicted by the flamboyant opulence of the hegemonic elites and their business associates, the grievances of the subalterns could radically develop rhetorics of survivalism under various disguises. The situation is aggravated if, as in the case of Nigeria, a significant proportion of the deprived and impoverished groups are fairly literate youths and urban dwellers that are politically enlightened and sensitized. The occasional incidents of degeneration of well-intended peaceful students' and civil society demonstrations into acts of arson and looting of public and private properties, as well as extortion of innocent road users is part of the tendency of the down-trodden to exploit violence as an economic opportunity. In a similar vein, a significant proportion of the petro-violence in the Nigerian oil producing region are either orchestrated or amplified by militant youths to extort petrobusiness or gain economic advantage over a rival community/group. Ikelegbe (2005:208) has aptly captured this extortionist dimension as the 'conflict economy in the Niger Delta, comprising an intensive and violent struggle for resource opportunities, inter and intra communal/ethnic conflicts over resources and the theft and trading in refined and crude oil, which has blossomed since the 1990s'. In this respect, one would also underscore the inextricable interest of sections of the local civil society, in particular, those of the environment and conflict resolution industry that thrive on the existence and persistence of petro-conflicts.

4. Poor institutional capacity for non-violent conflict prevention and management within the state system aggravates many conflicts involving the youths and other social agencies. The Nigerian state's

approach to counter-hegemonic conflicts involving youth and civil society groups, and disaffected factions of the elite is, to a large extent, characterized by tendencies of persecution, repression and brutality using state security forces. These tendencies are partly a consequence of the entrenched barrack culture and authoritarian legacy of past military dictatorships that form a vital part of the behavioural repertoire and *modus operandi* of the state. The situation is compounded by the large number of (ex-)serving senior military personnel that have played and continue to play key governance and conflict management roles in the 4th republic. The skills and tradition of non-violent conflict prevention and management scarcely exist in Nigerian state institutions and among state functionaries and security forces, with the result that most counter-hegemonic protests are seen from military lenses and tackled with military solutions. Too often, the use of military measures have complicated the conflicts and exacerbated state-society relations.

5. In addition, there are pervasive patterns of domestic and cultural violence in Nigeria, such as harmful traditional practices (e.g. female genital mutilation and infibulation, widowhood rites, early marriage, caste segregation and oppression, etc), and the inexorable clash between traditional institutions and forces of modernism, which impact adversely on children, women and youths. Violence rooted in traditional social structures in Nigeria are, however, often reinforced or aggravated by structures of poverty.

At the bottom of the too many violent conflicts in Nigeria is the high incidence of state failure. The state's abdication of or perhaps inability to meet its primary social obligations, notably development provisioning and maintenance of internal order, as well as its unconcealed appetite for misrule basically epitomize what many scholars have often conceptualized as state failure. It suffices to say that Nigeria is marked by an unacceptably high level of functional failure of the state linked to the correspondingly high level of political and legal impunity, which encourages largescale corruption and insensitivity of public functionaries to the plight of the populace. The high level of youth violence and restiveness, especially the organized activities of ethnic militias who increasingly challenge or attempt to usurp the authority and functions of the state could be seen as a response to the problem of state failure. The proliferation of small arms and light weapons, itself an expression of state failure, basically aggravates the imbroglio.

Conclusion: Responding to Youth Violence in Nigeria

How do we respond to the problem of youth violence in Nigeria? This is certainly not an easy puzzle for policy practitioners, conflict interveners and the larger peace industry. This chapter has, among other things, delineated the nexus of factors that dispose the youths to violent conflicts. Most of the delineated factors are structurally related to the dysfunctionality of the state and its reverberations to the wider society and beyond. A logical step towards solving the problems would therefore be to proactively transform the state by: (a) Re-engineering its functional capacity to formulate and deliver poverty reduction policies at all levels of government – federal, state and local governments. (b) Expanding and strengthening the capacity of the relevant government agencies responsible transparency scrutiny in public finance, contracts, tenders; project execution, monitoring and evaluation, and accountability at all levels of government. This is essential because of the colossal impact of prebendal corruption on social, economic, political and infrastructural development and mass welfare. (c) Involvement of local and international civil society groups in the government's anti-corruption campaign by creating formal institutional arrangements for collaborative investigation, verification, information sharing, prosecution of suspects, etc. (d) Strengthening the autonomy of key government institutions essential for political and economic reforms and democratic consolidation by placing the staffing (appointment), dismissal, funding and regulation of such bodies under appropriate legislative committees as opposed to the executive arm of government. This will improve transparency, fairness and efficiency. The agencies include the judiciary, transparency and anti-corruption bodies, public complaints commission, and electoral commissions.

The above measures will help to radically engender and safeguard good governance in Nigeria without which significant economic and sustainable development, including the much-desired development and implementation of pro-poor policies, will remain elusive.

Furthermore, to significantly grow and expand the economy to create more gainful jobs for the youths, there is the need to expand and strengthen the capacity of the state to regulate the private sector,

158

especially such strategic sectors like oil and gas, telecommunication, manufacturing, transport and aviation, building and construction, and service industries. The operational mandate, personnel strength and expertise, and facilities of existing agencies for private sector regulation such as the corporate affairs commission, relevant government ministries, Department of Petroleum Resources (DPR), etc should be expanded and streamlined to enhance efficiency. A corpus of new corporate legislations and guidelines should be introduced and enforced in the private sector to safeguard the interests of the sector's employees / potential employees, host communities, and the general public. The new regulations should focus on restructuring the following areas to enhance the advantages of local stakeholders and national economy: corporate social and environmental responsibilities (to be aligned with international 'best practices'), minimum wage for monthly and hourly paid jobs, conditions of service of employees, in particular, the disproportionately large number of contract workers they hitherto hire and fire with impunity, partial reinvestment of profits, value added, conditions for engagement of expatriate personnel, fair competition and profit repatriation.

Another important area of attention is the need for expanded investment in conflict prevention, conflict management and peacebuilding capacity-development programmes targeting various key institutions such as the state security forces (especially the police, army, navy and prisons), and top government functionaries. New recruits and serving officers of the state security forces should as a matter of urgency, be systematically exposed to training programmes on non-violent conflict resolution, peacebuilding, community policing, and security sector transformation. The new training programmes can be developed and incorporated into the curricula of the various academies and special programmes for training recruits and re-training serving officers.

For the various civil militia groups in different parts of the federation, a carefully negotiated weapon amnesty (with reasonable financial incentive) and a disarmament, demobilization, repatriation and rehabilitation (DDRR) programme is required (see Omeje, 2006).

Finally, there is a dangerous personality factor to many violent conflicts in Nigeria, which has implications for both political instability and the process of achieving peace and conflict prevention. In this regard, Wiebe Boer (2000:36) has observed that 'in each Nigerian community, there are select individuals, who have the clout to start or stop conflicts – these central figures could be politicians, religious leaders, youth leaders, or traditional rulers. Whoever they are, these individuals are able to pull the strings that make communities either function or dysfunction.' One is reasonably inclined to agree with Boer. Nigeria, like most African countries, is a profoundly hierarchical society and social relations within the hierarchical structures are often bound in socio-cultural traditions marked by top-bottom patterns of authority. Hence, it is not usually difficult for leaders of different groups, communities, organizations and political blocs and formations to mobilize, manipulate and channel their members to conflicts based on their personal inclinations and idiosyncrasies. Low level of literacy and poverty worsen the gullibility of the masses, who are often induced with petty pecuniary rewards and promises. The peace and conflict prevention industry should partly aim to focus peace education skill acquisition programmes and conflict mediation on the principal figures and personalities behind specific conflicts. This method has proved successful in deflecting and preventing a considerable number of violent conflicts in many war-affected and conflict-prone countries of sub-Saharan Africa but it is debateable whether the method could be effective as a means of sustainable conflict transformation.

Notes

*This chapter expands on an article I originally published in the *African Renaissance* entitled: 'Youths, Conflicts and Perpetual Instability in Nigeria', March/April 2005, vol. 2, no. 2, pp. 34-38.

1. This is a generic name for diverse ethnic Ijaw militants that are engaged in anti-oil protests and anti-state resistance in the Niger Delta regions by tapping into the spiritual power of the ancient Egbesu deity in their ethnic homeland. The Egbesu power believed to fortify those initiated into the Egbesu secret cult with the famous 'bullet proof charm' is a magical device that complements the militants limited firepower in relation to the main opponents – the state security forces.

References

Ake, Claude (1996) *Democracy and Development in Africa.* Washington DC: The Brookings Institution.

Boer, Wiebe (2000) 'To Build a Nation Where Peace and Justice Shall Reign', Unpublished report on OTI Conflict Resolution Initiative in Nigeria. USAID/OTI, Abuja, Nigeria, December.

Dike, E. Victor (2005) 'Youth Unemployment in Nigeria: The Relevance of Vocational and Technical Education'. Nigerian Village Square, Feb. 2005. http://www.nigeriavillagesquare.com/content/view/1035/55/. Website accessed on 12.12.06.

Ellis, Stephen (1999) *The Mask of Anarchy: The Destruction of Liberia and the Religious Dimension of an African Civil War.* London: Hurst & Company.

Ellis, Stephen & Gerrie Ter Haar, (2004) *Worlds of Power: Religious Thought and Political Practice in Africa.* London: Hurst & Co.

FGN (2002) 'Framework for Nigeria's Economic Growth and Development (2003 - 2007)'. Full text of the Federal Government home grown economic blueprint unveiled at the ninth Nigerian Economic Summit in Abuja, 16 October, 2002. http://www.nigeriavillagesquare1.com/Economicframework.htm Website accessed on 10.12.06.

Forsyth, Fredrick (1969) *The Biafra Story.* London: Penguin.

Harnischfeger, Johannes (2003) 'The Bakassi Boys: Fighting Crime in Nigeria', *Journal of Modern African Studies,* vol. 41/1, pp. 23-49.

Ikelegbe, Augustine (2001) 'The Perverse Manifestation of Civil Society: Evidence from Nigeria'. *The Journal of Modern African Studies.* 39/1: pp. 1-24.

Ikelegbe, A. (2005) 'The Economy of Conflict in the Oil Rich Niger Delta Region of Nigeria', *Nordic Journal of African Studies,* 14/2, pp. 208 – 234.

Kaplan, D. Robert (1994) 'The Coming Anarchy', *The Atlantic Monthly;* February, Volume 273, No. 2; pp. 44-76.

Kastfelt, Niels (ed.) (2005), *Religion & African Civil Wars.* London: Hurst & Co.

Omeje, Kenneth (2000) 'Military Rule and the Destabilization of Nigeria's Political Culture: The Politics of De-democratization'. C. I.

Onyesoh & K. Omeje (eds.) *Stabilizing Nigerian Polity Post - Military*, pp. 16-32.

Omeje, Kenneth (2004) 'The State, Conflict and Evolving Politics in the Niger Delta'. *Review of African Political Economy* 31/101, pp. 425-440.

Omeje, Kenneth (2005a) 'The Egbesu and Bakassi Boys: African Spiritism and the Mystical Re-traditionalization of Security', D. J. Francis (ed.) *Civil Militias: African Intractable Security Menace?* Aldershot: Ashgate, pp. 71-86.

Omeje, Kenneth (2005b) 'Oil Conflict in Nigeria: Contending Issues and Perspectives of the Local Niger Delta People', *New Political Economy*, 10/3: pp. 321-334.

Omeje, Kenneth (2006) *High Stakes and Stakeholders: Oil Conflict and Security in Nigeria.* Aldershot: Ashgate.

Suberu, Rotimi & Eghosa E. Osaghae (2005), *A History of Identities, Violence, and Stability in Nigeria.* CRISE Working Paper No. 6, Queen Elizabeth House, University of Oxford, UK. January.

Ukiwo, Ukoha (2005) *On the Study of Ethnicity in Nigeria. A History of Identities, Violence, and Stability in Nigeria.* CRISE Working Paper No. 12, Queen Elizabeth House, University of Oxford. June.

United Nations Division for Social Policy and Development (2005) World Youth Report. http://www.un.org/esa/socdev/unyin/wyr05.htm. See *also* http://www.un.org/events/youth2000/def2.htm. Website accessed on 10.12.06.

World Bank (2006) *Nigeria Data Profile.* The World Bank. http://devdata.worldbank.org/external/CPProfile.asp?CCODE=NGA&PTYPE=CP. Website accessed on 16.11.06.

Chapter 7

The Policy and Social Consequences of Privatization in Nigeria

Adeniyi Omotayo Adegbuyi

Introduction

Privatization refers to the sale of all or part of a government's equity in 'state-owned enterprises' (SOEs) to the private sector, or to the placing of SOEs under private management through leases and management contracts (Vuylsteke, 1988:8). Privatization was adopted on a worldwide scale in 1980s, covering both rich and poor countries, large and small nations, and governments subscribing to the full spectrum of the neo-liberal ideologies behind the policy. *The Economist* (1985:71) described the contemporary phase of privatization spearheaded by the International Financial Institutions (IFIs) in the global South as the 'greatest exchange ever between private citizens and their governments'. While the policy of privatization may have originated in the industrialized countries, some of its most devastating impacts have occurred in the developing world (Ramamurti, 1992:225). Over the years in many developing countries there has been a slowdown in economic growth, especially in the agricultural sector, which is the decisive sector of most developing economies. As part of the adjustments to the economic slowdown, many affected countries have curtailed the size of their public sectors, further turning to market-oriented reforms. Moreover, as a result of the declining economic growth in these countries, international donor organizations and creditors, such as the World Bank, IMF and Paris Club, have required certain structural reforms as a condition for economic assistance with privatization usually being a major component of the structural adjustment package.

Nigeria has been implementing the World Bank/IMF structural adjustment programme of which privatization is a major component since mid-1986. The main aims of the programme are to open new opportunities for foreign and local investors, increase private sector participation in the economy, expand capital market equity funding, inflow of foreign investment, job creation and engender continued deregulation, low cost of doing business, provide modern infrastructure, new technology and improved efficiency. Nigerians expected much from the exercise, but has privatization flourished in accordance with people's expectations? Who is profiting from privatization, the government or the people? Has privatization contributed positively to economic development? What are the ripple effects of privatization on local economies and social consequences on the people? This chapter is mainly conceived to address these relevant questions.

The chapter comprises five sections. In the first section, attempt is made to elucidate the meaning and aims of privatization in Nigeria. In the second section, the history and methods of the privatization policy in Nigeria are evaluated. The third section highlights the rationale of privatization in Nigeria while the economic and social costs of the programme on Nigerians are briefly analysed in the fourth section. The study is concluded in section five.

The Evolution of Privatization in Nigeria

Privatization has become a central feature of the economic policies of different countries. In addition to the IFIs-led economic reform considerations highlighted above, other factors that have contributed to the ubiquity of privatization in developing countries, the most notable being the generally held neo-liberal notion that privatized industries operate more efficiently than their publicly-owned counterparts. While privatization can bring about benefits under certain conditions, transfer of ownership of public enterprises to the private sector is by no means a sufficient condition for improved performance of firms and stimulating economic growth. Perverse outcomes of privatization leading to the perpetuation of soft-budget constraints and to nefarious asset stripping might occur under a soft or corrupt regime in the absence of robust market institutions, contract enforcement, and prudent regulations. The experience of many developing countries and transitional countries lend credence to such negative outcomes. In modern economic development history, state privatization programmes have been mostly based on the following neo-liberal rationale (Miller, 1997:399):

1. The size of government bureaucracy is too large.
2. Politicians and government bureaucrats cannot be trusted because they make decisions and formulate policies that typically benefit themselves or narrow constituencies. Their priorities often conflicts with and take precedence over those of effective business managers. This distorts the functioning of the free market and thereby limits the benefits of competition for society. Privatizing SOEs prevents politicians and bureaucrats from using them to further their own agendas.
3. The market is more efficient than the government in terms of allocating resources in the economy. Privatization is preferred because it promotes competition and thus increases the role of markets.
4. Government ownership and control of industries undermine individual responsibility and initiative on the part of employees and managers.
5. State-owned businesses are often riddled with bureaucracy and red tape and therefore responses slowly to the consumers needs in terms of quality and quantity of goods and services demanded, product diversity and choice, etc.

The process of privatization began in Nigeria in 1988, when the military ruler General Babangida announced that 95 state-owned companies were to be either partly or fully privatized. Of these, 73 were privatized; including insurance, banking and agro-industrial firms. For a variety of reasons, notably their decadent state and poor financial prospects, the remaining 22 firms, including several large public enterprises like Nigeria Airways were not immediately privatized. The phase of privatization programme introduced by the Babangida regime effectively came to a halt in 1993. Privatization remains a controversial issue in Nigeria. Public opinion is divided between those who support it as means of reviving decrepit utilities, and those who fear it will widen economic inequalities or undermine the necessary capacity of the prebendal state to disburse patronage.

After many years of indecision over the means of reforming Nigeria's major inefficient state enterprises, such as the National Electric Power Authority (NEPA) now Known as Power Holding Company of Nigeria Plc (PHCN) Nigerian Telecommunications (NITEL) and Nigerian National Petroleum Corporation (NNPC), in

1998 the General Abdusallami Abubakar administration launched a new privatization programme, although sales did not begin until the military gave up power in May 1999.

Following the privatization enabling law enacted by General Abubakar, which established Bureau of Public Enterprises (BPE), the Obasanjo administration began implementation of a three-stage programme for privatizing scores of state enterprises by 2003. The presidency appointed Dr. Julius Bala to head the BPE. He succeeded Mallam Nasir El-Rufai, who was then named Minister of the Federal Capital Territory Abuja. However, Bala was sacked in March 2005 due to what was perceived in federal government and IFI quarters as poor performance throughout the period he served as Director-General of the establishment. The sack saw the enthronement of Mrs. Irene Chigbue as the new Director General of BPE.

Ogwemoh (2004:5b), has tried to appraise the progress of the federal government privatization programme as follows: By the end of 1993 divestment had been concluded in 34 public companies through the stock market. Out of this number, 8 were first timers on the stock exchange after privatization; two of the 34 companies, United Nigeria Insurance Company Plc and United Nigeria Life Insurance Company Plc. (UNLIC) were involved in a merger. Federal Ministry of Defence also divested part of its holdings in Union Dicon Salt Plc.

In 2005 alone, the privatization agency, according to Mkpuma (2005:18), has privatized eight of the enterprises. Some of the enterprises are Afribank Nigeria Plc., NHL share in other hotels across the country, Apapa Port, Leyland Company, Bricks and Clay Companies, Central packaging Limited, National Fertilizer Company Nigeria Ltd. (NAFCON), as well as a few oil companies.

Strategies and Processes

Privatization takes different forms. In addition to simple ownership transfer, states can also benefit from the privatization of management without privatizing the ownership of assets. You can have privatization through management contracts leases and outright concession through which the private sector takes over responsibilities and services previously rendered by the public sector, particularly in sector where it is difficult to attract foreign investors (Bameke, 2003:16).

A good example of this is the National Hospital in Abuja, which was privatized under management service contract.

Other forms of privatization include the transfer of public assets via management buyouts, initial public offers; employees buy out (not common), [2] etc. A more concise analysis of the various methods and strategies of privatization are provided below: -

(a)   Selling of nationalized concerns of private shareholders
(b)   Share placement with institutional investors
(c)   Issue of share traded on the stock exchange
(d)   Joint venture with private sector having majority shares
(e)   Sale of assets of the privatized company
(f)   Relaxing state monopoly right to allow for competition (the type given to television and radio stations which brought private electronic media like AIT, DBN, MITV, Ray Power, etc into existence).
(g)   Allowing private contractors to tender for the provision of goods and services hitherto reserved for government enterprises as witnessed in the communication sector, where intercellular multi-links, Mobitel, Rel-tel are now on board with NITEL.
(h)   Selling majority share to core investors
(i)   Setting up an enabling Act for private enterprises to perform, produced and sell goods and services, as well as licensing some organizations to subdue monopoly (e.g. the emergence of GSM and other independent private operators).   Many private universities and polytechnics have also come on board under this arrangement.
(j)   Service delivery by proxy: Government has now called for tender for road construction and maintenance by private organizations for a fee to be paid by all users,
(k)   Sub-contracting revenue collection: Collection of government revenue is also being contracted out to private consulting firms.

Rationale of Privatization in Nigeria

Arguments for privatization in Nigeria include the following (Ibidunni, 2005:3):

a)   With the enterprises in the hands of private investors, it is argued that there will be economic efficiency.

b) Equity is very crucial in the provision of goods and services. The operators are always considering private income and wealth; hence all strata of the population are said to be taken into consideration.

c) Organization and management, through incentives, communication, consultation, collective bargaining and creativity make privatization result in better reward system.

d) It helps to reduce government regulation of the economy making room for greater deregulation and operation of market forces.

e) It encourages competition as private initiative in the privatized industries increase.

f) It reduces the burden on the dwindling resources of the government.

g) It will help restructure the Nigerian economy to allocate public fund to efficient users, create a self-sustaining culture, and attract foreign investors, while goods and services will reflect real values.

h) Over time the economy will shift from a consumption-oriented to a production-oriented one. This helps in the motivations of the work force and instilling of work ethics and greater discipline.

i) Employment opportunities and job creation, for instance many people did not know that GSM revolution has been made possible by privatization and that MTN, V-mobile, and Globacom, which recently came on board, have created over 25,000 jobs and over two-million mobile phone for Nigerians.

j) To eliminate government financial obligations to public enterprises thereby easing the strain on the budget and freeing economic resources for use in the provision of the much-needed infrastructure, development and social projects.

k) To create a better window in the global economy and allow participation in international trade.

l) To expand and deepen the capital markets.

m) To attract foreign direct investment, capital, technology and make managerial expertise available to Nigerians and the Nigerian economy. The analysis by Thomas Smith International (2005:26) shows that increased telecommunications penetration could be associated with higher foreign direct investment (FDI); for instance, a percentage increase in mobile penetration rates has been associated with a percentage higher rate of FDI/GDP in sub-Saharan Africa. By corollary, privatization helps to open up the economy for greater foreign and local participation. For instance, inflow of foreign investment in telecommunication between 2001 and 2002 is about N150 billion of which 90 per cent is from GSM.

n) To reduce the volume economic wastages in public offices.

o) To encourage economic growth and development and contribution to national development.

p)   Maximizing social benefits and infrastructure development.

The Economic and Social Cost of Privatization

Empowered by the Privatization and Commercialization Act of 1988, the Federal Government in all had 89 enterprises privatized between 1988 and 1993 in its first phase of the three-phased privatization programme. In the second phased (1999 – 2005), the Federal Government had privatized more than 32 enterprises. The enterprises include all government equity shares in commercial banks, insurance companies, hotels, flourmills, fertilizer companies, etc. The essence was to give better and more efficient structure to the Nigerian economy while the numerous benefits will accrue to the teaming population.

The evaluation in this section focuses on the social cost of privatization on the Nigerian populace. To many Nigerians privatization creates insalubrious climate to the economy and should earnestly be discontinued since it does not bring about immediate improvement to the economy.

The opponents of privatization are strong in their criticisms. According to Ezeife (2000:12), '…the present rush-sale of public assets to private interest …' is 'an unacceptable response' [my emphasis] to outside pressure'. Privatization according to Waziri (1990:7), is a conspiracy by a rich and privileged few against the masses, while Kingibe (1997:21) describe privatization in Nigeria as the 'systematic stripping by a privileged few of the assets of people built over the decades.' These commentators tend to dismiss privatization as being of little or no economic benefit and for creating an economic situation, which favours only a few individuals in the state system. It has also been criticized as impoverishing the nation and citizens, engendering insurmountable hardships and other economic woes within its nearly two decade of operation. These viewpoints resonate with the position of the dependency and underdevelopment theorists on the political economy of developing countries.

While the precise impact of privatization on employment may vary across industries and countries, most evidence point towards reductions in employment after privatization. This is best-summarised by the International Labour Organization (1999, chapter 2, p. 1 of web version) assessment of the programme outcome in the global South:

... the privatization and restructuring processes in water, electricity and gas utilities have in general resulted in a reduction of employment levels, sometimes affecting up to 50percent of the workforce. Employment cuts appear to be more severe under certain parts of the industry and total privatization or where there is a combination of privatization and restructuring. Moreover, employment increases after privatizations are rare and usually follow periods of large-scale retrenchment.

Empirical findings indicate that during the first decade of privatization, employment levels were affected by privatization (see Asaolu *et al* 2005: 65 – 74). One of the main obstacles to privatization and private concessions has been the trade union movement, which, as expected, is fearful of widespread job losses. Such fears are not without substance, given that most Nigerian parastatals are greatly over-manned. Retrenchment programmes have in most cases been implemented as a consequence of each privatization project and from the standpoint of the private capitalist sector, this seems more or less unavoidable if efficiency levels are to be improved.

A spokesperson for the Nigerian Investment Promotion Commission (NIPC) (Ezechukwu, 2000:29) cautioned, "the unions should not simply think of the direct effects on their members of rationalization by privatized firms but also consider the wider economic benefit which will also benefit their members". It is interesting to think of Nigerian union leaders as such strong proponents of free market economics. Unions are created to look after the needs of their members and this is what they will do, fighting redundancies tooth and nail in the wake of each privatization. However, while the government may argue that opposition to privatization has slowed down the sell-offs, slow progress merely exacerbates the situation. Where government is determined to pursue privatization it is important that it develops complementary social policies and schemes to help ameliorate the externality effects on workers as much as possible.

Some Nigerians do not see privatization living up to the expectations of salvaging the economy, judging from the incidence of heightening inflation, high and unsteady exchange rate, indiscipline, allegations of corruption in the implementation process of the privatization policy, among other anomalies. There are indications that the economy has been sorely affected by continued mismanagement and fiscal indiscipline. Even with the advent of fourth republic and the anti-corruption crusade, the situation does not seem to have significantly improved. Some other key features of the sacrifices made by the exercise have been drastic budgetary setbacks to critical social sectors, which have intensified social and economic problems. Especially affected is the related phenomenon of mass unemployment and underemployment; which has been further complicated by retrenchment of workers. Hence, in the final analysis the quantum of jobs that have materialized from the privatization policy is far outstripped by those lost through retrenchment of work force.

There is also the most contentious question as to whether the privatization exercise is not a breach of section (6) (c) and other similar provisions in chapter two of the 1999 constitution which states *inter-alia* that it shall be the goal of the government to provide social amenities, education and economic welfare for the citizen (Kekere – Ekun, 2002). If public utilities and organizations like NEPA, NITEL (now PHCN), NPA, MINT, Universities, Polytechnics, etc are transferred to people who now dictate the price, how will government discharge this obligation effectively to the citizenry? What legacies would this administration leave behind when all these valuable investments exchange hands?

Clearly, the effect of privatization on the Nigerian economy is worrisome if the existing economic indices and parameters already analyzed are anything to go by. Inflation, as a critical issue, is hardly addressed while the value of the local currency in the foreign exchange market continues to deteriorate. The standard of living remains poor for large sections of the populations. Uncertainty pervades the air in many sectors of the economy.

Furthermore, it is apparent that the federal government has increasingly privatized the relatively functional public enterprises, such as Federal Palace Hotel, diverse insurance companies and banks, Sheraton Hotel, etc whereas the more dysfunctional public corporations like Nigeria Railway Corporation and petroleum refineries are not privatized. This trend according to Ibidunni (2005:6) obviously undermines any good intention in privatization and mocks the entire process. If for instance, the oil refineries had been privatized, they would have been working at improved capacity and more efficiently. The nation would probably not have had any need to import fuel and, accordingly, local oil consumption would have been significantly insulated from fluctuations in the prices of oil in the international market. By extension, the needless strikes of labour would have been avoided and productive man-hours lost in the process would have equally been utilized to improve the nation's gross domestic product. In the same vain, privatization of NEPA (now PHCN) and deregulation of the energy sector would have led to a dramatic increase in industrial production in the country. It has the potential of unlocking the productive energy of Nigerians, especially those in the rural areas who have been unable to channel their energies into productive use due to lack of electricity.

Emphasis should be on selling public utilities, which, if transferred into private hands will become more efficient. All over the developed and industrializing world, the rail system is relatively the cheapest means of transportation. But Nigeria, the rail system has become a huge joke and is not reckoned as a means of transportation. The railways should have been considered among the first utilities to be privatized by the government. It is clear that if the railways had been functioning, the public outcry against incessant increases in fuel prices would not have been as fierce. People would have had an alternative and even cheaper means of transportation. The Federal Government should, therefore, look beyond the immediate self-serving gains of privatizing performing enterprises, and make hay to sell utilities that would in the near future make the economy to thrive and directly or indirectly benefit the Nigerian masses.

It is necessary to see another side of the privatization coin. The proponents of privatization maintain that it is the concern of the government, like its counterparts elsewhere in the world, to judiciously utilize scarce public funds and resources entrusted to its care and forestall actions that are inimical to economic growth and aspiration of the citizens. The habit of investing public resources in unprofitable ventures or organizations beleaguered with corruption and efficiency is antithetical to economic growth and development. In the end, it is difficult to exonerate the government from the responsibility for the poor performance of public corporations and the economy for a greater part of the post-colonial history. Most Nigerians, therefore, expect corrective measures to assuage the negative impacts of mismanaging the economy in the form of stringent economic discipline, proactive controls and supervision, and the recruitment of committed, competent, experienced and skillful employees to manage public establishments.

Conclusion and Recommendations

Most Nigerians would obviously not resist policies that add great value to the economy and significantly improve the standard of living of the populace, be it privatization, commercialization, liberalization, deregulation, etc. What the populace find distasteful is self-serving half-hearted measure whereby a privileged few in positions of power turn privatization to personal or family affair and dispose of valuable investments either to themselves, relatives, friends and business associate at a given away value.

Worthy of note in this regard are the following:

1. Nigerians reserve the right to seek information, explanation and enlightenment on any aspect of privatization from the government or its agencies because these establishments belong to all. Refusal to respond satisfactorily or outright denials unjust, unfair, undemocratic and seriously contradicts democratic tenets.
2. If privatization is to achieve the stated objectives, its execution should be in the best interest of the nation and for well-being of the citizenry. Greater commitment and dedication are also expected of the government, NCP, and BPE members and their actions must be devoid of corruption.
3. Anti-corruption campaign should be extended to all public offices with a sense of purpose and transparency. Appointments of public officers and senior managers must be devoid of all kinds of sentiments and nepotism but strictly on merit. This will help to ensure that such officers accountable and law abiding.
4. Proceeds of sold investments should be re-invested or used to address pressing needs and problems like food production, employment generation, education, health, water, shelter and other top social priorities.
5. The study conducted shows there are no enough laws to protect investment in Nigeria. For instance, it was alleged that the sale of NITEL was bungled because the nation does not have adequate laws governing the telecommunication industry. This further affected a lot of investors including First Bank of Nigeria. Therefore, there is need to review all enabling laws on privatization to become pro-active, context-specific and relevant.

6. Efforts should be made by government in concert with layouts to ensure a solid agreement with core investors to protect the interest of Nigerian workers in the event of privatization.

7. There is the need to instill greater discipline in the entire public service; necessary rules and regulations should therefore be put in place to checkmate excesses of core investors. This is highly necessary to curb the possibility of private monopolies and prevent situations where some capitalists dominate an industry and thereby hike prices of products and services indiscriminately.

Note

*This chapter is an expanded version of an article first published in the *African Renaissance* of September/October 2006.

References

Asaolu, T. O; Oyesanmi O., Oladele P. O. and Oladoyin A. M. (2005) 'Privatization and Commercialization in Nigeria: Implications and Prospects for Good Governance,' *South Africa Journal of Business Management*, 36(3)

Bammeke, S.A; (2003), 'Who is afraid of privatization in Nigeria?' *The Nigerian Accountant* April/June, vol. 36, no. 2.

Economist (1985) Privatization: Everybody Doing It Differently, Dec. 21: 71 – 86

Ezechukwu, D; (2000), 'Privatization will keep government at Bay' Lagos, *Policy Magazine* vol. 5, no.5, January 24 – 30, pp. 29-31

Ezeife, C. P. (2002) 'This Privatization?' *The Punch Newspaper*, 12 August, p.12

Ibidunni, O.S; (2005), 'Vision and mission of privatization in 21st century.' *A Multidisciplinary Journal*, vol. 2.

Ogwemoh, P. (2004), 'Privatized Enterprises, An Assessment of performance', Lagos, *Business Day*, Wednesday September: 15, p.5B.

Kekere-Ekun, A. (2002), 'Roles of Lawyers in privatization process', *The Guardian* September 22 p. 45

Kingibe, B. (1997) 'Privatization in Africa.' *The Guardian*, 30 September: p.21.

Miller, A. N; (1997) 'Ideological motivations of privatization in Great Britain versus Developing Countries,' *Journal of International Affairs* Winter 50, 2

Mkpuma, B. B; (2005), 'Chigbue's BPE: Six Month After.' Lagos, *Financial Standard*, vol. no. 36, September 12, p. 18.

Ogbu, C; and Yomi, O; (2002), 'Privatization will Save Democracy,' *The punch* Wednesday, August.

Thomas Smith International (2005), 'NCP lists benefits of reforms and privatization.' Lagos, *Financial Standard,* vol. 4 no. 32 November 21, p. 26.

Privatization: Opening a window of opportunities in Nigeria (on line serial) Retrieved April 28, 2006 from worldwide website: www.bpeng.org

Ramamurti, R. (1992) 'Why are Developing Countries Privatizing?' *Journal of International Business Studies,* vol. 23, no. 2 (2nd Quarter), pp. 225 - 249

Vuylsteke, C. (1988) *Techniques of Privatization of State-Owned Enterprises, vol. 1 Methods and Implementation.* Washington D.C: The World Bank, Technical Paper, no. 88.

Waziri, M. (1990) 'People's Right and Privatization,' *National Concord,* 5 March: p.7.

Chapter 8

Sustaining Poverty Reduction Efforts through Inter-Agency Collaboration in Nigeria

Chukwuemeka U. Okoye & Onyukwu E. Onyukwu

Introduction

Poverty is one of the most serious problems confronting Nigerians today. It is usually defined in either absolute or relative terms. Absolute poverty denotes a condition in which a person or group of persons are unable to satisfy their most basic and elementary requirements of human survival in terms of good nutrition, clothing, shelter, footwear, energy, transport, health, education and recreation. Without bothering about the many definitions of aspects of poverty, we would quickly point out that much of the earlier concepts of poverty have been limited in their capture of the dimensions of the phenomenon. In recent times scholars from all disciplinary areas have brought illumination into the debate, which now tells us that poverty can be approached from the angle of all human endeavors.

Accordingly, the concept of poverty has undergone at least four changes over the past decade (Shaffer, 2001:9). First, there has been a shift from a physiological model of deprivation, focused on the non-fulfillment of basic material or biological needs to a social model of deprivation, focused on such elements as lack of autonomy, powerlessness, lack of self-respect / dignity, etc. The social model is about incorporating issues of political and economic rights and social justice into the anti-poverty programmatic framework. Second, there has been renewed emphasis placed on the concept of vulnerability and its relationship to poverty (however defined). Third, the concept of inequality, and its relationship to poverty, has re-emerged as a central concern. Fourth, the idea that poverty should be conceptualised as the violation of basic human rights has been painstakingly argued of late by UN system agencies, among others. For a diagrammatic representation of the diversity in the conceptualization of poverty (see figure 8.1).

So any meaningful onslaught against poverty must be focused on many fronts, engaging both physical (as in the provision of physiological needs) and non-physical (as in the promotion of basic human rights) challenges. Poverty reduction policies must integrate all these dimensions in order to be seen to be complete. Efforts and resources needed to attempt to address the physiological needs of citizens alone is gargantuan enough, not to talk of waging an all-inclusive campaign against poverty, which is why all around the world there is a wide recognition that the socio-economic problems that policies address cannot be solved by governments acting on their own, nor are they exclusive domain of one sector (Brinkerhoff and Crossby, 2002).

Figure 8. 1: The Dimensions of Poverty

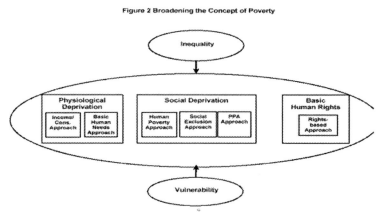

Source: Shaffer (2001:9)

The ability of governments in Nigeria to streamline and harness the enormous potentials for improved service delivery in all the existing public institutional structures of poverty eradication and in other stakeholder organisations is central to the achievement of the goals of poverty reduction and the millennium development goals (MDGs). A major task before the National Poverty Eradication Council (NAPEC) is to use the limited resources at its disposal to stimulate, nurture, promote, encourage and support collaborative arrangements that would constructively engage all relevant stakeholders, including those in remote rural environments in the implementation of poverty reduction strategies in the country.

Some of the pertinent questions that need to be addressed are:

i) How does the National Poverty Alleviation Programme (NAPEP's) design and strategies strengthen or support governance and economic structures and processes of local institutions (including community-based organizations - CBOs)?

ii) How can proper balance be maintained between NAPEP's choices of top-down and targeted approaches in the selection of relevant poverty indicators and the means of addressing them, and bottom-up choices in project identification and execution?

iii) What situational variables could constrain or facilitate cross-sectoral partnerships for poverty eradication?

iv) What are the effective mechanisms and processes for bringing together diverse agencies to cooperate around poverty eradication objectives?

iv) How can NAPEP apply strategic management techniques and tools for supporting its excellently planned cooperative action , and,

v) What steps can government/NAPEP, donors, the private sector and NGOs take to enhance the use of collaborations?

The design of NAPEP seems to have, deliberately or otherwise, recognized the breath and depth of the dimensions of poverty, illustrated above in figure 1 because it was clearly established with a consultative orientation, and roles are provided for a varied stakeholdership. The extent, however, these provisions are being translated into much gains in the programmes delivery of NAPEP is a matter, which only empirical evaluations of NAPEP activities would determine.

Key Approaches to Poverty Alleviation

Governments usually adopt a mix of approaches to tackle poverty. Usually this is done not by strict compartmentalization of anti-poverty activities. However, it is illuminating to distinguish four commonly adopted approaches as follows:

(a) *Economic Growth Approach* – This approach encourages broad based economic growth and focuses on capital accumulation, including human capital, which may influence outcomes in education, health, nutrition and housing needs of labour. Increased investments in the economy, would ceteris paribus, lead to increased output, employment and income through improvements in total factor productivity.

(b) *Basic Needs Approach* – This calls for greater emphasis on the distribution of output to citizens with a view to achieving broad based welfare gains and reducing inequality. In this respect, the provision of basic needs such as food, shelter, water, sanitation, health care, basic education, transportation etc to all citizens is perceived as the objective function to be maximized instead of investment and growth.

(c) *Rural Development Approach* – This approach is usually an attempt at redressing perceived imbalance in the incidence of poverty between urban and rural locations. This approach underscores the recognition that majority of the poor in developing countries live in rural areas, and that the opportunities for profitable employment are minimal, if non-existent, in these locations. It usually involves an integrated programme of infrastructural provision, which would help to give rural populations increased access to the basic necessities of life such as food, shelter, safe drinking water, education, health care, employment and income generating opportunities.

(d) *Target Approach* – This approach favours the directing of poverty alleviation programme to specific population groups in the country, mainly losers in the market place. It includes such programmes as the provision of social safety nets to the aged and other disadvantaged groups, micro credit to the enterprising but poor groups, school meals to children, etc.

Nigeria has implemented poverty alleviation measures along the lines outlined above, which sometimes, focuses on achieving the economic growth objective, basic needs, rural development and reaching out to targeted populations. Two distinct approaches to poverty alleviation have featured prominently in Nigeria's national development plans. These are the economic growth strategy that presumes the automatic trickle down of the benefits of growth to the poor, and the strategy of rural / agricultural development. Indeed, rural development could be viewed as having been central to Nigeria's poverty alleviation strategies. And the center-piece of the rural development policy has been agricultural development, complemented by social and economic infrastructure.

Poverty Reduction Strategies in Nigeria: A Historical Perspective

Poverty alleviation used to be a 'passive' content of development plans of government until sometime in the 1980s when an unprecedented erosion of peoples' living standards owing to the prevailing global recession necessitated the establishment of several poverty alleviation programmes. By the end of 1998, there were sixteen poverty alleviation institutions in the country. In 1994, the Government set up a broad-based Poverty Alleviation Programme Development Committee (PAPDC) under the aegis of the National Planning Commission. The primary objective of the PAPDC was to advise the government on the design, coordination and implementation of poverty alleviation programmes. Its work contributed immensely to the emergence of a new approach to the design and organisation of poverty alleviation programmes culminating in the establishment in 1996 of the Community Action Programme for Poverty Alleviation (CAPPA).

The CAPPA document drew largely from the past experience on poverty reduction efforts in the country and attempted to ensure that the poor were not only carried along in the design and implementation of poverty projects that affected them but that the poor themselves actually formulated and managed the poverty projects. Various agencies (Government, Donors and NGOs) involved in poverty alleviation in the country embraced the CAPPA strategy (Obadan, 2002). Thus, in 1996 a draft National Poverty Alleviation Policy document was produced by the Government through the National Planning Commission. Its thrust was the improvement in human welfare in the immediate and distant future.

Specifically, governments' efforts at poverty reduction had in the past been delivered through a number of multi-sectoral and sector-specific programmes aimed at improving basic services, infrastructure and housing facilities for the rural and urban populations, extending access to credit farm inputs, and creating employment. Most of the programmes were not strictly anti-poverty measures but, they expectedly, had positive impact on the poor.

The Pre-SAP Era

During the period preceding the introduction of the World Bank/IMF Structural Adjustment Programme (SAP) in 1986, poverty reduction was not the direct focus of development planning and economic management. Government only showed concern for poverty reduction indirectly. For example, the objectives of the first National Development Plan in Nigeria included the development of opportunities in health, employment and education as well as improvement of access to these opportunities. Similarly, the Fourth National Development Plan, which appeared to be more precise in the specification of objectives that were associated with poverty reduction, emphasized increase in the real income of the average citizen as well as reduction of income inequality, among other things (see Ogwumike, 1987 and 1998). Examples of the poverty-related initiatives are the *River Basin Development Authorities (RBDA), the Agricultural Development Programmes (ADP), the Agricultural Credit Guarantee Scheme (ACGS), the Rural Electrification Scheme (RES), and the Rural Banking Programme (RBP)*. Despite the significant degree of success made by some of these programmes, most of them could not be sustained.

Many of the programmes mentioned above failed, over time, as a result of deviations from their original focus. Other notable poverty reduction related programmes that were put in place in Nigeria before the advent of the Structural Adjustment Programme (SAP) include *Operation Feed the Nation (OFN)* set up in 1977, *Free and Compulsory primary Education (FCPE)* set up also in 1977, *Green Revolution Programme* established in 1980, and the *Low Cost Housing Schemes*. Both the OFN and Green Revolution were set up to boost agricultural production and improve the general performance of the agricultural sector among other things. These programmes made some laudable impacts; they enhanced the quality of life of many Nigerians. The programmes, however, could not be sustained due to lack of political will and commitment, policy instability and insufficient involvement of the beneficiaries in these programmes (CBN Enugu Zone, 1998).

The SAP Era

Conscious policy effort by government towards poverty alleviation began in Nigeria during the era of SAP. The severe economic crisis in Nigeria in the early 1980s worsened the quality of life of most Nigerians. The government made determined effort to check the crisis through the adoption of SAP. However, the implementation of SAP further worsened the living conditions of many Nigerians, especially for the most vulnerable groups. This made the government to design and implement many poverty alleviation programmes between 1986 and 1993. Under the guided deregulation of the economy that spanned the period, 1993 to 1998, more poverty reduction programmes were put in place by government.

Many of these programmes had varied impact on poverty alleviation. For example, the establishment of the *Directorate of Food, roads and Rural Infrastructure (DFRRI)* was not only a radical departure from the previous programmes, but also recognized the complementarities associated with basic needs such as food, shelter, potable water, etc. DFRRI had tremendous impact on the rural areas in terms of road construction and food production (CBN, 1998). DFRRI, however, could not achieve many of its objectives due to several factors such as lack of standards for project harmonization and effective mechanisms for co-ordination among the three tiers of government and between DFRRI and the levels of government (CBN Bauchi Zone; and Enugu Zone, 1998).

The National Directorate of Employment (NDE) was meant to design and implement programmes to combat mass unemployment; and articulate policies aimed at developing work programmes with labour intensive potentials. Its programme components included the Vocational Skills Development Programme (VSD), the Special Public works Programme (SPW), the Small Scale Enterprises Programme (SSE) and the Agricultural Employment Programme. The NDE was, however, poorly funded and as such could not cope with the needs of the ever increasing number of job applicants in the country.

The *Better Life Programme (BLP)* was set up to enhance the quality of life of rural women, among other objectives. The Better Life Programme tried to harness the potentials of rural women and thereby impact positively on their economic activities and incomes. The BLP improved the quality of life of many women through the distribution of various inputs, granting of easy credits, and the establishment of various educational/enlightenment programmes. The programme was not only hijacked by position–seeking individuals but the resources set for the programme were diverted to other uses.

The *People's Bank of Nigeria (PBN)* was set up to encourage savings and provide credit facilities for the underprivileged. Similarly, *Community Banks (CB)* were established to provide banking facilities for rural dwellers as well as support micro–enterprises in urban areas (Oladeji and Abiola, 1998). Although the two banking schemes had some successes, they were bedeviled by several malpractices including corruption. Thus, gross mismanagement curtailed their impact.

The *Family Support Programme (FSP)* was set up to provide health care delivery, child welfare, youth development, and improved nutritional status to families in rural areas. Similarly, the *Family Economic Advancement Programme (FEAP)* was established to provide credit facilities to cooperative societies to support the establishment of cottage industries in both rural and urban areas. The programmes were also designed to create employment opportunities at ward levels, encourage the design and manufacture of appropriate plants, machinery and equipments, and provide opportunities for the training of ward–based business operators. In a nutshell, both FSP and FEAP were designed and set up to improve the quality of life of rural dwellers.

Other programmes such as *National Agricultural Land Development Authority (NALDA)*, the *Agricultural Development Programmes (ADP)*, and the *Strategic Grains Reserves Programmes (SGRP)* had in one way or the other impacted positively on the agricultural sector and by implication reduced poverty. Similarly, in the health, education and housing sectors several poverty reducing programmes were implemented. Examples include the *Primary Health Care Scheme* and the *Guinea Worm Eradication Programme*. Although the guinea worm eradication programme recorded a tremendous success, the effectiveness of the primary health care programme was grossly reduced due to inadequate funding, lack of equipment, essential drugs and trained manpower (see Egware, 1997).

The Democratic Era of the Fourth Civilian Republic

Since 1999 the key poverty-reducing actions/programmes of the Federal Government are as follows:

i) Upward review of salaries and wages in the civil service;
ii) Production of a comprehensive economic empowerment strategy document (NEEDS);
iii) Wide-ranging reforms in the agricultural, health, education, water/sanitation, and communications sectors whose short term impacts have been adjudged to be controversial but which hold some hopes of reducing poverty in the long run if consistently nurtured;
iv) The constitution of the Ahmed Joda Panel in 1999 and the Ango Abdullahi Committee in 2000. The immediate concern of the Panel/Committee was the streamlining and rationalization of existing poverty alleviation institutions, and the coordinated implementation and monitoring of relevant schemes and programmes. These culminated in the introduction of the National *Poverty Eradication Programme (NAPEP)* and the establishment of the National Poverty Eradication Council (NAPEC) in 2001;
v) Implementation of a Poverty Alleviation Programme (PAP), from January 2001 as an outcome of the Ahmed Joda Panel report on the streamlining and rationalization of poverty alleviation institutions in Nigeria. Soon after inauguration, the Ahmed Joda Panel worked on streamlining and rationalising of poverty alleviation institutions and agencies. Before PAP there were 16 poverty alleviation institutions in Nigeria. Consequently, six of these agencies were wound up, nine were merged and six others were re-structured. Pending the formulation and adoption of a more permanent programme, an ad-hoc programme to provide jobs to 200,000 unemployed, popularly called PAP 2000, had been introduced in January, 2000.

National Poverty Eradication Programme

The implementation of PAP generated a deluge of accusations of shoddiness and corruption which damaged its credibility. Subsequently a Technical Review Committee headed by Professor Ango Abdullahi reviewed PAP and produced the draft National Policy on Poverty Eradication. Thereafter, a White Paper Committee that included membership from relevant Ministries and Agencies articulated Government's position on the National Policy document and combined it with other existing policy documents, to come up with the blueprint on the National Poverty Eradication Programme [NAPEP].

Established in 2001, NAPEP has been conceived through a consultative process that involved all stakeholders in poverty eradication in Nigeria namely: the Federal, State and Local Governments, civil society organisations, research institutions, the organised private sector, women groups, and concerned individuals. The aim was to address the most manifest aspects of absolute poverty, and to eradicate them in the shortest possible time. It was recognised that there are certain fundamental reasons for the inadequacy of anti-poverty measures over the years. These include the absence of a policy framework, inadequate involvement of stakeholders, poor implementation arrangements, and lack of proper co-ordination. All of these seem to have received attention in the conceptualization and design of NAPEP. This background preparation is what differentiates this latest poverty eradication effort of Government from all past efforts. NAPEP's mandate is to monitor and coordinate all poverty eradication efforts in Nigeria in order to harmonize these efforts and ensure better delivery, maximum impact, and effective utilization of resources. Log books and indices for monitoring, data collection and analysis have been carefully designed and selected on the basis of ease of use and quantification. Furthermore, an elaborate data recording system was established alongside a Structured Databank and Management Information System.

NAPEP is composed of four schemes intended to be implemented by Ministries, Parastatals and Agencies of the Federal Government, in close collaboration with States, Local Governments, and Communities in a bottom-up approach. The place of important stakeholders like financial institutions, the organised private sector, NGOs, CBOs and traditional rulers are well recognized in the scheme. The four schemes of NAPEP are:

- *Youth Empowerment Scheme (YES).* This deals with capacity acquisition, mandatory attachment, productivity improvement, credit delivery, technology development and enterprise promotion.
- *Rural Infrastructure Development Scheme (RIDS).* This has to do with the provision of portable and irrigation water, transport (rural and urban), rural energy and power supply.

- *Social Welfare Services Scheme* (SOWESS). This deals with interventions in special education, primary healthcare services, establishment and maintenance of recreational centres, public awareness facilities, youth and student hostels development, environmental protection facilities, food security provisions, agricultural input provisions, micro and macro credits delivery, rural telecommunication facilities, provision of mass transit, and maintenance culture.
- *Natural Resources Development and Conservation Scheme (NRDCS).* This deals with the harnessing of agriculture, water, solid minerals resources, conservation of land and space (beaches, reclaimed land, etc) particularly for the convenient and effective utilization by small-scale operators and the immediate community.

At the top of the organizational structure for NAPEP is the National Poverty Eradication Council which is headed by the President of the Federal Republic of Nigeria with membership of about 13 Ministers holding portfolios relevant to poverty alleviation. The NAPEC coordinates the poverty-reduction-related activities of all the relevant Ministries, Parastatals and Agencies. It has the mandate to ensure that the wide range of activities involved are centrally planned and coordinated in ways that make them complement one another so that the objectives of policy continuity and sustainability are achieved. The day to day management of NAPEP is the function of the National Coordinating Committee under the chairmanship of the National Coordinator of the programme. Membership of the coordinating committee spreads across different ministries, bodies like Nigerian Union of Journalists, labour organistion, chambers of commerce and the representative of registered political parties in the country (Garuba, 2003).

In terms of institutional structure for clear specification and smooth flow of authority, responsibility, M&E, no other poverty reduction agency is comparable to NAPEP. NAPEP data and information flow upwards from the Local Government Level to the State Coordinating Committees and up to the National Coordination Committee. Information flow is from the bottom up, with each subsequent level reviewing, refining and standardizing data and completing assessment reports. A National Impact Review, which includes reviews of M&E structures, is being put in place by the

National Coordinating Committee (NCC). The National Poverty Eradication Council (NAPEC) shall review NCC reports in an effort to assess government directed poverty reduction efforts. State Poverty Eradication Councils (SPECs) are also in place and expected to function to coordinate the mandate of NAPEP across states.

NAPEP plays monitoring and evaluation functions. The monitoring strategies and guidelines of NAPEP rely on the onsite monitoring of all relevant initiatives periodically to confirm project location, gauge project implementation according to agreed plans, ensure the status of project delivery, note functionality of facilities provided, assess impacts on livelihood of communities, ensure equitable distribution and fair spread of basic necessities of life through coordination, and review the actual poverty status of communities with a view to setting further targets for total eradication of absolute poverty in Nigeria. Field monitoring teams specializing in the areas of financial monitoring, impact assessment, and technical assessment are expected to conduct their work in cooperation with national and state coordinating committees. Standardized log books will be developed in order to facilitate data collection and collation across the three levels of government. Indices of monitoring will be extracted from broad performance blocks including quality, project objective and target achievement, scheduled completion, financial prudence, and maximized impacts as well as the multiplier effects.

Overall it can be seen that the structure and process of NAPEP are supposedly dynamic, with varied windows for engaging a diverse array of stakeholder interests – monitors, investors, farmers, researchers, resource persons, coordinators, financial experts, et cetera. Obviously, without these participants, the NAPEP machinery would crash.

Commendable Features of NAPEP

We have already mentioned briefly some positive attributes that set NAPEP apart from previous poverty reduction programmes of governments in Nigeria. More specifically, the NAPEP Blueprint has the following commendable features (Aliu, 2001:12-13):

i) it adopts the participatory bottom-up approach in programme implementation and monitoring. The involvement of professional bodies, workers' union and Manufacturers Associations in the National Coordinating Committee of NAPEP, the body responsible for the execution of the directives of the National Poverty Eradication Council is considered progressive;

ii) it provides for a national framework that lays emphasis on appropriate and sustainable institutional arrangement;

iii) it provides for pro-active and affirmative actions deliberately targeted at women, youths, farmers and the disabled;

iv) it provides for inter-ministerial and inter-agency co-operation;

v) it provides for the participation of all registered political parties, traditional rulers, and the communities;

vi) it provides for technology acquisition and development particularly in the real sectors, agriculture and industry;

vii) it provides for capacity upgrade for existing skills acquisition and training centres;

viii) it provides for the provision of agricultural and industrial extension services to rural areas;

ix) it provides for institutional development for marketing of agricultural and industrial products; and,

x) it provides for integrated schemes for youth empowerment, development of infrastructure, provision of social welfare services and exploitation of natural resources.

In addition, the NAPEP initiative is just focused on poverty reduction.

Can NAPEP, given its structure and *modus operandi*, be able to assist Nigeria to meet the MDG goal of halving the incidence of poverty by the year 2015? With regard to collaborations and partnerships, it is evident from a careful consideration of the foregoing and their elaborations in the NAPEP blueprint that much of the problems that attended previous efforts have been properly addressed in the design of the present initiative. However, the statement of good intentions and enunciation of measures towards poverty reduction are only necessary but not sufficient conditions for poverty alleviation. One way forward is to recognise the problems and look beyond to operational and incidental matters that may arise at the level of implementation *vis-à-vis* some pertinent issues that may not have been adequately covered in the blueprint. It is also pertinent to note that it would take a very committed workforce, generous funding, regular capacity upgrading and highly innovative operational strategies, as well as very active engagement of other stakeholders to activate and make effective all those provisions.

A Critique of Poverty Alleviation Efforts in Nigeria

General Problems

A number of factors have contributed to the failure of past poverty-related programmes and efforts. The major ones have been described by Kankwenda *et al*, 2000; Ogwumike, 1998; and Egware, 1997 and include: programme inconsistency, poor implementation, corruption of government officials and public servants, poor targeting mechanisms and failure to focus directly on the poor. More specifically, we can identify the following shortcomings:

(i)   Lack of targeting mechanisms for the poor and the fact that most of the programmes do not focus directly on the poor.

(ii)   Political and policy instability have resulted in frequent policy changes and inconsistent implementation which in turn has prevented continuous progress.

(iii)   Inadequate coordination of the various programmes had resulted in each institution carrying out its own activities with resultant duplication of efforts and inefficient use of limited resources. Overlapping functions ultimately led to institutional rivalry and conflicts.

(iv)   Severe budgetary, management and governance problems afflicted most of the programmes, resulting in facilities not being completed or broken down and abandoned, unstaffed or ill-equipped.

(v)   Lack of accountability and transparency, making the programmes to serve as conduit pipes for draining national resources.

(vi)   Over-extended scope of activities of most institutions, resulting in resources being spread too thinly on too many activities. Examples are DFRRI and Better Life Programmes which covered almost every sector and overlapped with many other existing programmes.

(vii)   Inappropriate programme design reflecting lack of involvement of beneficiaries in the formulation and implementation of programmes. Consequently, beneficiaries were not motivated to identify themselves sufficiently with the successful implementation of the programmes.

(viii)   Absence of target setting for Ministries, Agencies and Programmes.

(ix)   Absence of effective collaboration and partnership among the three tiers of government.

(x)   Absence of agreed poverty reduction agenda that can be used by all concerned – Federal, State, and Local Governments, NGOs, and the International Development Partners.

(xi)   Most of the programmes lacked mechanisms for their sustainability.

A number of these problems and constraints are remediable through more concerted partnership building and collaborations.

Problems Specific to NAPEP

In spite of the commendable design characteristics of NAPEP, which may have circumvented many of the problems identified in section 5.1, observers have been pointing at some lacuna that may devalue the progamme delivery of NAPEP. They include the following:

i. It is believed that although there seems to be adequate provisions for wide stakeholder involvement in the implementation of NAPEP projects, the same cannot be said about the conception and design of the programme activities. It is still the usual top-down approach. Where participant-driven, bottom-up approach is emphasized in the design of a programme, motivation for participation on the part of people becomes intrinsic (Garuba, 2003).

ii. Another set of problems that have been observed in the NAPEP initiative include poor policy formulation and coordination, poor target setting for agencies involved on NAPEP projects, absence of demonstrable levels of collaboration and commitment among the three tiers of government, non-involvement of traditional authorities and community groups in project selection and implementation, absence of an agreed poverty reduction agenda that can be used by all concerned (the Federal, state and local government agencies (Aliyu, 2001).

iii. The political motivation for establishing NAPEP has been suggested as a possible source of interference, which might undermine the institution's credibility and effectiveness. Its top-ranking officers are political appointees, and therefore subject to political pressures. However, we have argued that, if communities find their politically appointed local government coordinators corrupt, they can petition the

190

government for the official's removal. Communities are currently not part of the in national M&E systems of NAPEP (Sirker, 2003).

iv. A lacuna in the design of NAPEP is the non-representation of certain interests that are considered critical in some of its organs. For instance, the role of adult and non-formal education in poverty alleviation had not been fully appreciated by the designers of the programme. The central adult education agency in Nigeria is the National Commission for Mass Education, Adult and Non Formal Education. One would have expected the agency to be represented on all the major strategic committees of NAPEP while the state agencies for mass education should be more visible in the implementation of the programme at state level. For instance, the Executive Secretary of this agency should have been made a member of both the National Poverty Eradication Council and the National Coordinating Council. This is a fundamental oversight. Since adult education bodies are not well represented in the design and implementation of NAPEP, there will be problem of harmonisation of adult education and poverty alleviation programmes.

vi. One other significant flaw in NAPEP is the lack of focus on community education. This is one area where adult education could have come in handy as public / community education is one of the important foci of education for poverty alleviation.

vii. For adult education to serve as an effective instrument in Nigeria's present initiative on poverty alleviation, repackaging and repositioning are required. There has to be harmonization of adult education and poverty alleviation programme. The activities of all adult education providing agencies should constitute an integral part of NAPEP with certain percentage of the programme fund devoted to execution of special literacy and adult education project. Adult Education should be community based to allow for participant driven arrangement. Special community education programmes in form of Literacy for Poverty Alleviation (LPA) and Poverty Awareness Campaign (PAC) should be mounted. While LPA will emphasize functional literacy, skill improvement, entrepreneurial skill, management of small business and extension education, the focus of PAC would be on public enlightenment on the causes of poverty, poverty alleviation programmes and how to benefit from the programmes. NAPEP will need many NGO and CBO partners to do these things effectively.

viii. The programme has also not made tangible the special case for women beyond the talk about affirmative action. Given the fact that more women than men are poor and that the dynamics that engender this imbalance remain strong in our society, a special programme on poverty alleviation for the female gender is highly desirable. In addition, the involvement of civil society organizations in NAPEP activities has not been as expected. CSOs should have been well represented on the National Poverty Assessment committee. This committee evaluates the implementation of NAPEP activities and reports to the Poverty Alleviation Council.

ix. Perhaps, as a result of the Abdulahi and Joda committees not appreciating the newer dimensions of poverty such as deprivation and human rights, they did not mention Ministry of Justice as one of the core poverty alleviation agencies. This has minimized the frequency with which activities akin to this conceptualization of poverty are thrown up.

Benefits of Partnerships and Collaborations

We have seen from the critique of NAPEP that much remains to be done by way of inclusiveness and partnership building in poverty reduction programmes in Nigeria. This is because, so far, most of the reservations expressed about NAPEP relate to its not being inclusive enough. Collaborations and partnerships, where they are properly instituted and coordinated could precipitate the following benefits:

i) Leads to expanded set of linkages that connects public sector organizations to such other stakeholders as private firms, NGOs, community associations on the one hand, and the target poor population groups on the other hand. This, ceteris paribus, ensures maximum effectiveness and efficiency in the programmes delivery.
ii) Encourages inclusiveness in decision making, which promotes empowerment, social mobilisation, participatory democracy and education.

iii) Discourages concentration and facilitates delegation and devolution in poverty eradication activities to non-state or quasi-state actors.
iv) Economic growth alone is not sufficient for poverty reduction. Therefore, growth must be accompanied by a deliberate policy of

redistribution and equity, promoted by participation. In this direction, broad-based growth dynamics that involves the poor and generates employment is recognised to have tremendous impact on poverty reduction.

v) The government can target the delivery of some services and resources to reach poor areas and to communities living in poverty, but it cannot succeed without building on the assets of existing community-based organisations, civil society groups and their activities where possible.

vi) Collaborative monitoring could help solve the problems of corruption that have bedeviled other anti-poverty programmes of government. The manifestations and problems associated with corruption have various dimensions. Among these are project substitution, plan distortion, misrepresentation of project finances, diversion of resources to uses to which they were not meant, even conversion of public funds to private uses, etc. The effect of corruption is both direct and indirect on poverty increase.

vii) Lack of social responsibility usually manifests in the vandalisation or willful destruction of facilities that benefit the poor. It is expected that the bottom-up approach to project identification with attendant association of beneficiaries with the projects, will minimise assets vandalisation. In order to ensure transparency and accountability in the management of poverty reduction programmes and projects, all the stakeholders should be involved in the monitoring and evaluation of such projects.

viii) Participation/collaboration has intrinsic democratic governance value because increased participation by stakeholders in programmes design and delivery could enhance accountability, transparency and responsiveness to public policy and ultimately help operationalise and reinforce democratic governance.

ix) Citizen participation in policy oversight and service quality monitoring in poverty eradication projects is empowering. This is particularly relevant in agricultural, environmental and community health projects in remote locations where government resources may not reach easily.

Roles of Key Agencies Involved in NAPEP

The NAPEP is not a direct implementing agency. It is responsible for coordination and monitoring of all poverty reduction programmes under the schemes being implemented by the various ministries and agencies. The 14 core poverty alleviation ministries identified by the Ahmed Joda Panel and the Abdulahi Committee reports include:

(i) Agriculture and Rural Development
(ii) Education
(iii) Water Resources
(iv) Industry
(v) Power and Steel
(vi) Employment, Labour and Productivity
(vii) Women Affairs and Youth Development
(viii) Health
(ix) Works and Housing
(x) Environment
(xi) Solid Minerals Development
(xii) Science and Technology
(xiii) Finance, and
(xiv) National Planning Commission

Similarly, thirty-seven (37) core poverty alleviation institutions, agencies and programmes were identified.
The responsibilities of the key implementing ministries and agencies are defined as follows:

Federal Ministries and Agencies shall:

i.   implement relevant programmes and projects while NAPEP coordinates and monitors the execution of these projects;

ii.   establish relevant structures at federal, state and local government levels;

iii.   ensure effective collaboration with various state and local governments in programmes and projects implementation;

iv.   be required to provide quarterly reports to NAPEP Secretariat for deliberations by the National Coordinating Committee;

v.   ensure that targets set for them by NAPEP are met within the stipulated time frame;

vi.   ensure that funds released by NAPEP for programmes and projects are not used for personal emolument and travels but are used only for the specific programmes the fund is meant for;

vii.   make their services available all over the country;

viii.   ensure that all counterpart funds required by the international donor agencies are channeled through NAPEP; and

ix.   continue to play their supervisory role of agencies under them.

State Governments Shall:

i.   ensure effective collaboration and consultation with federal government in projects planning and execution;

ii.   ensure effective collaboration and consultation with all its local governments in projects planning and execution;

iii.   ensure effective division of labour so as to avoid duplication of projects between federal, state and local governments;

iv.   ensure that all its services are provided to its citizens without political biases;

v.   ensure good working relationship with the state coordination committee, and;

vi.   ensure that it is fully represented in the State Coordination Committee.

Local Government Area Councils Shall:

i.   ensure effective collaboration and consultation with federal government in projects planning and execution;

ii.   ensure that all their services are provided to their indigenes without political discrimination;

iii.   make efforts to provide markets, motor parks and other recreational facilities in rural areas;

iv.   ensure good working relationship with local government Monitoring Committee.

Political Parties Shall:

i.   ensure the mobilisation of party members to participate and support the programme; and

ii.   ensure that the parties are fully represented at the national, state and local government committees of NAPEC.

Agencies, institutions and organisations may play direct or indirect / passive roles in poverty alleviation efforts. Non-state actors such as NGOs, CBOs, cooperative societies, and others can play several important roles in NAPEP as service deliverers, project managers, impact analyst, monitor, dialogue promoter and/or advocate and lobbyist, information disseminator, and intermediary and spokesperson. The current and potential roles of agencies of private enterprise collaborating with public institutions in poverty alleviation, not necessarily the private firms themselves, but institutions that those firms nurture for the advancement of their common interests - e.g. the Manufacturers Association of Nigeria (MAN), Bankers' Committee which has promoted SMIEIS, farmers associations, traders associations, and others are crucial for the success of NAPEP.

The role specifications above for government agencies are rather general and are same as their usual statutory expectations within the government/civil service hierarchy. It is therefore difficult to decipher any role that gives unique operational advantage to NAPEP. Until critical masses of projects that make demand on these roles emerge, we cannot objectively assess the adequacy or otherwise of those specified roles.

Evidence on Current Patterns of Collaboration in NAPEP Projects

Experience from the past poverty alleviation programmes has shown their relative inability to involve the beneficiaries in their planning and implementation. One of the commendable features of NAPEP, however, is the adoption of the bottom-up approach to programme implementation and monitoring (Aliu, 2001:12). We, however, imagine that the bottom-up prescription precludes the involvement of beneficiaries in the identification of projects and programmes. This is more so as 'NAPEC is mandated to ensure that the wide range of activities are centrally planned, coordinated and complement one another so that the objectives of policy continuity and sustainability are achieved' (FRN, 2001:5). A veiled suggestion in this statement is that NAPEP may willfully fail to devolve planning without any blame because certain matters (like ensuring policy consistency and coordination) can only be handled centrally. Even at the interface between NAPEP projects and beneficiaries it may be reasonable for us to worry about the specifics of the extent to which NAPEP has brought in collaborators and partners to jointly take decisions on aspects of project implementation and monitoring.

Institutional collaborations under NAPEP activities are of two broad types. NAPEP collaborates with non-state actors with focus on poverty-related advocacy and empowerment. There is also another kind of collaboration in which the focus is on policy planning, implementation and service delivery. Similarly, partnerships on NAPEP projects are of two types. The first type involves partnership between the federal and other sub-national governments. The second type involves partnerships between different types of state and non-state actors, including the beneficiary groups.

As an example of the later, we note the case of Rivers State NAPEP which runs the Managed Attachment Programme (MAP) where beneficiaries are attached to relevant companies for capacity enhancement. It is, however, instructive to observe here that while many of the carpenters, electricians, and welders etc trained through this arrangement, there were no corresponding arrangements to establish the trainees in their own businesses. This led to a situation where though the beneficiaries had their capacity enhanced, they were not sufficiently empowered to become 'masters of their own' through lucrative engagements. If this persists, the advantage and demonstration effects of such partnership may be lost, thereby discouraging potential collaborator beneficiaries.

Lagos and Rivers States NAPEP have collaborated with Globacom and MTN (private sector telecom service providers) to set up GSM call centres for unemployed youths. Such public-private partnerships have not been common in the poverty eradication efforts in Nigeria and should be encouraged in other areas such as agriculture, health, etc. In the health sector, for example nurses and midwives wishing to set up in designated remote or disadvantaged locations could be partnered with by NAPEP.

Still in Rivers State, the provision of matching fund by the state government to support NAPEP projects is another positive collaborative outcome in the genre of the first category of collaborative arrangements. In the state, Gokana LGA boosted the ₦5 million microcredit lifeline that NAPEP proposed to give to some 250 widows with an additional sum of ₦2 million. By 2005, it was about the first such collaboration between NAPEP and a LGA in Nigeria. The Multi-Partner Microfinance Scheme (MPMS) – involving NAPEP, Kogi State Government and Oceanic Bank was launched in Lokoja in 2006, the first in the North Central Zone of the country.

These are encouraging signs that the NAPEP strategy is working. The question is how can these isolated cases be scaled-up and made to spread to all other states and local government areas with minimal prodding. In spite of the excellent organizing principles around which NAPEP's strategies have been built, there are concerns about its ability to fully operationalise its plans particularly in regard to collaborative and joint working among stakeholder agencies, institutions and individuals. This is because, sometimes, even when Nigerian governments manage to make good plans, they still face overwhelming implementation challenges.

Some Factors that Would Make Partnerships and Collaborations Work

The following steps can be undertaken to make cross-sectoral and multi-actor arrangements to operate effectively:

i. *Program Objectives of NAPEP and other collaborators must converge.* Some NGOs and their members may harbour the secret desire to treat received funds as 'national cake', bolstered by the moral hazard created by poor credit recovery records of past poverty alleviation institutions in Nigeria. There is always need to lower the power differentials among the various actors in poverty eradication project implementation as a result of differences in resource levels.

ii. *Collaborative partnerships need not start with a formal* agreement ab-initio. Sometimes one party needs to 'rest the waters' by mounting activities that permit the parties to a potential partnership not to commit each other until trust and agreed-upon modes of interaction could be developed via MoUs. Public enlightenments, workshops/seminars on potential benefits of joining efforts with NAPEP could elicit expression of interest from many potential collaborators. If used imaginatively, such fora could introduce the kind of flexibility that may open up new ideas in anti-poverty projects, since potential partners would be driving the process of project identification. This is an important issue, which has traditionally been left largely to donors in their relationship with Governments, NGOs and CBOs, but this strategy could be adopted by NAPEP.

iii.   *Coordination and Linkages*
NAPEC and the whole line-up of lower level monitors and promoters could provide effective linkage and coordination of NAPEP partnerships. It has to be reminded that these linkages and coordination should be cross-sectoral as well as cut across state, LGA, and community boundaries for the overall NAPEP machinery to realize its objectives. Enhanced participation will lead to better anti-poverty policy implementation targeting and lower service delivery costs.

iv.   *Institutionalizing Trust and Minimizing Rent Seeking*
The level of trust between NAPEP and its State government partners, especially where a state government is controlled by another political party, is an important determinant of the strength of the partnership. It influences their willingness to initiate and sustain joint anti-poverty activities. Federal authorities may fear that an aggressive state government could take advantage of its matching contributions to earn political capital, and vice versa. This was a common experience in the second republic and there are, no doubt, similar motivations under the present dispensation. Indeed, similar motivations may exist in varying degrees in partnerships involving other actors.

Recommendations

Having proffered some general suggestions for improvement of certain aspects of NAPEP in earlier sections of this chapter, we would limit our recommendations to issues that have to do with collaboration and partnership building and sustainability. The following suggestions are therefore proffered with a view to sustaining existing partnerships and generating new ones for more effective poverty eradication activities by NAPEP.

i.   Poverty reduction especially in rural areas will require greater collaboration with CBOs but there would be need to strengthen the management capabilities of these community based initiatives such as community based organizations and community development associations through seminars and workshops to enable them participate effectively in poverty reduction activities at the community level. This will require the involvement of sub-national governments (especially local councils) in the formulation and execution of such poverty alleviation programmes. This also calls for effective coordination and avoidance of duplication of efforts especially in states and local governments where the ruling political party is not in power.

ii. Incentives are fundamental to the feasibility of using partnership mechanisms for policy implementation and to ensure the sustainability of poverty reduction policy outcomes. Part of the reasons for giving incentives is to elicit the interest and collaboration of local non-state actors who are sometimes suspicious of government. NAPEP should design positive incentives to cultivate partnerships with other actors. This may involve some level of resource transfers to say NGOs for such activities as capacity building events. You may need incentives to bring rural NGOs to work with public sector agricultural research and extension institutions to speed the transfer of technology in rural areas and even for the provision of HIV/AIDS services. Direct capacity building support could be given by NAPEP to potential partner organisations in form of both funding and technical assistance.

iii. The presidency has a responsibility to continue to reiterate and demonstrate its commitment and political will to achieve the MDGs through the instrumentality of NAPEP. It should continue to take interest in the implementation of NAPEP programmes as a way of retaining the interest of potential partners.

iv. Legal and regulatory frameworks may be limiting state-civil society partnerships. For instance, government may not be permitted to align with NGOs or CBOs that do not have legal status but in certain communities where capacity for project management is limited, such NGOs or CBOs may indeed be the only informed and experienced collective that can partner in development projects. It may be necessary to provide a subsidiary legal window to engage such non-state actors.

v. Development partners should be encouraged to use their vast experience in the promotion of partnerships to assist NAPEP in stimulating collaboration with civil society organisations and private sector groups. DFID, USAID and others are well known support organisations that could help broker and incubate such partnerships at all levels.

vi. Deliberate efforts need to be made within NAPEP to increase support for administrative structures, procedures and mechanisms that will facilitate the establishment and operation of collaborative arrangements. For instance, this may mean increasing information dissemination, expanding opportunities for civil society access to NAPEP officials, establishing venues for dialogue (town hall meetings, public hearings), forming working groups, etc.

vii. NAPEP should consider the idea of stimulating non-government agencies further in their efforts to collaborate among themselves rather than just with NAPEP by giving them incentives as long as they are pursuing goals similar to those of NAPEP.

viii. The National Assembly has a duty to increase its oversight functions on poverty eradication processes, programmes and projects, and to specifically express its predisposition towards collaborative linkages.

ix. Private Enterprises (multinational corporations, small and medium enterprises, and micro enterprises) can make significant contributions to the poverty reduction process mainly because they can become the major source of new jobs. The recent experience of the country, in this respect, from private telecommunications companies is a good case. New efforts should be made to involve them more in NAPEP activities than is currently the case.

x. The communiqué and syndicate reports of the first retreat for Executive Governors and State coordinators of the NAPEP, June 24-25, 2001, issued under the aegis of the Presidency, raised some very crucial issues concerning political allegiance and continuity of NAPEP programmes, projects and Services. One of their resolutions/recommendations is that NAPEP should not be limited to the life span of any particular Government or Administration in power but should be sustained to elicit desired objective and impact. This is an area where the collaboration of the legislature should be strongly sought so as to progressively make laws on aspects of NAPEP activities that would outlive a particular government. The legislature should be seen as one of the core poverty alleviation institutions in Nigeria, given its role in the making of laws that can confront poverty.

xi. Perhaps, consideration could be given to making poverty alleviation an explicit constitutional matter in view of the fact that no one administration can meaningfully bind its successor to its programmes. This also reinforces the need to give expression to poverty alleviation objectives in national development plans with the strategies consolidated into the nation's overall development/policy management framework.

Conclusions

Over the last three decades Nigeria has recorded considerable strides in the development of institutions to fight poverty. The design characteristics and operational strategies of the current poverty reduction programme, NAPEP, have overcome many of the shortcomings of its predecessors. In particular, coordination, monitoring and evaluation, and people participation have improved. However, as a result of limitations in the conception and approach to poverty by NAPEP, there seems to be a disproportionate focus on physiological and social deprivation while very little attention is paid to rights-based considerations.

Going by the institutional structure of NAPEP which supports the execution of its programmes, unless collaborations and partnerships are nurtured with stakeholders in all sectors and across the different levels of government, the anti-poverty activities of NAPEP may not be achieved. It is therefore necessary for NAPEP to device approaches to see active partnership with agencies within core poverty reduction ministries, as well as with the private sector, NGOs, CBOs, traditional authorities and donor community.

Note

*The original manuscript of this chapter was presented at the National Conference and Exhibition on Poverty Alleviation, held at the Shehu Yar'Adua Centre, Abuja, 25 – 26 April 2006.

References

Aliyu, Abdulahi (2001). *National Poverty Eradication Programme: Conception, Implementation, Coordination and Monitoring*, Abuja. Government Press.

Brinkerhoff and Crossby (2002). *Managing Policy Reform*. Bloomfield, Kumarian Press.

Central Bank of Nigeria, Enugu Zone (1998) A Profile of Regional/Zonal Poverty in Nigeria: The Case of Enugu Zone. In

Measuring and Monitoring Poverty in Nigeria, Proceedings of the Seventh Annual Conference of the Zonal Research Units.

Egware, L (1997) 'Poverty and Poverty Alleviation: Nigeria's Experience'. In *Poverty Alleviation in Nigeria,* Selected Papers for the 1997 Annual Conference of Nigerian Economic Society.

Ogwumike, Fidelis O (2002) 'An appraisal of poverty reduction strategies in Nigeria' *CBN Economic & Financial Review,* vol. 39 no. 4.

Ogwumike F. O. (1998) 'Poverty Alleviation Strategies in Nigeria'. In *Measuring and Monitoring Poverty in Nigeria,* Proceedings of the Seventh Annual Conference of the Zonal Research Units of CBN.

Ogwumike, F. O. (1995) 'The Effects of Macro-level Government Policies on Rural Development and Poverty Alleviation in Nigeria,' Ibadan, *Journal of the Social Sciences,* vol. 1, no. 1, pp. 85 – 101.

Garuba Ayo (2003), *Adult Education and Poverty Alleviation Programmes in Nigeria: A Case for Harmonization.* Federal College of Education, Yola, Nigeria.

Obadan, M (2002) 'Poverty Reduction in Nigeria: The Way Forward'. *CBN Economic and Financial Review,* vol. 39 no. 4.

Shaffer, Paul (2001). 'New Thinking on Poverty: Implications for Poverty Reduction Strategies', Paper Prepared for the United Nations Department for Economic and Social Affairs (UNDESA) Expert Group Meeting on *Globalisation and Rural Poverty.* United Nations, November 8-9. pp. 44.

Sirker, Karen (2003) ed. Report of the *Community-based Monitoring & Evaluation System Methodology Design Workshop* (June 11-14, 2002 and follow-up (January-March).

Chapter 9

Banking Regulation and Reforms in Nigeria: The Consolidation Experience

Stanley Ukeje, Chukwuma Agu & Onyukwu E. Onyukwu

Introduction

Financial sector soundness has continued to be viewed as a key indicator of the general health of any economy. Effective financial intermediation by definition implies direct interdependence of the real and financial sectors of any economy. While there may be arguments in the literature as to the effectiveness and propriety of funds in growing the real sector, there is very little argument on validation of money by output. Indeed, traditional economic thinking relates financial sector changes only to the extent to which they have inherent impacts on real sector performance and the production of goods and services in an economy.

The imperative of creating financial sectors that support real growth was one of the major driving factors underlying the World Bank Structural Adjustment Programme (SAP) adopted by many African countries in the 1980s and early 1990s. Particularly, with the underlying recommendations of the financial repression theory and the attendant corruption in many public institutions, there was the incentive to introduce private sector participation in financial intermediation. Many African countries embraced this wholeheartedly, leading to the proliferation of banking and other financial institutions in many African countries.

The initial outbursts that attended the liberalization of the financial industry and the entry of private sector participants were quite short-lived. The nature of the risks faced by the banking populace and many African economies at large quickly changed from that of repression and lack of access to high risk of failure. Much of the new private sector entrants into banking services were weak, poorly capitalized and lacked experience on the macroeconomic implications and actions of microeconomic agents. The spate of banking crises in the 1990s remained one of the most potent proofs of this lack of experience and resources.

The response of both regulatory bodies and the government to much of the failures in the financial sector was reactionary and belated. In Nigeria, for example, the government set up the Nigeria Deposit Insurance Corporation (NDIC), which managed failed banks with a view to recover some of its assets and settle part of its obligations to depositors and shareholders. Under the regulation, a depositor is entitled to only a fixed (often meager) sum in the event of the collapse of the bank. The Abacha regime also set up the failed banks tribunal that arrested and tried key actors (particularly bank managers) whose actions or inactions could have contributed to distress in the banks. All these efforts, however, only lagged the incidence of distress and punished perceived offenders in the event of distress but lacked the capacity to effectively compensate losses incurred by economic agents in the event of financial sector distresses. There were little provisions made for early warning signals and legal provisions for preemptive actions on the part of regulators to check distress in the banking sector.

After nearly two decades of reactionary banking regulation, the Central Bank of Nigeria in 2005, under the leadership of Professor Chukwuma Soludo, initiated a 13 point agenda with the key challenge of fostering sound banking sector. A key provision of the agenda is the shoring up of the paid up capital of banks from a minimum of N2 billion to a minimum of N25 billion (more than ten fold increase). Referred to in popular parlance in Nigeria as banking sector consolidation, the programme of reviewed capital base of banks has attracted much discussion among the populace, intellectuals and other stakeholders in the banking industry.

But what exactly is this banking sector consolidation in Nigeria? What are its major objectives and to what extent has it been able to achieve those objectives? What are the overall macroeconomic and social impacts of the programme, as well as the possible transmission mechanisms for these impacts? This chapter is a contribution to the evolving body of knowledge on the nature, provisions and impact of the banking sector consolidation programme in Nigeria. It examines the underlying rationale for the consolidation, as well as the processes and outcomes (real or intended). Clearly, it is still early days to assess the overall impact of the consolidation programme. However, it is still significant to analyze the empirical components of the programme as a means to determine its performance trajectory and prospect.

Most of the data used in the analysis of this chapter are from secondary sources. The chapter is divided into six sections. Section 1 is the introduction. Section 2 x-rays the macroeconomic context of Nigeria and situates the structural characteristics of the banking sector within the overall macroeconomic framework. Section 3 explores the historical evolution of the Nigerian banking sector while section 4 focuses on the banking sector reforms that kicked off in 2004. Section 5 highlights the key outcomes of the reforms while the study is concluded in section 6.

Macroeconomics of Nigeria and the Banking Sector

Nigeria's overall economic performance, especially prior to 2003, was low, volatile and disappointing. Addison (2002) shows that while long-run average growth rate per-capita for the 15 fastest growing economies in his sample was an average of 4.1 per cent per annum, Nigeria's per capita growth was only a disappointing 0.2 per cent per annum between 1960 and 2000. Proxying private sector access to domestic credit by the share of credit to the private sector as a share of GDP, it was also noted that the fast growing nations transfer four times as much domestic credit to the private sector than does Nigeria and the wealthiest nations even transfer five and half times as much domestic credit to the private sector (Addison 2002).

Historically, Nigeria has been one of the most volatile macro-economies in the world. In the same study, Addison (2002) shows that Nigeria is one of the ten most volatile countries in a sample of 87 countries covering the period 1960 – 2000. Table 9.1 below shows volatility in selected macroeconomic indicators in Nigeria relative to the countries in the sample.

Table 9.1: Measures of Macroeconomic Volatility, 1960-2000

		1961-2000 a/			1991-2000 b/		
	Sample Size	Nigeria Rank	Median (%)	Nigeria (%)	Nigeria Rank	Median (%)	Nigeria (%)
Real Growth per-Capita c/							
GDP	87	9	4	8	68	3	2
Private Consumption	108	9	6	14 x/	4	5	20 x/
Private Investment	34	5	22	67 x/	3	19	67 x/
Revenue d/	71	3	11	41	2	10	47
Price Inflation							
Terms of Trade e/	90	3	10	27	3	7	28
Consumer Prices	114	21	7	19	9	3	25
Real Exchange Rate ($/N) f/	84	4	7	31	2	5	35
Policy							
Monetary Growth	125	32	14	20	33	9	16

Source: Addison, 2002

a. Countries with 15 or more observations in the period. Most countries (80 per cent) had observations for 20 years or more.
b. Countries with 9 or more observations in the period. For revenue, it was 8 or more observations.
c. Post-1981 data are under review.
d. Nigerian data include stabilization account drawings in 1995 and 1999.

e. Nigeria is 1ˢᵗ out of 110 countries for the standard deviation of terms of trade in levels, 1960-00.

f. Long-run average is for 1979-2000. IMF did not provide data prior to this period.

x. These data are under revision from 1983 onward and may be revised in the next draft.

The high volatility reflected in the table above for most aggregates indicates an underlying structural weakness in the Nigerian economy. Being an oil economy, Nigeria's 'fortunes' fluctuate with the international price of crude oil for the most part. Components of gross output like consumption and investment grow or dip with the country's performance in oil sales. According to Soludo *et al* (2003), periods of high oil prices and therefore high returns are often treated as permanent with the government making irreversible commitments to both labour and capital while periods of low returns are treated as temporary. With weak and largely undiversified taxation source, the government has often had to live above its means. Volatility of domestic prices is affected not just by oil prices but also by the highly diversified structure of domestic imports and the weak production base.

Both the low performance and the high volatility of the Nigerian economy have impacted adversely to the effectiveness of major macroeconomic policy instruments. In the monetary sector, major macroeconomic targets are often missed with wide gaps. Appendix 1 shows targets and outcomes of major macroeconomic aggregates in Nigeria between 2001 and 2005 (we have also included the indicators of relative performance of the targets). As shown in the Appendix, actual values of major macroeconomic (particularly monetary) variables have historically been multiples of the targets set by the authorities. On the average, over the six years between 2000 and 2005, broad money (M2) outcomes have been 176 per cent of its target values while aggregate credit turned out approximately 123 per cent of its target values. The worst offenders have been narrow money and credit to the government. For narrow money, the cash-based nature of transactions makes it quite difficult for even the Central Bank to control the quantity of currency in circulation. Credit to government, on the other hand, is mainly affected by fiscal indiscipline, which has been a major difficulty for monetary policy in the country (see Nnanna, 2001).

The poor growth performance and volatility of the macro-economy affected the entire financial system and financial intermediation process in Nigeria in profound ways. First, there was a complete breakdown in the relationship between economic growth and performance of the real sector and that of the financial sector. The risks associated with investment in the real sector grew astronomically relative to the returns. For an economy with dwindling growth and consequently poor returns on investment and where none of the core real sectors is thriving, the incentive for channeling mobilized funds into the real sector diminished substantially. Meanwhile, growth implosion also seemed to have 'coincided' with the liberalization of the financial sector and the withdrawal of direct instrument of control. Without a heavy reliance on either moral suasion or incentives for investment of funds in the real sector, private agents who took control of the banking sector began to search for more rewarding investments.

Many banks found profitable investment in foreign exchange trading, short-term loans for imports, purchase of government bonds and other securities. With these, many of them were able to bridge the disconnect between the profit expectations of their shareholders and the poor performance of the larger economy with dwindling profitability in real sector investments. This meant that while a number of the banks were growing and declaring jumbo profits, overall economic growth was not impacted. In no time, a unique nature of dualism between financial and real sector activities developed, with the former having real boom while the latter lagged far behind. Table 9.2 below shows the correlation of output growth with selected monetary aggregates.

Table 9.2: Correlation of Growth in Major Monetary Variables with Growth in Real Output, 2001 – 2005

Variable	Correlation with Output
M2	-0.37
Aggregate Bank Credit	-0.18
Credit (net) to Government	-0.40
Credit to private sector	-0.01
Inflation rate (%)	0.60

Source: *CBN Annual Report and Statement of Accounts,* 2005

Survival in the difficult environment for the banks therefore meant a lot of ingenuity in exploring investment opportunities outside of the real sector. Investment in agriculture and manufacturing was risky, but so also was investment in services. The volatility in the economy was accentuated by volatility in the polity. Banks responded to these uncertainties by taking interest rate to the rooftops, and committing to only very short term loans even under the extremely high interest rates. Even as at the time of this research, nominal lending rate is still in excess of 20 per cent for most commercial banks.

In a competitive environment, competition may often imply undercutting activities by players in the industry. The need to survive despite the risks led to very risky behaviours on the part of the banks. Conceptually, liberalization produces credit boom. In the ensuing bid to win favour of clients, banks compete stiffly and this drives banks to increase risky investment and loans. Less skilled staff are taken on board in an effort to increase market share and the outcome is even more low quality assets being acquired. In Nigeria, people with less than 10 years banking industry experience occupy senior management positions in banks and some of them are responsible for important decisions. Doubts about the quality of corporate governance affects investor confidence and some banks' share value. The experience in Nigeria is that the values of some banks' share remain low, because of the calibre of their directors. There was also competition with deposit rates. When deposit rates rise faster than deposits, the net transfer of funds to depositors by banks increase and, thereby expose the banks to greater liquidity problems. Of course, weak and poorly capitalized banks are often more aggressive in offering higher deposit rates and, thereby instigate even stronger banks to emulate them. In the course of this, financial vulnerability of the whole banking sector increases as depositors demand a net transfer of funds from banks, which they are unable to meet because they cannot recover their assets from borrowers or from their liquid assets.

Two other features of Nigeria's macroeconomic history that affected developments in the financial sector are worth noting. The first is oil price shocks, part of which impact has been alluded to previously. The other is the impact of policy summersaults. Oil prices dropped from period highs of between US$40 and US$42 per barrel in 1981 to as low as ten dollars per barrel in the 1990s. In Nigeria, this had adverse impact on GDP, external and domestic debt service, and government revenue and expenditure. Most of the newly licensed banks relied heavily on government deposits (which they in turn use to purchase government instruments) for survival. Implosion in government revenue meant less deposits and therefore less access to liquidity for the banks. Quite a large amount of failures in the early 1990s owed greatly to this.

Policy inconsistencies affect the value of assets held by banks. In Nigeria, import and sometimes export bans, exchange controls, nationalization and privatization, credit rationing, placement and withdrawal of public sector deposits from deposit money banks, and many others affect the quality and value of assets held by banks and thereby introduce crisis into the sector. In many instances, regime changes and introduction of new measures were quite sudden, unannounced and largely unpredictable. These macroeconomic policy regimes often did not provide suitable response that will ameliorate adverse effects on agents and so, in many cases, the balance sheet of banks were adversely affected.

Banking Development and Regulation in Nigeria – An Historical Overview

In 1886, the Post Office Savings Bank, later Federal Savings Bank, was set up as the first banking institution in Nigeria. But the first deposit money bank, the African Banking Corporation, which was later acquired by the British Bank of West Africa (today's First Bank Plc), was founded in 1892. Enthusiasm to participate in the new modern economy led to the setting up of many banks by Nigerians between 1927 and 1951. There was no banking regulation in force during the period and as a result, twenty-two of the twenty-five indigenous Nigerian banks in existence failed. In response, the banking ordinance of 1952, set standards, and provided for a required reserve fund, schemes of assistance for indigenous banks, and made provision for banking examinations. At this time there were two indigenous banks – National Bank of Nigeria (now Part of Skye Bank) and African Continental Bank (ACB) now part of Spring Bank) and three foreign banks, Bank of British West Africa (now First Bank), Barclays Bank (now Union Bank) and the British and French Bank (now Afribank).

A currency Board had been established in 1912 for British West African colonies. In 1958, the Central Bank of Nigeria (CBN) was established by an Act of parliament and began operation on 1st July 1959. Among other things, it had a mandate to regulate the banking industry and was independent of the government. In 1968, the Banking Act introduced further regulation of deposit money banks and the Central Bank of Nigeria was itself brought under the control of the Federal Government. Since the Central Bank of Nigeria was established in 1958, banks in Nigeria have been subject to regulation.

Under the indigenization policy of the 1970s, 60 per cent of the interests (equity) in foreign-owned banking enterprises in Nigeria were acquired by the Federal Government in order to control the commanding heights of the economy, as stipulated in the policy document. Many states (sub-national governments) had also established banks in the 1970s and as such the Nigerian Banks became largely public sector-owned up to 1986.

In 1986, Nigeria adopted some economic liberalization policies as part of the Structural Adjustment Programme (SAP), which was introduced to address the severe economic problems the country had faced in the 1980s. As a result, the banking sector was liberalized and many new banks were licensed, particularly private sector-owned banks. From less than twenty banks with about 100 branches in the early 1980s, at the end of 1988, the banking system consisted of the Central Bank of Nigeria, forty-two commercial banks and twenty-four merchant banks with about 1500 branches. The number of banks in the country continued to grow throughout the 1990s.

In further expansion of the banking sector, the Federal Government, in 1990, introduced the Community Banking Scheme (a kind of unit savings bank) to cater for the micro-finance needs of small-scale enterprises. Subsequently, the Federal Government privatized her shares in the commercial banks it had acquired dominant interests in the 1970s as a result of the indigenization policy. Thus, starting from the late 1980s up to the 1990s, the banks in Nigeria had largely acquired private sector character, which presented new regulatory challenges in the system. When banks were liberally licensed, the risky behaviours among bank managements increase, thereby exposing depositors to losses and banks to insolvency.

The Banking and Other Financial Institutions Act (BOFIA) 1991 and the Nigerian Deposit Insurance Corporation (NDIC) Act were enacted to guide the sector. Nevertheless, by 1995, many of the banks were in distress. This called for the reform of the banking sector, to which the government's response was first to set up the Failed Banks Tribunal, through which all those implicated in the large-scale abuses that had characterized the banking sector were prosecuted. A key assumption of the NDIC Act was that depositors are not in a position to affect the behaviour of bank management. Their inability stems from insufficient information and the difficulty of affecting the incentive structure facing bank management. The Act sought to protect depositors to a limit of N50,000.00 (approximately US$400) in the event of bank failure and liquidation. As a result, the most vulnerable group, small depositors have often recovered their deposits through the Nigerian Deposit Insurance Corporation (NDIC). As has been argued in the literature, it is possible that deposit insurance makes depositors less mindful of the behaviour of banks in which they have deposits (Diamond and Dybvig, 1983; and Dewatripont and Triole, 1994).

By 2003, there were eighty nine banks with a total of 3,382 branches. The banking sector was characterized by low capitalization (minimum capital for new commercial banks was N2bn (about US$16m) and many existing banks had less than that sum as capital). The total capitalization of all the banks in the country was less than US$146bn, (which is the size of the capitalization of ABSA, a South African Bank). Very few banks were dominant and many depended on public sector deposits and foreign exchange dealing. Quite a number were insolvent and illiquid, under weak corporate governance and held poor loan assets. The result of the assessment of the operational performance of licensed banks by the Central Bank of Nigeria, using CAMEL parameters showed that the symptoms of systemic distress were present in the sector. The banking sector's credit to the domestic economy was only 24 per cent of GDP, compared to 272 per cent for developed countries and average of 87 per cent for African countries. As a result of the illiquidity and insolvency of a number of banks, the Central Bank of Nigeria appointed seven banks as Settlement banks, in order to prevent a situation where banks overdrew their settlement accounts with it frequently. But this was far from being adequate for the problems facing the sector.

Table 9.3: Rating of Nigerian Banks, Using CAMEL Parameters

Category	Year		
	2001 Number	2002 Number	2003 Number
Sound/ Satisfactory	73	67	64
Marginal/Unsound	17	23	23

Source: *CBN, Annual Report and Statement of Accounts*, 2005.

The Banking Sector Reforms of 2004

The institutional and structural features of an economy, and in particular, its banking sector, to a large extent, determine its susceptibility to crisis (Hardy, 1998). The Act establishing the Central Bank of Nigeria (the apex financial regulatory institution) and the Bank and other Financial Institutions Act (BOFIA) empower the Central Bank to make regulations regarding prudential operation of banks. Licensed banks are required to abide by any such regulations. For international best practices in the sector, the Central Bank of Nigeria participates in, and subscribes to the Basel Accords. The 1988 Basel Accord (Basel I), focused on credit risk and classified banks asset into five, according to credit risk. Banks were then required to hold capital equal to a percentage of their risk-weighted assets. Basel II (1997 Accord), uses a 'three pillars' concept – (i) Minimum Capital requirements, (ii) supervisory review and (iii) market discipline, to promote greater stability in the financial system. The Central Bank of Nigeria has the responsibility to bring the Accords to bear on banking operations in Nigeria.

On 6th July 2004, with the accession of a new management, the Central Bank of Nigeria announced a 13 point agenda for reform. In terms of objective, the reform has three broad components. The first relates to the restructuring and realignment of institutions in the banking sector for increased reliability and efficiency of service. The second relates to the improvement of the capacity and focus of the Central Bank itself as a regulating institution to be able to effectively carry out its functions. The third is a one-point monetary policy agenda meant to reduce banks' reliance on public sector funds and correct the perverse incentive structure that has been created over the years arising from access to cheap funds with the attendant macroeconomic imbalance. We briefly take a look at some of the issues raised in the banking sector reform agenda.

The banking sector reform derived from the national development strategy, the National Economic Empowerment and Development Strategy (NEEDS), which was designed in 2003 by the National Planning Commission. NEEDS outlined the major problems affecting the financial system to include a shallow capital market, dependence of the banking system on public sector as a significant source of funds and foreign exchange trading, submission of inaccurate information by deposit money banks to monetary authorities, prolonged delay in repayment of bank loans and advances and the absence of harmony between fiscal and monetary policies (FGN, 2004). To address these problems, NEEDS enunciated a policy thrust aimed to deepen the financial system in terms of asset volume and instrument diversity; drastically reduce and ultimately eliminate the financing of government deficits by the banking system in order to free up resources for lending to the private sector; review capitalization of financial institutions in the system; and develop a structure of incentives to enable the financial system to play a developmental role by financing the real sector of the economy. Some of the strategies it identified include a comprehensive reform and improvement of the financial infrastructure (including laws and information systems); rationalization, restructuring and strengthening of the regulatory and supervisory framework in the financial sector, as well as addressing low capitalization and poor governance practices of financial intermediaries that submit inaccurate information to the regulatory authorities.

Reform of Deposit Money Banks

The requirement in the reform that relates to deposit money banks is basically twofold:

- Requirement that minimum capitalization for banks should be raised to N25bn (approximately US$200m) not later than 31st December 2005.

Banks that fail to meet the capital requirement will lose their banking licence.

- Consolidation of banking institutions through mergers and acquisitions. Indeed, this second requirement was more of an outcome of the first.

By far, the above two requirements relating to the banks were the most profound and prominent in immediate impact among the provisions of the reform. Almost every agent in the economy was in one way or the other affected by these requirements. The degrees of such affectation differ from one group of actors to another, but in almost all cases, there was some form of impact. Almost immediately, a number of banks that have been operating as private limited liability companies had to either merge or go to the capital market in search of funds. The volume of activity and awareness about the capital market immediately soared among the general public.

At the expiration of the Central Bank deadline, the number of banks declined from 89 to 25. Appendix 2 shows the 25 banks that made the list of qualified banks, including the pre-reform institutions that formed each emergent bank plus shareholders' funds as at October 2006. A number of other banks (14 in number) had their banking licences withdrawn.

Reform of the Central Bank and Banking Regulation

Even though most stakeholders, for reasons of unaccountable vested interest, do not seem to be welcoming of the new measures, it is apparent that the most significant provision of the reform agenda of the Central Bank relates to its own operations and capacity to monitor the banking sector. Of the thirteen-point reform agenda, nine were on Central Bank operations, stance towards monetary policy and regulation of deposit money banks. These relate to issues of operating laws and environment, internal monitoring and zero tolerance on misreporting and infractions in the regulatory framework; adoption of a risk-focused regulatory framework; automation of the process by which banks renders returns to the Central Bank and strict enforcement of the contingency planning framework for systemic distress. Others include working towards the establishments of an Asset Management company as an important element of distress solution; promotion and enforcement of dormant laws, especially those relating to the issuance of dud cheques, and the vicarious liabilities of members of the Board, in cases of bank failure, as well as revision and up-dating of relevant laws and drafting of new ones for the effective operation of the banking system. The apex Bank also provided for closer collaboration with the Economic and Financial Crimes Commission (EFCC) in the establishment of the Financial Intelligence Unit, and enforcement of the anti-money laundering and other economic crime measures. The enforcement of greater transparency and accountability will be the hallmark of the system. Finally, it provided for the establishment of a hotline and confidential internet address for all Nigerians wishing to share any confidential information with the Governor of the Central Bank of Nigeria on the operations of any bank or financial institution.

Prior to the emergence of the more comprehensive reform programme, previous administrations at the Central Bank evolved a programme code-named 'Project EAGLES'[1]. The project aimed to reposition the Central Bank as an effective monitoring and regulatory institution. This became imperative because the Central Bank had gradually got enmeshed in routine administration that it was barely able to face its developmental challenges. Prior to the reform, the responsibility of monitoring of deposit money banks, given their sheer number, was becoming a burden to the Central Bank. On-site visits, which was one of the most effective means of the Bank confirming data and information it receives on the operations of the banks was quite expensive in human, time and financial resources.

While much of the items in the repositioning of the Central Bank are process-based making it slightly difficult to evaluate their impact in the short run, some outlines of changes and impact on the regulatory framework have emerged within the short time of the implementation of the programme. The new reform programme incorporated and expanded 'Project EAGLES' and continued the programme of increasing the efficiency of individual staff. The Central Bank instituted online reporting of the activities of banks. With the consolidation and the consequent reduction in the number of bank groups, as well as online reporting, the pressure for physical monitoring of many banks was partially lifted from the regulatory body. The new regulatory and monitoring regime has also made it possible to quickly track sources of distortions in the reporting and data systems flowing to the Central Bank. There are also indications that the Central Bank is presently much better focused on core macroeconomic responsibilities rather than micro challenges of tracking private agents or business units.

Macroeconomic Policy and Currency Reforms

Two of the provisions of the reform programme relate to phased withdrawal of public sector funds from banks and currency reforms and restructuring. As mentioned earlier, public sector funds formed the bulk of deposits in banks. Also, a disproportionate share of credits to the economy goes to the public sector. With a long legacy of indiscipline and weak infrastructure for monitoring of fiscal policy, financing of deficits has been indiscriminate over time. Indeed, one of the major reasons repeatedly proffered by the Central Bank for the consistent missing of targets it sets is what operators have termed 'fiscal dominance' – where fiscal actions of the government makes nonsense of monetary policy measures taken by the Central Bank. As noted in the preceding analysis, most banks court public sector funds with lavish offers. In turn, they use such funds to trade in government securities and foreign exchange with huge returns. With very little rules guiding public sector access to financing from the banking sector, credit to the public sector most often crowded out credit to the private sector with the attendant retardation in growth of the private sector. This provision, therefore, aimed to strengthen rules and rule enforcement on banks' access to public sector funds and vice versa, reducing such access to only the very necessary.

Prior to 2006, coins were near extinct in the Nigerian currency system. In addition, replacement rates for the lower denominations were quite high and the costs sometimes swamped the gains obtained from such replacements. Indeed, the culture of providing balance in small transactions was almost gone from the system. The outlook of the national currency (the Naira) also needed shoring up. Part of the reforms, therefore, provided for the reintroduction of coins by the conversion of some of the lower notes into coins. There was also some attempt to change the outlook of the lower currencies, making them easier to recognize and use, and also to strengthen their durability.

Preliminary Assessment of the Reform

From the preceding analysis of the Nigerian macro-economic context, it is evident that a fundamental reform of the banking sector was an urgent necessity. The reform package enunciated by the Central Bank in 2004 could, at best, be seen as a policy response to the observed necessity. However, far-reaching reforms of this nature are usually underscored by a number of institutional and structural challenges. For instance, Central Bank Governors in the recent past have been in the main, core stakeholders, usually with strong ownership interests in the sector's network of banks. This was, however, not the case with the new Central Bank Governor who, unlike most previous Governors that have emerged from the top echelon of the banking system, came with an illustrious academic-technocratic background and thus had no personal vested interest in the banking industry. Hence it is not surprising that there was intense resistance to the Central Bank reforms from many of the key stakeholders – bankers, shareholders, politicians, etc.

Right from the time of the promulgation of the reforms, there was a significant stir in the overall economy. Arguably, the banking sector reform has impacted more on the economy than the rest of the NEEDS programme. Virtually all aspects of the economy has been affected – the capital market, micro-credit institutions, etc.

The stability of the banking sector since the beginning of 2006 has had a positive knock-on effect on the economy. One positive outturn is exchange rate stability. The banks are key players in the foreign exchange market. With consolidation, the behaviour of banks has changed dramatically. The observed desperation displayed by banks in the foreign exchange market in the past has changed in a radical way. As a result, the official and black market rates have almost merged as the black market premium is now less than 3 per cent. This development has lasted for not less than a year.

The Central Bank presently spends more time managing monetary policy than policing deposit money banks. New policy initiatives, which has been made possible include, lowering the inflation rate to a single digit, introduction of new monetary policy framework –lower cash reserve requirement (CRR) is now 3 per cent, having come down from 5 per cent; introduction of a Monetary Policy Rate to replace the Minimum Rediscount Rate (MRR) and Standing Facility (SF) for banks to manage their liquidity. The foreign exchange market has been restructured such that the Central Bank of Nigeria now operates a Wholesale Dutch Auction System (W-DAS) instead of the previous retail Dutch Auction System in which banks bid for definite customers. Also, foreign exchange bureau or Bureau D' Change (BDCs) now are allowed at the Central Bank window, hence, even banks now operate BDCs.

Most of the 25 banks are public limited companies and, in addition to Central Bank regulation are, therefore, subject to additional regulators – the Securities and Exchange Commission (SEC), Nigerian Stocks Exchange (NSE) and the Corporate Affairs Commission (CAC). Supervising 25 strong banks is certainly easier than supervising 89 mostly weak and poorly capitalised banks. Now the Electronic Financial Analysis and Surveillance System (E–FASS) is in place and through it, operating banks provide online real-time data to the Central Bank.

The size of the balance sheet of the 25 licensed banks and their profitability has made it possible for some of them to obtain credit from foreign banks, thereby increasing the savings available for investment in the country. For example, Guaranty Trust Bank issued a US$300m Eurobond, which was oversubscribed by US$221m. Foreign portfolio investors have been putting money into Nigerian Banks since the consolidation exercise in response to their favourable rating by rating agencies. UBA has just been rated A+ by both Agusto & Company and Fitch rating agencies. The rating is based on the balance sheet, profitability, risk management framework, strategy, quality of management, operating environment and the future development of business vision.

Depositor confidence has increased and savers are now responding to bank offerings, so much so that Nigeria is finding it difficult maintaining the reserve money requirements of its policy support instrument (PSI) since the bank consolidation exercise. Banking supervision is gradually being moved away from on-site and off-site supervision towards a risk–based supervision system. The hope is that bank customers would be enabled to form opinion about the risk behaviour of banks. This will bring pressure to bear on bank management and reduce the risk exposure of bank deposits.

Deposit Money Banks have accepted the challenge of going beyond the N25bn minimum shareholders fund. Those who have met a shareholder fund benchmark of (U.S $1.00bn) have, in partnership with pre-qualified foreign banks been given portions of Nigeria's foreign reserves (not more than US$500m each) to manage. Since then, banks have been increasing their capitalization by going to the capital market and by private placement. Improved professionalism of the consolidated banks have made it possible for Nigeria to be de-listed from the International Financial Action Task Force (FATF) list of countries where money laundering is not being vigorously discouraged. Overall, the banking system in Nigeria can be said to be fairly stable now, more than in the decade before 2004.

The volume of currency in circulation is still relatively high in Nigeria. This is a challenge which the banking system has to tackle. Presently, the reserve money in Nigeria is almost entirely made up of the currency in circulation, yet the minimum lending rate which stands at 19 per cent is disproportionately high compared to the savings rate of 3 per cent. Thus the banks are not mobilizing savings enough in a country where the majority is poor and the prevailing inflation rate stands at 8 per cent and above.

Conclusion

The banking sector reforms were founded on the understanding that globally, size matters in the banking business, particularly given new trends in internationalization of finance and the pressure of globalization. The desire to create capable global players with local roots in the Nigerian banking sector was a strong motivation for the reforms. In a number of ways, this has paid off as some Nigerian banks have for the first time made it into the list of first 100 banks worldwide. The sense of renewed confidence in the banking sector and the overall macro-economy is almost palpable. In addition, the Central Bank has repositioned itself with increased capacity to be able to provide effective oversight to the new banking structure.

Implementing the reforms faced strong challenges, mostly from those whose entrenched interests left them fighting for long held privileges. To counter the resistance, the Central Bank relied on the judicious use of incentives and sanctions to compel stakeholders to conform to the new guidelines. For example, authorization was provided for the accredited banks to deal in foreign exchange and also be depositories for public sector funds and part of the nation's foreign reserve. The Central Bank also provided experts to help the accredited banks with the complex legal and transactional bottlenecks of mergers and acquisitions that were desperately necessary for the 18 months capitalization deadline to be met. It also provided a general amnesty for past misreporting, distorting and misrepresentation of facts, but insisted on a zero-tolerance of any such acts of misconduct in the future.

Although a significant measure of success has been recorded, there are still some major challenges. In particular, the Central Bank needs institutional strengthening to progressively deliver on Guitian's three-pillar paradigm for banking sector soundness – (a) official oversight (prudential standing), (b) internal governance (risk management in each individual bank), and (c) market discipline (sound banking practices). These pillars have to be complemented by ensuring that in the banking system, there are responsible owners and managers and professional authorities (especially, auditors and accounting standards), prudent macroeconomic management, and good international cooperation. The establishment of an Asset Management company may help prevent generalized distress in the banking sector as bad loans can more easily be transferred to the company by banks. Efforts to put it in place need to be intensified. Both the banks and regulatory authorities need to develop suitable stress indices that will help forecast banking sector problems and thereby forestall sectoral decline and inefficacity. For this to be done effectively, the endemic dearth of data and data unreliability has to be solved. With foreign investors in Nigerian banks, and the banks borrowing for on-lending to domestic customers, the system is increasingly exposed to international economy. This demands considerable attention to the rapid change in maturity structure of international loan liabilities and banks' domestic credit assets and the incorporation of these into early warning mechanisms.

Note

1. EAGLES is a Central Bank of Nigeria acronym for Efficiency, Accountability, Goal Orientation, Leadership, Effectiveness and Staff-Oriented

References

Addison, Douglas, (2002) *Policy Options for Managing Macroeconomic Volatility in Nigeria.*

Central Bank of Nigeria (2005), *Annual Report and Statement of Accounts.* Abuja, CBN.

Dewatripont, Mathias and Tiole Jean (1994) *The Prudential Regulation of Banks,* Cambridge: MIT Press.

Diamond, Douglas W. and Dybvig, Philip H. (1983) 'Bank Runs, Deposit Insurance, and Liquidity', *Journal of Political Economy,* 91(3), pp. 401-419.

Djiwandono, S. J. (1998), *Banking System Soundness and Macroeconomic Management: The Recent Indonesian Experience.* www.pacific.net.id/pakar/sj/banking.html.

Elumelu, Tony O. (June, 2005), *Investment, Finance, and Banking in Nigeria: Evolution and New Opportunities.* Paper presented at the 2005 U.S-Africa Summit of the Corporate Council on Africa, Baltimore, USA.

Gavin, M. and Hausann, R. (1998) 'The Roots of Banking Crises: The Macroeconomic Context', in *Inter-American Development Bank, Working Paper,* no. 318.

Guitian, Manuel (1994) 'Rules or Discretion in Monetary Policy: National and International Perspectives', in *Frameworks for Monetary Stability: Policy Issues and Country Experiences,* Washington: International Monetary Fund.

Hardy Daniel C. (1998) 'Are Banking Crises Predictable.' *Finance & Development,* December 1998. IMF.

International Monetary Fund (1993) *International Capital Markets, Part II: Systemic Issues in International Finance.* Washington: International Monetary Fund.

International Monetary Fund (2000) *Monetary and Financial Statistics Manual.* IMF, Washington DC.

Mishkin, F (1991), "Anatomy of financial crisis" *NBER Working Paper,* no. 3934.

National Planning Commission (2004), *National Economic Empowerment and Development Strategy (NEEDS.).* Abuja, NPC.

Nnanna, O. J. (2001) *Monetary Policy Framework in Africa: The Nigerian Experience.* Central Bank of Nigeria, Abuja, July 2001.

Soludo, Chukwuma C. (2006) 'Beyond Banking Sector Consolidation in Nigeria'. Paper presented at the Global Banking Conference on Nigerian Banking Reforms at Dorchester Hotel, London.

Soludo, C. C., Oji, G. O., Agu, C., and Amakom U., (2003) 'Nigeria: Macroeconomic Assessment and Agenda for Reforms.' *Report on the Performance of the Nigerian Economy,* written for the United States Agency for International Development in Collaboration with IBM Consulting, US.

Sundararajan, V., *et al* (2002) *Financial Soundness Indicators: Analytical Aspects and Country Practices* IMF Occasional Paper 212.

Appendix 1: Comparing Targets and Outcomes of Major Macroeconomic Indicators, 2000-2005

Year		M2 /a	M1 /a	Aggregate Bank Credit /a	Credit (net) to Govt /a	Credit to private sector /a	Inflation rate (%) /a	GDP /a
2000	Target	14.6	9.8	27.8	37.8	21.9	9	3
	Actual	48.1	62.2	-23.1	-162.3	30.9	6.9	3.8
	Actual/Target (%) /b	329.5	634.7	-83.1	-429.4	141.1	76.7	126.7
2001	Target	12.2	4.3	15.8	2.6	22.8	7	5
	Actual	27	28.1	75.8	79.7	43.5	18.9	3.9
	Actual/Target (%)	221.3	653.5	479.7	3065.4	190.8	270.0	78.0
2002	Target	15.2	12.4	57.9	96.6	34.9	9.3	5
	Actual	21.6	15.9	64.6	6320.6	11.8	12.2	3.5
	Actual/Target (%)	142.1	128.2	111.6	6543.1	33.8	131.2	70.0
2003	Target	15	13.8	25.7	-150.3	32.3	9	5
	Actual	24.1	29.5	29.1	58.4	27.1	23.8	10.2
	Actual/Target (%)	160.7	213.8	113.2	-38.9	83.9	264.4	204.0
2004	Target	15	10.8	22.5	29.9	22	10	5
	Actual	14	8.6	12	-17.9	26.6	10	6.5
	Actual/Target (%)	93.3	79.6	53.3	-59.9	120.9	100.0	130.0
2005	Target	15	11.4	22.5	-10.9	22	10	5
	Actual	16.03	15.5	14.5	-37	30.8	11.6	6.2
	Actual/Target (%)	106.9	136.0	64.4	339.4	140.0	116.0	124.0
Average		175.6	307.6	123.2	1570.0	118.4	159.7	122.1

Source: CBN, *Annual Report and statement of Accounts, 2005*

Notes: /a. M2 is broad money; M1 is narrow money, while GDP is gross output. All variables are in percent growth except where otherwise specified.

/b. Actual/Target values were obtained by dividing the outcomes with targets to obtain the proportion of the outcome to the target.

/c. Average of Actual to target values for each variable over the time covered by the table.

Appendix 2: Shareholders' Fund, Revaluation and Loan Loss Reserve as at October 2006

S/No	Bank Name	Members of the Group	Paid-Up Capital =N='000	Reserve Fund =N='000	Revaluation Fund =N=000	Loan Loss Reserve =N=000	Total =N='000
1	Afribank	i) Afribank International Ltd (Merchant Bankers) ii) Afribank Nigeria Plc	2,554,216	23,544,667	1,093,524	10,736,101	37,928,508
2	Access	i) Access Bank of Nigeria Ltd; ii) Capital Bank International Ltd; iii) Marina International Bank Ltd	6,978,162	21,915,731	0	12,663,486	38,864,919
3	Diamond	i)African International Bank Ltd; ii)Diamond Bank Ltd; iii) Lion Bank Plc	3,801,804	31,167,766	0	4,838,303	39,807,873
4	Ecobank	i) Ecobank Nigeria Plc	5,413,557	20,349,301	0	2,359,203	28,122,061
5	ETB Bank	i) Devcom Bank Ltd; ii) Equatorial Trust Bank Ltd	6,500,000	19,868,015	62,687	5,977,747	32,408,449
6	FCMB	i) Cooperative Development Bank Plc; ii) FCMB Bank Plc; iii) Midas Bank Ltd; iv) Nigeria-American Bank Ltd	4,751,215	20,618,149	0	7,480,152	32,849,516

7	Fidelity	i) Fidelity Bank Plc; ii)FSB International Bank Plc iii) Manny Bank Ltd	8,231,84 3	18,531,7 69	0	7,776,14 8	34,539,76 0
8	First Bank	i) FBN Merchant Bankers; ii) First Bank of Nigeria Plc; iii) MBC International Bank Ltd	5,238,69 0	51,378,5 38	2,379,30 2	34,387,1 81	93,383,71 1
9	FirstInlan d	i) First Atlantic Bank Ltd; ii) IMB Bank Plc iii) Inland Bank Plc; iv) NUB Bank Ltd	4,844,31 5	24,923,7 42	579,892	13,407,2 25	43,755,17 4
10	Guaranty Trust	i) Guaranty Trust Bank Plc	4,000,00 0	32,420,0 42	0	4,995,35 7	41,415,39 9
11	IBTC-Chartere d Bank	i) Chartered Bank Plc; ii) IBTC Ltd; iii) Regent Bank Ltd	6,028,60 4	29,192,5 47	0	6,850,74 8	42,071,89 9
12	Interconti nental	i) Equity Bank of Nigeria Ltd; ii) Gateway Bank iii) Global Bank Plc; iv) Intercontinen tal Bank Plc	5,361,79 4	48,146,6 96	0	13,914,6 86	67,423,17 6
13	NIB	i) Nigeria International Bank Ltd	2,793,77 7	23,297,0 60	0	2,799,03 3	28,889,87 0
14	Oceanic	i)Internation al Trust Bank Ltd; ii) Oceanic Bank	4,656,80 3	37,906,2 74	0	1,705,23 9	44,268,31 6

		Plc					
15	Bank PHB	i) Habib Nigeria Bank Ltd; ii) Platinum Bank Ltd	9,652,53 7	23,829,0 06	0	4,534,34 5	38,015,88 8
16	Skye Bank	i) Bond Bank LTD; ii) Cooperative Bank Plc; iii) EIB Bank Ltd; iv) Prudent Bank Plc; v) Reliance Bank Ltd	14,149,5 01	17,319,5 20	0	10,520,1 15	41,989,13 6
17	Spring Bank	i) ACB International Bank Plc; ii) Citizens Bank International Ltd; iii) Fountain Trust Bank Ltd; iv) Guardian Express Bank Ltd; v) Omega Bank Plc; vi) Trans International Bank Ltd	18,968,4 31	19,008,8 25	2,037,87 1	19,456,4 65	59,471,59 2
18	Stanbic Bank	i)Stanbic Bank Ltd	1,480,00 0	24,171,4 87	0	753,915	26,405,40 2
19	Standard Chartere d	i) Standard Chartered Bank Ltd	2,500,00 0	23,642,8 39	0	- 1,809,74 4	24,333,09 5
20	Sterling Bank	i)INMB Bank Ltd; ii)Magnum Trust Bank Ltd; iii) NAL Bank Ltd; iv)NBM Bank LTD; v) Trust Bank of Africa Ltd	5,276,42 4	15,492,1 71	540,000	8,889,57 2	30,198,16 7

21	UBA	i) Broad Bank Ltd; ii) Union Bank of Nigeria Plc iii) Union Merchant Bank; iv) Universal Trust Bank	3,530,000	32,428,386	9,019,141	7,953,000	52,930,527
22	Union Bank	i)Continental Trust Bank ii) Standard Trust Bank iii) United Bank for Africa Plc	5,575,611	91,603,223	313,906	44,509,625	142,002,365
23	Unity Bank	i)Bank of the North ii) Centre Point Bank Plc iii) First Interstate Bank Ltd; iv) Intercity Bank v) New Africa Bank Plc; vi) New Nigerian Bank Plc vii) Pacific Bank Ltd; viii) Societe Bancaire Ltd ix) Tropical Commercial Bank	22,105,341	3,988,126	4,344,929	12,115,698	42,554,094
24	WEMA Bank	i)National Bank Plc ii) WEMA Bank Plc	5,679,762	20,521,671	0	12,663,486	38,864,919
25	Zenith Bank	i) Zenith Bank Plc	4,632,762	90,691,419	0	5,309,248	100,633,429
Total			164,705,149	765,956,970	20,371,252	250,945,848	1,201,979,219

Source: CBN Banking Supervision Unit; *Annual Report and Statement of Accounts,* 2005.

229

Chapter 10

Understanding Corruption in Nigeria

Paul Okojie & Abubakar Momoh

Introduction

Corruption is an issue of household conversation in Nigeria. The mass media play a leading role in setting out the moral and political arguments against corruption. They also play an important part in exposing corruption in high places and in the other sectors of the economy, although the context and incentive for promoting and protecting whistleblowers does not exist in Nigeria. Nigerians have experienced long periods of political and economic insecurity in the country and corruption has often been cited by military coup plotters as one of the major causes of their unconstitutional intervention and overthrow of government (Ademoyega, 1981).

As an oil rich nation, Nigerians should be experiencing great economic prosperity, but instead, it is in a perpetual economic crisis, to an extent that the country is considered to be on the verge of becoming a failed state (Okojie and Momoh, forthcoming). The country regularly earns huge revenues from oil. Between 2002 to 2006, Nigeria earned 8.8 trillion Naira (local currency) from oil exports (Komolafe, 2007), yet 70 per cent of its population is classified as poor with 35 per cent living in absolute poverty (International Fund for Agricultural Development, 2004).

According to Wenar (2007): 'in the 30 years after 1970, the percentage of Nigerians living in extreme poverty (less than US$1 per day) increased from 36 per cent to almost 70 per cent – from 19 million to 90 million people. [This is over half of the total population put at 140 million by the 2006 population census]. Oil revenue has not impacted positively on the average standard of living of the people, and, indeed, the period of oil boom has seen a great decline in living standards. Moreover, inequality in Nigeria simultaneously skyrocketed. In 1970, the total income of those in the top 2 per cent of the distribution was

230

equal the total income of those in the bottom 17 per cent. By 2000, the top 2 per cent made as much as the bottom 55 per cent.'

By virtue of its foreign exchange earnings, Nigeria is not classified as a poor country. According to the World Bank categories, Nigeria is recognised as a 'blend' country. This places Nigeria among the group of countries that are ineligible for the World Bank's debt reduction scheme and is restricted to borrowing from the Bank's commercial stream where access to credit depends on 'good policy performance' (Moss, Standley and Birdshall, 2005). However, the country was recently granted substantial debt relief by the Paris Club of Western creditors.

The Centre for Economic Development has argued that a more realistic assessment is for Nigeria to be judged by the poverty of the majority of its citizens, although this is not a view shared by the World Bank, which believes the country's poverty is self-inflicted and that it should not be seen to be rewarding poor economic performance.

Characterisation of Corruption

There are various forms of corruption, ranging from the venial – referred to in Nigeria as 'dash' 'Egunje,' 'settlement' or 'kola' to wholesale embezzlement of public funds, influence peddling and the abuse of public power. This chapter focuses on the systematic use of public office by the governing elites for self-enrichment - phenomenon described by many analysts as 'grand corruption.'

Corruption is not like any other crime. Corruption has an Octopus effect. As a 'devilfish' it has a predatory mollusc, ' which can creep over hard surfaces using their arms; when they travel through water they move by jet propulsion, taking in water and ejecting it forcibly through a funnel as their muscular mantle contracts. They vary in size from a few centimetres to the giant Octopus of the Pacific Ocean, which can grow to over 10m (Canadian Museum of Nature, nd). Corruption is like an elephant, hard to describe but easy to recognise.

There is no agreed definition of corruption. Many definitions and charaterisations of corruption have taken behavioural, psychoanalytical or economistic perspectives (cf. Mensah, 1986; Odekunle 1997; Olopoenia, 1998; and Osoba, 1997). This is both a lament and a recognition that an activity that has so many tentacles is not easy to define.

This chapter concentrates only on grand (as opposed to petty) corruption. Corruption is said to be grand when public policy-making, its design and implementation are compromised by corrupt practices and when public office holders indulge in barefaced looting of public treasury. Examples of grand corruption abound in privatizations, government procurement, and labour policies. Examples are the use of 'public office for private benefit, which involves the compromise of government procedures or the capture of a government institution's rulings (United Nations Office on Drugs and Crime).

While the harm caused by petty corruption is not discounted, corruption is always a matter of proportionality. Grand corruption is usually systematic and its effect is greater on the polity, notably in the form of economic failure, poverty, hunger, death and in extreme cases, it can cause the collapse of the state. A classic example is Zaire under Mobutu Sese Seko. President Mobutu owned palaces, villas, personal zoos and held billions of dollars in European banks. Although the genesis of the civil war and the eventual collapse of Zaire date back to the time of independence from Belgian Congo, the circumstances that plunged that nation into collapse cannot be divorced from Mobutu's grand corruption. In his captivating history of the Congo, Edgerton (2002) wrote:

> ... as vast sums of money came to Mobutu from the bribes given him by large foreign corporations, including many in the United States, and as the percentage he took from the profits of all economic ventures in the country rose rapidly, he soon became wealthy enough to use money as his weapon of choice. He would make corruption the keystone of his administration, untold thousands eagerly joined in.... Mobutu's self-enrichment program relied on direct bribes from foreign governments and security agencies, payments by investors, diversion of Zairean government funds, embezzlement of export earnings, and the massive diversion of foreign loan and aid. Estimates of the amount of money Mobutu stole from the Congo vary widely. The lowest estimates are 4-5 billion U.S. dollars, with some as high as $15 billion. He built and lavishly furnished over a dozen grand palaces in the Congo, led in grandeur by the one at Gbadolite, deep in the tropical forest of northeastern Congo near his birthplace. It boasted a fifteen-thousand- bottle wine cellar... He also had many properties in Europe on the French Riviera, in Brussels, Switzerland, Paris, and Madrid, not to mention Cape Town, Marrakech, Dakar and Abidjan.

Describing how Zaire descended into pillage, Edgerton (2002) explained that:

> State employees supplemented their inadequate and irregular salaries by postal and judicial fraud, false billing, extortion, embezzlement, outright theft, padding payrolls with false names, forgeries, import, export and exercise fraud, illegal taxation, and taking second or third jobs. Bribery became universal. No one could arrive or leave from an international airport without paying a host of bribes, and military barricades set up on roads around the country extorted money from every traveller able to pay. Admission to a secondary school or university was based on bribery, not outstanding grades. Even university students joined in the corruption saying, "If there is anarchy, profit from it."

Examples from Nigeria show a similar pillage on a grand scale under the Abacha regime (Okojie and Momoh, forthcoming). Large sums of money were found in Abacha's house after his sudden death on June 8 1998. In one incident, his widow was caught at Kano Airport with 38 crates of US dollars which she intended to take abroad to deposit in one of their overseas bank accounts (Okojie and Momoh, forthcoming). General Sani Abacha's corruption was similar in scale to Mobutu's. The accusation against him ranged from direct looting of the Central Bank of Nigeria to receiving bribes from foreign companies and kickbacks by inflating the cost of contracts, masking his involvement through Nigerian companies that were effectively under the control of his family members, forcible appropriation of assets of Nigerians, storing of money in vaults, use of fronts and lackeys to bid for contracts or government financial patronage. As with Mobutu, the proceeds of the crimes were transferred to numbered bank accounts in overseas countries (Ige, 2002). The scale of Abacha's corruption merits the term *Mobutuism*, meaning the systematic pillage of a country's wealth by its leaders in the manner perpetrated by Mobutu. This sobriquet should only be used in circumstances of widespread pillaging of public funds that go beyond merely using public office for private gain in a single instance.

Containing Grand Corruption

The current Nigerian government believes that grand corruption is being tackled and lay responsibility for Nigeria's reputation as a corrupt nation at the door of previous administrations. It points to measures instituted since 1999 to prosecute corrupt officials. The new policy will be examined below.

Ribadu (2004a), the head of Nigeria's principal anti-corruption agency, the Economic and Financial Crimes Commission [EFCC] holds previous administrations responsible for the country's economic mismanagement, corruption, lack of accountability and transparency. He laments Nigeria's poor economic rating, which, in spite of oil wealth, is among the 20 poorest countries in the world. Can the Obasanjo administration so easily exonerate itself from these problems? This question is considered in this chapter.

History of Corruption in Nigeria

The history of corruption in Nigeria goes back to colonial times. Embezzlement and misappropriation of funds took place under the watchful eyes of the British colonial administration. It was so widespread that at some point the British contemplated delaying the country's move towards self-rule. There were various reports of misfeasance by politicians and trade unions. In one inquiry report, the Secretary of the Colliery Workers' Union, one Okwudili Ojoyi, was accused of a lavish life style supported by the misuse of his members' funds (Tignor, 1993). Local and regional administrations were mired in corruption. The British colonial administration constantly received reports of how local councillors and politicians used elected office to enrich themselves and to gain political advantages over their political rivals. Most of the reports in the public domain concentrated on the activities of local and some national politicians in Southern Nigeria. The colonial administration was particularly concerned about corruption in key municipalities such as Ibadan, Lagos, Onitsha and Port Harcourt. These were the fast emerging cities.

The first cited report was an inquiry in 1951 into misconduct in local government in Ibadan, in the old Western Nigeria, followed by another one, two years later (1953) into the Lagos Town Council. By 1955, there was more frequent use of inquiries to investigate corruption. There were four such inquiries into local government administration in the old Eastern Nigeria alone. The full list of the corruption inquiries conducted under the British colonial administration is listed in the endnote (see also, Butcher, 1951).

Although the British colonial administration sought to discourage these illicit activities, they were partial in targeting culprits. Reports they were receiving showed that corruption in the Northern part of Nigeria was as widespread as in the South, but there was not a single publicly conducted inquiry into the allegations of wrong-doing in Northern Nigeria. Agitation for independence among the Northern aristocracy was less fervent and the British did not want to expose them to what they regarded as the humiliation which a public corruption inquiry brings. The British feared that this could radicalise their powerful allies in the North and bring about a common cause between the politicians in the South and North in the demand for independence (Tignor, 1993).

Often, allegations of corruption were brought to the attention of the British colonial administration by political opponents. This political rivalry served the interest of the British who were willing to oblige with an inquiry, especially against the radicals agitating for political independence. The British wanted them to be exposed as venial and untrustworthy.

The British colonial administration used corruption inquiry to serve two purposes – to address issues of criminality and moral turpitude and to score points against opponents of colonial rule in Nigeria.

The African Continental Bank Affair (A.C.B)

The affairs of the African Continental Bank (A.C.B) became a cause célèbre for the British. This was, by far, the most important public inquiry into corruption by the colonial administration in Nigeria. It was so serious that the Chief Judge of the Nigerian Supreme Court, Sir Stafford Foster-Sutton, was appointed to conduct it. Prior to this, it was common for the Colonial Office to send an official from the UK to conduct an investigation. For example, the Town Clerk of Norwich, England, Bernard Storey conducted the inquiries into the Lagos Town Council even though he admitted his ignorance of Lagos politics. Similarly, another Town Clerk from Abingdon, near Oxford, England, was given the task of investigating corruption allegations against the late Adekoye Adelabu of Ibadan in the old Western region. He too admitted lack of knowledge of the politics of Ibadan.

Dr Azikiwe and the A.C.B

At the centre of the allegation was Dr Nnamdi Azikiwe, a nationalist and an arch campaigner for independence and who is regarded by Nigerians as the 'Father of Independence.' It was the first time that a major political figure was exposed to a full scale public investigation over abuse of public office. Dr. Azikiwe was at the time, the Premier of the old Eastern Nigeria. The essence of the allegations is that he used public funds to prop up his private bank and businesses. The Tribunal of Inquiry noted:

> Statements were laid before us to show that the position of the (African Continental Bank) and the Zik Group of Companies as at 31st March 1955. From these it was clear that the state of solvency which then existed throughout the whole organization (with one exception) could only result in the liquidation of the Bank and the companies in the group.

According to Sklar (1966), 'the investment and deposit of £2million, previously held by the Marketing Board in the form of 3 per cent savings bonds, gave the bank a new birth of vitality and the wherewithal to extend large amounts of credit.

Tignor (1993) traced the origins of the ACB. The bank was purchased in 1944 as a private enterprise by Dr Azikiwe long before he held public office. He justified the establishment of a bank under the direct control of Nigerians to counteract dependence on foreign owned bank whose policies were constraining the development of black enterprises. He saw it as a bulwark against the domination of the banking sector in Nigeria by foreign banks. Tignor (1993) expands on the facts of the allegations:

> The A.C.B. initially operated on a small-scale: in 1950 its capital was a mere £9,623 and its savings and deposit accounts were only £106,724. Two years later, British financial officials enacted legislation whereby all banks in Nigeria were given until 1955 to meet certain minimum capital and reserve requirements. The A.C.B. used many stratagems to

achieve legal compliance, but although depositors and debtors were cajoled into placing their funds in the bank for a single day at the end of the accounting periods so that these monies could be counted as liquid, such tactics were merely palliatives. What saved the A.C.B. was the Eastern Regional Financial Corporation's decision, taken in May 1955, to invest £877,000 in the bank's equity, and its capitalisation had increased to £911,946 by 1956. The investment of such a large sum from governmental surpluses in the East at a time when Azikiwe was the regional Premier offended many persons.

The Strafford Forster-Sutton Inquiry as a Trail

The Justice Strafford Foster-Sutton inquiry report was to set the trail which is now familiar to Nigerians. A public inquiry is used to expose wrongdoing in public office. The inquiry receives widespread publicity, but in the long term, it does not achieve the desired outcome, that makes public office holders to regard accountability, transparency and good governance as the purpose of holding a public office.

Based on previous studies, there is no significant evidence that anti-corruption policy in Nigeria has brought about a change in attitude and/or willingness on the part of public office holders to act with probity and in public good. This is judged by the number of those accused of corruption who subsequently were able to hold public office in spite of their previous exposure. Evidence from colonial times show that exposure does not necessarily affect the political fortunes of the exposed. The publication of the Justice Strafford Foster-Sutton inquiry report did not bring about the resignation of Dr Azikiwe, as the Premier of the old Eastern Nigeria, on the contrary, he went on to become the first civilian [non-executive] President of Nigeria at independent in October 1960.

There are, of course, a few noticeable exceptions, Joseph Tarka and Chief Anthony Enahoro,   two prominent members of the cabinet under Gowon's military regime in the 1970s. Their political careers suffered because of the allegations of corruption against them. Their experience is the exception, rather than the rule. Even so, Chief Enahoro went on to become an active member of the National Party of Nigeria (NPN), the ruling party in Nigeria in 1979. The Nigerian public have become accustomed to seeing politicians with tainted record of public service being put back in positions of trust.

Post-Independence Experience

The first five years of Nigeria's independence from British colonial rule was a period of political conflicts, instability and maladministration. These factors were used by the military to justify their intervention in government in 1966. The leader of the 1966 coup, Major Chukwuma Kaduna Nzeogwu, explained that the purpose of the military was to 'establish a strong united and prosperous nation, free from corruption and internal strife. Our method of achieving this is strictly military but we have no doubt that every Nigerian will give us maximum cooperation by assisting the regime ... (Nzeogwu, 1966). He noted that the real enemies of Nigeria were the contractors/politicians who inflate the cost of contracts by 10 per cent or more for their personal gain.

Public shock and disbelief accompanied the exposure of corruption in the old Western Nigeria following the investigation of the management of public utilities in that part of the country. The Coker Commission of Inquiry (1962) was the first such major one after the A.C.B affairs. It exposed how senior political figures systematically abused public trust. The Coker Inquiry found that the ruling party in western Nigeria, the Action Group, used public utilities to funnel money into the coffers of the party. Although scandalised, the public did not believe this type of misdeed was confined only to the Western region. As with the British under colonial administration, the federal government saw an opportunity caused by the disarray in the Action Group (A.G.) to set up the Coker Inquiry (1962). Its aim was not considered sincere. As with the A.C.B. affair under British rule, there was a lack of balance in the anti-corruption policy.

Although revelations of the misdeeds were shocking, reaction to them differed in different sections of the country. Those in the Action Group (A.G.) controlled areas tended to see the inquiry as an instrument used by the party's enemies to ferment troubles and disorder in Western Nigeria. The Action Group's opponents in Northern and Eastern Nigeria took gleeful delight at the turn of events. They were more interested in the party's grief than in the economic consequences of the revelations. Yet, there was common knowledge in Nigeria as evidenced by the broadcast by Major Chukwuma Kaduna Nzeogwu that all the political parties both at regional and federal levels were equally guilty of the practises of which the Action Group had been accused. This assertion is further supported by the spate of corruption inquiries conducted under the aegis of the first military government in 1966.

In judging the different reactions to the Coker Inquiry to be very significant in the different parts of the country, the authors came to the conclusion that reactions were a consequence of what can be regarded as the '*tribalisation of probity*.' This means condemnation of the accusers based on tribal sentiments and dismissal of all corresponding allegations of impropriety as tribally (and therefore politically) motivated. The principals of the Action Group were Yoruba. Members of the coalition government at the federal level that set up the Coker inquiry were Hausa/ Fulani and Ibo that represented parties with different tribal bases - the Northern People's Congress (NPC) and National Council of Nigerian Citizens (N.C.N.C), respectively. The N.C.N.C was the junior partner in the coalition government at the federal level. They were bitter rivals of the Action Group and not unnaturally, hoped to reap political dividends from the Action Group's travails. When Dr Azikiwe was the subject of investigation over the A.C.B affairs, he accused the Action Group and other 'disgruntled elements' in his party for instigating the complaint in order to damage him politically. He did not admit to any wrongdoing. The 'tribalisation of probity' is a neutralisation technique (Sykes and Matza, 1957), enabling the accused to question the accuser's motive and using the defence of *tu quoque* to cast doubts on the accusers' sincerity. This is often expressed with a sense of victimhood.

After exposure, the accused returns to his comfort zone – this gender expression is deliberate as the majority of the reprobates are men. The deep sense of victimhood and reversed sense of injustice is chorused by his kinsmen. The tribalisation of probity enables the exposed to deflect attention away from his moral failings and to turn on his accuser by suggesting malice in their motive. There follows a period when the accused drops out of the limelight – waiting for eventual political rehabilitation because he is a major political operator in his comfort zone.

Most Nigerians did not believe the Action Group was the only corrupt political party when the Coker inquiry was set up, but there were not many voices demanding the investigation of the other political groups. This is not to suggest that the focus on the Action Group (A.G.) in 1962 was whimsical, but it was a missed opportunity for the civilian administration to restore probity in public life. Partiality in the exposure of corruption, whether imagined or real, breeds cynicism and undermines the credibility of a serious anti-corruption policy.

Nigeria has registered a growth in the incidence of corruption since independence; neither the Justice Strafford Foster-Sutton inquiry report nor the others since has had the desired effect.

The soldiers who removed the civilians for corruption themselves fell into the same temptation. There was therefore no discernible moral distinction between civilian and military governments.

Undimmed Hope

Nigerians frequently read shocking reports of scandals in high places. This is almost the daily diet of the print media. They are the principal source of information about corruption in Nigeria. They get their information from anonymous whistleblowers and petitioners. The hope for an end to corruption in the country is high. This is evident by the countless letters to newspapers and magazines where the writers call on public servants to act on development issues.

There has been two specific periods in the nation's history when there have been a near euphoric support for anti-corruption crusade taken by the military. The first was under General Murtala Mohammed's rule. His brisk approach to corruption was seen by all as purposeful and goal-oriented. He used decrees to short-circuit legal processes that might frustrate the government's anti-corruption crusade. His shock tactics enjoyed a wellspring support even though they violated specific civil and political rights.

The second was during the Buhari/Idiagbon military rule. They too thought the solution to corruption is to be found by draconian measures. Their administration saw politicians as venial and irredeemably corrupt. No other government ever since has been as high-handed as the Buhari/Idiagbon's in seeking to squeeze corruption out of the political system.

The Buhari/Idiagbon regime stated that they were forced to act against President Shagari's civilian government because of corruption and the rigging of the 1983 elections (Momoh and Adejumobi, 2002). The popular view was that Shagari's government had taken corruption to a scale unheard of in Nigeria before. In less than six years, a number of political figures associated with the National Party of Nigeria (NPN), the ruling party, had become unimaginably rich, some even owned their private jets supposedly acquired at public expense (Okojie, 1989).

Factors Contributory to the Erosion of Trust

The erosion of public support for politicians and public institutions was gradual. The loss of support and of legitimacy was brought about by a combination of events. This is exemplified by the episode in 1975 under Gowon's regime when the country's seaports were suddenly choked with ships waiting to berth with cargoes of cement (*Tribunal of Inquiry into the Importation of Cement into Nigeria, 1976*). In the 1970s Nigeria accumulated huge foreign reserves from oil revenue. The country's leaders repeatedly stated that money was no obstacle to development. Their major problem was how to spend it!

The report of the inquiry into how the country managed to order so much cement revealed chaos at the heart of government. It also exposed the ability of a few well placed individuals to inflict great harm on the national economy in pursuit of their personal gain. Through the combination of ineptitude and corruption a few self-seeking individuals with allies in the central bank were able place orders for bags of cements far in excess of the country's need.

Infamy

There is no section of Nigerian institution that is untouched by corruption, be it the police, the judiciary, the legislature, the list is long. In one instance, the Chief Justice of Nigeria was asked to recuse himself from a case on the grounds that he had accepted favours from one of the litigants in a civil case (*The News*, 4 July 2005).

Politicians and civil servants have a credibility problem. Embezzlement, fraud, bribery misappropriation of public funds and influence peddling is common in all spheres of public life. The Inspector General of Police, Tafa Balogun was recently deposed and prosecuted on charges of corruption that included having savings of $120m in his bank accounts, in addition to owning several properties.

Can the Tide of Corruption be Stemmed?

According to a calculation done by the authors, the Nigerian federal government has had over twenty public inquiries into corruption between 1960 and 1999. The list is incomplete as it does not include inquiries by state governments into corruption at the subnational state level. There are more investigations against senior politicians than those which are as yet unpublished because of section 308 of the 1999 constitution, which protects certain groups of public officers.

There was a brief moment in Nigeria when there was probably an appreciable fall in the reporting of corruption. This was during the Buhari/Idiagbon rule. A fall in the reporting of such incidence does not mean an absolute drop in the level of corruption even under the military government. As already indicated, the administration took draconian measures against corrupt politicians. It sentenced some corrupt politicians to ninety years imprisonment. The administration exposed many scandals as it happens when there is a regime change in the country. It purged the civil service of corrupt and incompetent officials. It 'launched a War Against Indiscipline in spring 1984. This national campaign, which lasted fifteen months, preached the work ethic, emphasized patriotism, decried corruption, and promoted environmental sanitation' (Pike, nd).

The government used decrees to effect its anti-corruption policy. Initially, these measures enjoyed popular support. Eventually, opinion turned against the government. Its policy was seen to be tainted with partiality. It was believed that politicians from the North enjoyed the administration's covert protection. Though in a high profile case, the administration entered into a risky enterprise with Israeli agents to kidnap a wanted corrupt top politician, Dr Umaru Dikko, who was then in exile in London. He was a prominent politician from the North. He was drugged and put in a crate destined to be flown back to Nigeria, but the plot was foiled and the Nigerian government denied any involvement (*New York Times*, nd). This led to a diplomatic row between the United Kingdom and Nigeria, leading to withdrawal of High Commissioners and scaling down of diplomatic activities between both countries. The perceived partiality of the anti-corruption policy turned the support of sections of the federation for the regime into cynicism.

Corruption Since 1999

The head of Nigeria's Economic and Financial Crimes Commission (EFCC) stated that the Obasanjo administration has managed to keep corruption under control. While not under-estimating the scale of the problem, he believes that Nigeria was, for once, beginning to get a measure of the problem. Since 1999, there has been a more systematic approach to reduce corruption with evidence that the government relying more on a body of laws than on piecemeal probes or inquiries. Agencies have been set up to be pro-active in detecting corruption.

In an important policy statement in Berlin in 2003, President Obasanjo articulated his government's anti-corruption policy which he believes would take Nigeria 'out of the pond of corruption to the island of integrity'.

It is his belief that before 1999, Nigerians were wedded to the old way of doing business which was entirely mired in corruption:

> The story of my country Nigeria is fairly well known. Until 1999, the country had practically institutionalized corruption as the foundation of governance. Hence, institutions of society easily decayed to unprecedented proportions as opportunities were privatized by the powerful.

His diagnosis of corruption in Nigeria is unsparing:

> This process was accompanied, as to be expected, by the intimidation of the judiciary, the subversion of due process, the manipulation of existing laws and regulations, the suffocation of civil society, and the containment of democratic values and institutions. Power became nothing but a means of accumulation and subversion as productive initiatives were abandoned for purely administrative and transactional activities. The legitimacy and stability of the state became compromised as citizens began to devise extra-legal and informal ways of survival. All this made room for corruption. At the root of the corruption quagmire in Nigeria, is the failure and virtual collapse of governance, the contamination of democratic values, the erosion of accountability procedures, and the prevalence of bad leadership. The erosion of public confidence in the country's political and economic institutions promoted a culture of contempt for the rule

of law and ultimately and unfortunately, a societal tolerance for a myriad of conducts previously considered abominable.

He presents an optimistic and hopeful future that would propel Nigeria into a new economic re-birth without the scourge of corruption:

In recognition of the fact that only a well-designed public sector accountability reform package targeted at improving the governance indicators positively can reverse the wrong trajectory of our national integrity journey, I declared the campaign against corruption as a fundamental mission of our government. My personal commitment to heralding a new transparent, accountable and zero corruption tolerant Nigeria is borne out of my profound personal conviction that only the commitment of the highest political authority to a national anti-corruption strategy will yield an integrity dividend that is deep, wide and far-reaching. During our first term, our Administration established a number of institutional and structural measures signaling a new attitude to governance. Some of these measures resulted in the establishment of new institutions with specific mandates on promoting transparency in government budgetary and financial operations. Such measures taken by my administration include:

1. Open and competitive tender arrangements for government contracts.
2. The establishment of a 'Due Process' mechanism that vets and eliminates excess 'fat' from government contracts.
3. Massive anti-corruption campaigns involving all public officials and the President.
4. Public sector reforms to reduce, if not completely eliminate, the opportunity for corruption, especially through the comprehensive monetisation of benefits to public officers.
5. A committed focus on privatisation and auctions for government licences such as was the case with the telecommunication sector liberalization.
6. Increasing the likelihood of exposing instances of poor governance and corrupt practices as well as sanctioning such acts through the establishment of an independent anti-corruption agency and an Economic and Financial Crimes Commission.
7. The establishment, in the President's office of a Policy and Programmes Monitoring Unit to build a comprehensive policy

data-base, follow-up on all decisions of the President, and monitor programmes at in ministries and parastatals.

The speech contained the architecture of his policy for a clean government and a better managed economy.

Even before I was sworn in as President in my first term in 1999, I had prepared a comprehensive Anti-Corruption Bill drawing heavily on my experiences as a founding member of TI. Among other things, this draft Bill had included a clause that would have made it possible to investigate the source(s) of wealth of public officers who seem to live above their known means. I agonized as the former National Assembly kept this Bill in the cooler for over a year and eventually passed a rather watered down version of it, which does not empower investigation of people known to be living above their means.

He credits the EFCC with reducing the number of scams by Nigerian fraudsters:

The widely known scam letters promising shares of proceeds of illicit activities that often emanated from some fraudulent Nigerians, and some other nationals posing as Nigerians, is fast losing its wide spread appeal. Through the efforts of the EFCC, tighter controls and enforceable sanctions have been applied on a number of cases and these have in turn signalled the undiluted commitment of the government to containing the corruption virus.

He commended the Economic and Financial Crimes Commission (EFCC) for:

... a vigorous campaign to arrest known fraudsters, many of who are still held in custody, awaiting trial. The leadership of the Commission has shown strong commitment to tackling the financial crime, money laundering and other economic misconducts that have created difficulties for the country with the OECD-Financial Action Task Force (FATF); [and wished] that the international community will appreciate and reward our efforts. The truth is that, it is much tougher to fight corruption in a developing society than it is in the developed world.

He believes the award of government contracts was a principal source of corruption and believed his policy would bring about a more transparent outcome in the process:

> Historically, it is in the award of contracts by various governments in Nigeria that the poor transparency image, of the country is mostly ascribed. The Administration therefore set up the Budget Monitoring and Price Intelligence Unit (BMPIU) that commenced a process of contract award review, oversight and certification now commonly known as 'Due Process'. It is a simple mechanism that certifies for public funding only those projects that have passed the test of proper project implementation packaging. Such packaging must have adhered stringently to the international competitive bid approach in the award process. Through the instrument of certification, value for money is once again returning as the fundamental premise for public expenditure. In the two years of the implementation of the Due Process, reasonable progress in promoting fair-play and competition resulting in huge savings through reduction in contract sums to the tune of $500 million. There have also been a number of cancellations of contracts awarded by spending units that failed to comply with laid down open, competitive bid parameters. Respect and public confidence in the contract award process is gradually returning. I can say that today, all ministers and heads of unit know that it is almost a waste of time to inflate contracts. It will be detected and the consequences can be grave.

Assessment

Has the Obasanjo administration policy been successful? How should success be measured? Is Ribadu's claim that Nigeria has turned the corner well founded? The administration's success or the lack of it can be measured in a number of ways. Of course, there is no error free method to determine success. By its nature, corruption is a subterranean act. Unless reported or detected, it remains clandestine. In the absence of a systematically conducted survey, certain measures can be applied, however crude. For example, the greatest source of information about corruption is through the print media. Occasionally, information comes to public notice through detection by one of the several anti-corruption agencies in Nigeria. The country has seen the establishment of at least four new agencies to tackle various aspects of the problem; these are:

1. The Independent Corrupt Practices and Other Related Offences Commission (ICPC)
2. Economic and Financial Crimes Commission (EFCC) 2000 as amended by the Corrupt Practices and Other Related Offenses Act 2003
3. Extractive Industries Transparency Initiative (EITI) 2002
4. Economic and Financial Crimes Commission (EFCC) 2003
5. Budget Monitoring and Price Intelligence Unit (BMPIU) 2003

These agencies form part of the economic reform agenda in Nigeria. Some of the initiatives were generated by local exigencies while others were due to external influences, an example being the push by the UK government to encourage transparency in the extractive industry. The oil industry has long been mired in corruption. The initiative by the UK government was to ensure that multi-national corporations do not collude in corrupt practices that damage economic development. The initiative requires the extracting industries to publish the amount they pay to the government in the hope that this would introduce transparency into the process. The operating slogan by Publish What You Pay (PWYP) has the clear aim of taking the lid off the murky accountancy of the extractive industries.

In 2003, the federal government launched the National Economic Empowerment and Development Strategy (NEEDS), a strategy for reducing poverty based on a better management of economy. The focus of the initiative includes:

1. Reforming (restructuring and capacitating) government institutions.
2. Growing the private sector by reducing the influence of government in the economy and accelerating the privatisation, deregulation and liberalisation programme.
3. Beginning to implement a social charter to improve people's access to health, education, welfare, employment, security and participation.
4. Value re-orientation, including anti-corruption, freedom of information and enhancing the role of civil society (*Department for International Development*, 2003).

In the government's own assessment of these aims, Senator Abdallah Wali the Minister and Deputy Chairman, the National Planning Commission claimed that the government had achieved its target of employment generation, poverty reduction, wealth creation and value orientation. Surprisingly, the government claims to be reducing corruption as the table below illustrates. These claims may be surprising to most Nigerians who still largely perceive the government as irrelevant to their conditions of poverty and deprivation.

Table 10.1: Curbing Corruption in Nigeria

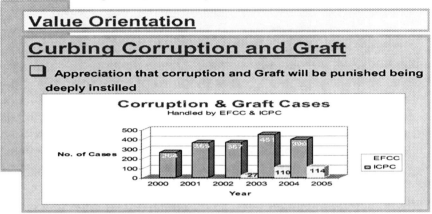

Source: National Planning Commission, 2006.

A more realistic account of the current situation is that Nigeria is still experiencing extreme poverty: over 70 million people live on less than US$1 per day; one in five children die before the age of five; 7 million children are not in school and around 3 million people are living with HIV or AIDS. None of these realities is reflected in the government's appraisal of the situation.

The ICPC and EFCC

The government has given two agencies the principal responsibility of policing corruption. The first to be established under the post 1999 civilian administration was the Independent Corrupt Practices and Other Related Offences Commission (ICPC). The role of the agency is to police corruption in the various state bodies. Its work is overseen by a retired Judge who chairs a board of commissioners drawn from the countries 6 geo-political zones. The ICPC relies solely on petitions from members of the public on issues concerning fraud or finance in the public sector. As a result, it relies on whistleblowers.

Regrettably, it lacks the effective means of protecting the whistleblowers, thus affecting the willingness of the public to disclose the vital information it needs to do its work. ICPC's remit is tightly defined. It acts on petitions it receives from members of the public relating to public office holders only or public servants-politicians, civil servants, workers in Ministries, Parastatals, departments, agencies and institutions of government. It only investigates private individuals if the petition reveals that a private individual has acted in concert with a public official in connection with the corrupt practice.

The ICPC's procedures are very legalistic; an investigation could take between a month to one year. On completion of its investigation, subject to the grounds of prosecution being established, the public officer is referred to the office of the Attorney General of the Federation for prosecution. The ICPC does not have its own in-house lawyers to conduct the prosecution. It is obliged by law to rely on the office of the Attorney General conduct the prosecution. Most of those prosecuted so far as a result of the ICPC investigations are local government chairmen and senior police officers. ICPC has carried out investigation on some state governors as a result of petitions, but they have not been able to prosecute them because of their immunity under Section 308 of the 1999 Nigerian Constitution.

The reliance on petitions from members of the public has advantages and probably more disadvantages. The petitions are submitted by those unaware of the need to provide sufficient evidence to enable the ICPC to conduct an effective investigation. Often, the petitioners fail to recognise the significance of attaching relevant documents to their petition. In the absence of this, the experience of the ICPC investigation team is that when the suspect becomes aware of the petition, it triggers his taking of evasive action to frustrate the investigation. For example vital documents may be either concealed or destroyed or other steps taken to render evidence inaccessible.

One of ICPC's previous Chairman, Justice Mustapha Akanbi, thought ICPC's process should be re-balanced so that the ICPC could adopt a more pro-active approach in prosecution of suspects. The ICPC has another role, which is to educate the public about corruption. Justice Emmanuel Ayoola, its current Chairman, sees the limits of investigations and prosecutions. Although these are necessary on an on-going basis, the long-term solution is to bring about a change in attitude and to raise the standard of behaviour among public office holders.

The EFCC

The Economic and Financial Crimes Commission (EFCC) was established in 2003. Unlike the ICPC, it has an Executive Chairman who is able to make decisions unencumbered by the obligation to consult with Commissioners. The EFCC's brief is to handle financial crimes which may be domestic or cross-border. In particular, it has been asked to tackle the 'advance fee crimes' (known as 419 being the section of the relevant legislation which prohibits the offence) for which Nigerians had acquired a notorious reputation. Thus the EFCC handles financial and economic crimes or cases of 419 relating to private individuals both Nigerians and non-Nigerians.

As originally conceived, there was a clear demarcation of responsibilities between the ICPC and the EFCC. Thus matters of corruption relating to public officers fell within the jurisdiction of the ICPC.

It is, perhaps not so easy to delineate issues of financial crimes. It is believed that the EFCC has not always maintained jurisdictional boundaries and that it has acted in areas that are the preserve of the ICPC. By broadening its remit, it has inadvertently overshadowed the ICPC. It is believed that it has usurped some of ICPC's role and that it enjoys projecting itself as the premier anti-corruption agency in the country. Its activities are constantly reported in the media who relish scandals. While the media attention carries with it certain benefits, e.g. maximum public awareness of actions against wrongdoers in public places, it risks the grave possibility of undermining due process. The disclosure of information regarding investigations in progress could create the impression of guilt even before a suspect is brought before the courts. This amplification of deviance is difficult to reverse even if after court of law subsequently find a suspect not guilty (Hall *et al*, 1978).

The EFCC's methods generate controversy. Its critics say it does not draw sufficient distinction between allegations and criminalisation. It is accused of behaving as if its suspects are guilty of the allegations even before the completion of the investigation stage. A further source of criticism is its practice of placing suspects in 'EFCC custody' without the option of a bail.

Critics point to the different practices between the EFCC and the ICPC. EFCC draws maximum publicity to its investigations, while the ICPC prefers to conduct its investigation quietly without exposing the facts to the public gaze. The authors suspect that it is the EFCC's melodramatic approach that has resonance with the public. In the turf war between the ICPC and the EFCC, the ICPC feels that some of its cases are wrongly attributed to the EFCC. Why are there so many agencies dealing more or less with the same matter? Has the time come for the EFCC and ICPC to be merged into one organisation to avoid the duplication of efforts, confusion, energy and costs? The EFCC enjoys huge advantages in its mode of operations. It has wide powers to act against suspects and it receives funds from the Nigerian government and from international donors. It also receives technical training and support from the international donors; its staff are better paid than those of the ICPC who, until 2006, were on civil service pay scale. The ICPC is funded almost entirely by the Nigerian government. By all account, the EFCC staff are not only better trained, they also enjoy better prospects for continuing professional development. Not surprisingly, they are better motivated than their ICPC counterparts.

Both the ICPC and the EFCC have reported low success rates in securing convictions against those they have prosecuted. The low conviction rate is not affected by the high cost of investigation and prosecution. According to the EFCC, the cost of investigating and prosecuting a high profile case is between five to ten million Naira.

The low conviction rate could be accounted for by a number of factors, such as the nature of the crimes which are notoriously difficult to prove, the lack of evidence because of the concealment of vital information; and issues relating to poor preparation. The anti-corruption agencies blame the courts and the lawyers for their poor success rates.

They have criticised defence lawyers for excessive delay in the criminal process. Ribadu (2004b), the head of the EFCC, points out that defence lawyers use interlocutories cynically to delay proceedings. He believes the use of these delay tactics brings the law into disrepute. The government has obliged by seeking methods to fast track cases.

As already indicated, the ICPC and the EFCC have contrasting methods. The former is considered to be bureaucratic and fastidious in complying with due process. The latter is seen as a more crusading organisation against corruption. Do they compliment each other?

EFCC's tactics are the ones that attract the most controversy and criticisms, especially from the powerful. This is the reverse of the perception about crimes of the powerful. According to Pearce (1976) the crimes of the powerful are not exposed to the rigour of the law because they are able to use their social status to protect themselves. The EFCC targets to hunt down the criminals in high places.

Is the EFCC Achieving Successful Strikes?

To be the subject of EFFC's attention, many observe, is a frightening experience. The corrupt are acutely aware of the EFCC's existence. As already indicated, the EFCC has proclaimed some successes in reducing corruption.

However, reduction in corruption cannot be measured in absolute terms. A battery of tests has to be applied before determining a country's overall improvement rate. The evidence from the colossal malpractices that characterised the 2007 elections in Nigeria does not tend to support the much-vaunted progress.

Transparency International, for example, advocates the use of national Integrity System (NIS) in order to achieve a more balanced measure. Their measure consists of twelve indicators. By contrast, the World Bank's (2006) Worldwide Governance Indicators (WGI) contains eight measures: voice and accountability; political stability and absence of violence; government effectiveness; regulatory quality; rule of law and control of corruption.

Using the WGI framework, only a modest progress can be said to have been achieved. This progress includes the fact that the Paris-based Financial Action Task Force (FATF) no longer regards Nigeria as a money laundering country. In spite of this optimistic assessment, Ribadu is yet to subject his claim to a rigorous statistical analysis.

It is still left to the investigator to consult the Transparency International Corruption Perception Index (CPI) [2007] for an independent assessment of Nigeria's rating. According to its CPI for 2006, Nigeria's score is 2.2 out of a possible 10. In the scheme of things, this means Nigeria no longer has the sobriquet of one of the 'most corrupt countries in the world.' For a country that has stubbornly remained near the bottom of   the CPI scale for decades, a 2.2 score, achieved for the very first time in 2006, seems relatively a noticeable achievement. However, the CPI itself is a crude measure and may in fact distort the true national picture.

The anti-corruption effort in Nigeria must be subjected to a more rigorous test before accepting the rosy picture currently portrayed by the EFCC and the National Planning Commission.

For progress to be recorded, it must be shown that a country's key institutions, laws and practices ... contribute to integrity, transparency and accountability... (Transparency International, 2007).

This means that more than a fall in the reporting of the incidence of corruption is required. According to Kaufmann (2007), positive and negative changes can take place in the short-term (i.e. some deteriorations and improvements can be expected at the same time). Nigeria is at that stage when a more rigorous evaluation is needed to determine what attitudinal change has taken place since President Obasanjo launched his anti-corruption crusade eight years ago.

More than Anecdotal Evidence

On our desk as we write this chapter are two reports in a weekly magazine in bold headlines 'Crooks in the Senate'(*Newswatch*, 20 October 2003) and 'Thieves in the Corridors of Power: Fraud, Bribery, Squandermania in High Places (*Newswatch*, 27 October, 2003) . These were published in 2003 in a respectable Nigerian weekly magazine, *Newswatch*. A trawl of newspapers and magazines in Nigeria, four years later, found that embezzlements and misappropriation of public funds in high places is still the routine. On 20 April 2007, the same magazine reported in a cover story: 'PTDF: The Report that nailed Obasanjo, Atiku'. Exactly a week later, it reported in another cover story, 'Federation Accounts: The Missing Billions.' More recently, a report in the *Nigerian Tribune* [15 May 2007], stated that a panel set up by the Federal Government to probe allegations of maladministration and financial improprieties against the Chief Executive of the National Insurance Commission [NAICOM] Chief Emmanuel O. Chukwulozie recommended his removal from office.

Is the Current Anti-Corruption Policy Doomed to Fail?

Nigerians are subjected to several campaigns in which they are informed that corruption is morally repugnant. For example, a promotional pamphlet by Zero Corruption Coalition (2006) aimed at the general public declares that 'Corruption Makes Us Poor'. The pamphlet invokes the patriotic appeal 'Let's Stop It!'

In a recent appeal, Ribadu (2007c), the head of the EFCC has urged Nigerians to 'stop corrupting the police'. He believes it is not only morally reprehensible to do so, but that it contributes to the undermining of the criminal justice system. Ribadu believes by bribing the police, the public deprive themselves of the moral right to accuse the police of corruption.

The idea that it is the public that corrupt the 'honest police' is of course not credible. Equally, it is unrealistic to expect corruption to be ended by anti-corruption agencies alone. There is a civic obligation on citizens as part of their law abiding duty, to resist the temptation to bribe their way out of the consequences of their breaking the law. The common view is that Nigerians readily resort to the use of bribes to avoid the inconvenience of the law. Both the police and judges are known to be on the take. A general view is that corruption exists in every sector of Nigerian society.

The reports of corruption in the media in Nigeria show that political leaders and senior civil servants are the least likely to pay heed to the 'zero tolerance' campaigns. Indeed, in his Berlin speech, President Obasanjo pointed out the greater difficulty in fighting corruption in developing countries than in mature economies.

Tremlett (2006) describes the system of *'enchufe'* in Spain – a practice that would be easily recognisable in Nigeria. Pallast's critique of the corrupt alliance of politicians and business groups in the US and Europe give cause to cast doubt on the President's assertion. Paul Volcker's Report on the Oil for Food Inquiry (Le Billon, 2005) and the cancellation of the British Aero-Space Saudi Arms Inquiry should be sufficient to quell the belief that the mature economies are less motivated by 'private gain'.

Sustaining Anti-Corruption Crusade in the Long-Term

Anti-corruption crusade can, after a while, become a drone. The public will stop listening to the homilies if the incidence of grand corruption remains high. As he ends his presidency, President Obasanjo's anti-corruption policy is being assessed and scrutinised. The fulcrum is the fulcrum of his crusade. From its inception, the President made the EFCC answerable to him. This gave the EFCC an undoubted advantage. In the Nigerian constitution, the presidency enjoys unprecedented powers and this has worked to the benefit of the agency. However, its close ties with the presidency has raised serious questions about its methods and neutrality.

In an article entitled, *'Politicizing the War against Corruption'*, President Obasanjo has been accused of using the EFCC as a veritable tool in his vendetta against his opponents. To this extent, the EFCC has been accused of excessive zeal and of breaching its statutory powers.

The EFCC has a global reach through collaboration with foreign security agencies. It is trusted by the foreign agencies as an effective anti-corruption body. This view is not always shared by some of those it targets. It has taken upon itself the power to investigate state finances – a process that could lead to the removal of state governors from office; it has done this successfully in three instances – but by methods regarded by its critics as questionable. It can order the freezing of state bank accounts in the course of its investigations, a decision that could potentially paralyze programmes in the state concerned. Not surprisingly, it has been accused of abusing its powers by coercing state legislators to commence impeachment proceedings against state governors that the agency considered to be corrupt. One of the allegations levelled against the agency is that legislators had been threatened with arrests and detention unless they agreed with the agency's demands.

Critics have questioned its right to examine state accounts – a right that it is believed falls within the jurisdiction of the Auditors-General and the Houses of Assembly. The head of the EFCC has been accused of making pronouncements about investigations his agency is conducting, thus jeopardising possible prosecution and failing to respect the presumption of innocence.

A frequent complaint is that the EFCC's approach is unbalanced and that it deliberately avoids investigating areas that are sensitive to the presidency. It is also alleged that it is less than strident in its investigation of matters affecting the presidency. The example often cited is the allegation that the president held shares of up to N200m in a private firm called Transcorp. In spite of the president's claim that he raised the capital through the commercial banks, critics believe that the EFCC's investigation had been less than thorough. While the truth cannot be proven, there is a persistent belief that the agency's link with the presidency is a hindrance when dealing with the presidency or his associates.

A further accusation against the agency is the lack of action against three governors, referred as the triumvirates who are alleged to be involved in questionable dealings but who are protected because of their close association with the presidency. The so-called untouchables are the governors of River State (Odili), Delta State (Ibori) and Nassarawa state (Adamu).

Ribadu has made announcement about the number of state governors likely to be prosecuted for corruption when they cease to hold public office on 29 May 2007. In one announcement, he claimed that there were 32 state Governors under suspicion and that he had evidence against them. It is alleged that this made many state governors to support what came to be known as Obasanjo's 'Third term' agenda, a bid by the President to change the constitution to enable him to contest the office of the presidency for a third term. The state governors were alleged to have supported the 'agenda' in the belief that they would be shielded from possible prosecution in the event of President Obasanjo's re-election. It was further alleged that as a result of the support for the president's third term bid, the number of governors on Ribadu's corruption list dropped to 19, and then to 4. While the authors cannot vouch for the accuracy of these claims, the view is generally held that the list had been modified according to support for the third term agenda. The authors are aware that there are numerous claims and counter-claims and at the moment it is difficult to say how many governors are likely to be prosecuted for corruption when they leave office on 29 May 2007.

Nevertheless, the EFCC has announced steps it has taken to prevent suspected governors from leaving Nigeria when their terms of office have ended. For example, it has asked foreign embassies in Nigeria to cancel the visas issued to suspected governors. Ribadu has also submitted a list of 142 public officials to the Secretary of the federal government in order for an administrative review panel to be set up. Without a doubt, many public officials are likely to be subject of indictment when they cease to enjoy the Section 308 of the 1999 Constitution's protection.

The Apogee

The President's opponents cite the PTDF inquiry and the 2007 elections as two significant factors that show that his reform agenda was phoney.

In the PTDF affair, the EFCC presented a report to the Senate in which the Vice-President was accused of corruption. This resulted in the President and the Vice President making allegations and counter-allegations about how they managed the affairs of PTDF. The facts are in dispute; however, the Senate has exonerated the President, but not the Vice President. Some are of the view that the investigation into the PTDF was motivated by the President's feud against his Vice President.

By far, the most damaging event to the president's credibility, domestically and internationally, is his handling of the elections in Nigeria in April 2007. The foreign observers of the elections were unable to endorse them as being free and fair. The list of accusations against the conduct of the elections is long:

13. Elections materials were deliberately delayed or delivered late to many polling booths, particularly in many parts of Eastern Nigeria, where voting did not start until about 3pm. And in most cases voting took place only in towns and urban centres and not in rural areas.
14. Not enough ballot papers were sent to many polling booths.
15. Officials of the electoral agency (INEC) did not appear in many polling booths, thus preventing voting from taking place.
16. Fake/wrong voter registers were sent to some polling booths, thus preventing many people from finding their names where they registered.
17. Ballot boxes were snatched at gun point, and polling agents were scared away at gunpoint.
18. In many instances, votes were not counted at the polling booths.
19. Polling agents were forced to sign results after stuffed ballot boxes were returned by hoodlums.
20. Fake INEC Form FC 8, was given to party polling agents to sign without their knowing they were fake.

21. Thumb printing took place three to four days to the elections - a malpractice involving INEC staff and the PDP (the ruling party). Foam soaked in ink was used to stamp ballot so that the thumbprint will not be captured in case of litigation in court.
22. Polling agents of opposition political parties were not allowed into Local Government Collation centres.
23. Voting was still taking place in many states while INEC was declaring winners in Abuja.
24. In Imo state, the Governorship and House of Assembly elections held the same day and at the same polling booths. INEC, however, cancelled the Governorship election because of 'wide-scale irregularities' but approved the results to the House of Assembly election. This, it was said, was due to the fact the All Peoples Grand Alliance (APGA) candidate had won the election to the disappointment of the PDP, which having no official candidate in the governorship election backed the Progressive Peoples Party's (PPA) candidate. At the re-run of the Governorship election, the PDP-backed candidate was, as many expected, declared winner by INEC. Imo is the only state where the ruling PDP had no official governorship candidate in the election for the simple reason that the party decided not to back the candidature of Senator Ifeanyi Ararume who won a Supreme Court ruling against the PDP as winner of the party's governorship primaries.

The PTDF affair and the conduct of the elections have seriously damaged the government's good governance agenda.

Conclusion

To be effective, anti-corruption policy must satisfy certain tests in order to continue to enjoy public support, especially in the medium to long-term:

- The credibility of the policy initiators.
- The credibility of those who administer the policy.
- Impartiality in the enforcement of the relevant laws.
- Independence and impartiality of the anti-corruption agencies.
- Acting on well-founded allegations following a professionally sound investigation and report.

- Strict application of the due process, allowing the accused a fair opportunity to respond to the allegations, including fair hearing and fair treatment of the accused.
- Speedy and scrupulous investigation of the allegations.
- Protection for whistleblowers.
- Avoidance of prejudicial statements about investigations still in progress, including the use of subtle threats and torture to elicit evidence.
- Massive sensitization campaign on the implications and consequences of corruption.
- Effective use of the principle of 'naming and shaming' in the anti-corruption campaign.

All of the above have to be adhered to in order to sustain anti-corruption on a long-term basis. Recent political events in Nigeria may have seriously set back the anti-corruption crusade for a long time to come.

Notes

A list of Inquiries into Corruption Before and After Independence

1. Eastern Region of Nigeria, *Report of the Commission of Inquiry into the working of Port Harcourt Town Council*, Enugu, 1955.

2. Eastern Region of Nigeria, *Report of the Inquiry into the Administration of the Affairs of the Onitsha District Council*, Enugu, 1955.

3. Eastern Region of Nigeria, *Report of the Inquiry into the Allocation of Market Stalls at Aba*, Enugu, 1955.

4. Eastern Region of Nigeria, *Report of the Inquiry into the affairs of the Eastern Ngwa District Council*, Enugu, 1955.

5. Eastern Region of Nigeria, *Report of the Inquiry into the Administration of the Affairs of the Igbo-Etiti District Council*, Enugu, 1956.

6. Nigeria, *Report of the Tribunal Appointed to Inquire into Allegations Reflecting on the Official Conduct of the Premier of, and Certain Persons holding Ministerial and Other Public Offices in, the Eastern Region of Nigeria*, London, 1956-7, Cmnd.5.

7. Report of the Foster-Sutton Tribunal of Inquiry, p. 30, quoted in Sklar, R.L (1963) Nigerian Political Parties, Power in an Emergent African Nation, Princeton: Princeton University Press.

8. Western Region of Nigeria, *Report of the Commission of Inquiry into the Administration of the Ibadan District Council*, Abingdon, 1956. Source:

Tignor, R.L. 'Political Corruption in Nigeria Before Independence', *The Journal of Modern African Studies*, 31, 2 (1993), p. 184.

References

Ademoyega, A. (1981) *Why We Struck: The Story of the First Nigerian Coup*. Ibadan, Evan Brothers.

Butcher, H. L. M. (1951), Report of the Commission of Inquiry into Allegations of Misconduct against Chief Salami Agbaje, the Otun Balogun of Ibadan, and Allegations of Inefficiency and Maladministration on the Part of the Ibadan and District Native Authority. Canadian Museum of Nature (nd) 'Octopus'. http://www.nature.ca/notebooks/english/octopus.htm (accessed 27.04.07).

DFID (2007) 'Nigeria: Overview' http://www.dfid.gov.uk/countries/africa/nigeria.asp (accessed 17.05.07); See also, http://www.nigerianeconomy.com/downloads/part4.pdf

Edgerton, R.B. (2002) *The Troubled Heart of Africa: A History of the Congo*, New York: St Martin' Press.

Federal Government of Nigeria (1976) *The Tribunal of Inquiry into the Importation of Cement into Nigeria*, Lagos.

Hall, S. *et al* (1978) *Policing the Crisis*, Houndmills: Macmillan

IFAD (2006) 'Enabling the rural poor to overcome poverty in Nigeria' (http://www.ifad.org/operations/projects/regions/PA/factsheets/ng.pdf) . (accessed 07.05.07)

Ige, B. (2002) 'Abacha and the bankers: cracking the conspiracy' Forum on Crime and Society, Vol. 2 No.3, December.

Ikejiani, O. *The Unrepentant Nationalist: My Journey through Life*, An Autobiography Enugu: The Forth Dimension.

Komolafe, B. (2007) 'Nigeria earns N8.8 trillion from oil in 5 years', Vanguard, Lagos, 7 May (cover story) [http://www.vanguardngr.com/articles/2002/cover/may07/07052007/f30 7052007.html, [accessed 7.05.07].

Le Billon, P. (2005), 'Corruption, Reconstruction and Oil Governance in Iraq'. *Third World Quarterly*, 26, 4-5, pp. 685-703.

Mensah, E. (1986) 'Methodological Problems in the Study of Corruption' in Femi, O. ed. *Nigeria: Corruption in Development*, Ibadan, Ibadan University Press.

Momoh, A and Adejumobi, S. eds. (2002) *The National Question in Nigeria: Comparative Perspectives*, Aldershot: Ashgate.

Moss, T, Standley, S & Birdshall, N. (2005) 'Double Standards on IDA & Debt: The Case for Reclassifying Nigeria' published by the Centre for Global Development http://www.newstartnigeria.org/content/briefings/CGD%20other%20briefing.pdf (accessed on 7.07.07).

Newswatch October 20 2003. 'Crooks in the Senate: How Mantu, Zwingina Operated their bribery syndicate' – Headline.

Newswatch, October 27 2003. 'Thieves in the Corridors o Power: Fraud, Bribery, Squandermania in High Places' – Headline.

Newswatch, 2 April 2007.

Newswatch 9 April 2007.

New York Times online, 'World news about Nigeria'. Breaking news and archival information about its people, politics and economy from The New York Times http://topics.nytimes.com/top/news/international/countriesandterritories/nigeria/index.html?s=oldest&offset=120& (accessed 12.05.07).

Nigeria, Report of the Coker Commission of Inquiry into the affairs of Certain Statutory Corporations in Western Nigeria, Lagos, 1962.

Nzogwu C. K. (1966) 'Declaration of Martial Law' – The January 1966 Coup. http://www.dawodu.com/nzeogwu2.htm (accessed 11.05.07).

Obasanjo, O. (2003) Speech by President Obasanjo in Berlin at the 10th Anniversary celebration of Transparency International, Berlin, November 2003, titled: Nigeria: from Pond of Corruption to Island of Integrity. (http://www.nigeriavillagesquare1.com/Articles/obj3.html, (accessed 29.04.07).

Odekunle, F. (1991) 'Controlling indiscipline and corruption in Nigeria: Fundamental and Short term Measures', mimeo.

Okojie, P. 'Africa and Poverty' *Journal of African Marxists*, February 1989, Issue II.

Okojie, P & Momoh, A. 'Corruption in Nigeria and the Crisis of Development' in Sarah Bracking (ed.) *Corruption and Development* (forthcoming, Nov. 2007), Hampshire: Palgrave Macmillan.

Olopoenia, A. Z. (1998) *A Political Economy of Corruption and Underdevelopment*. Faculty of Social Science Lecture, Series no. 10, University of Ibadan.

Osoba, S. (1997) 'Corruption in Nigeria: Historical Perspectives' in *Review of African Political Economy*, no. 69, pp. 371-386.

Palast, G. (2003) *The Best Democracy Money Can Buy: The Truth About Globalization Corporate Cons and High Finance Fraudsters*. Penguin Plume, Florida.

Pike, J. (nd) 1983 Coup, *Global Security*.
http://www.globalsecurity.org/military/world/war/nigeria2.htm (accessed 10.05.07).

Politicizing the War against Corruption
http://www.efccnigeria.org/index.php?option=com_content&task=view&id=1134&Itemid=2 (accessed 13.05.07).

Ribadu, N. (2004a) 'The Role of EFCC [Economic and Financial Crimes Commission) in Sanitising the Nigerian Economic Environment in a Democratic Setting'. Paper presented at the Adamawa Economic Conference and Financial Exhibition, December 9-10, 2004. (www.efccnigeria.org/index.php?option=com_docman&task=doc_download&gid=14, accessed 07.05.07)

Ribadu, N. (2004b) 'Obstacles to Effective Prosecution of Corrupt Practices and Financial Crimes Cases in Nigeria', being paper presented at the 1sr Stakeholders Summit on Corrupt Practices and Financial Crimes in Nigeria Organized by the House Representatives Committee on Anti-Corruption, National Ethics and Values at the International conference Centre, Trade Fair Complex, Kaduna, 23-25 November, 2004.
http://www.efccnigeria.org/index.php?option=com_docman&task=cat_view&gid=77&limit=10&limitstart=10

Ribadu, N. (2007c) 'Stop corrupting the Police'
http://www.efccnigeria.org/index.php?option=com_content&task=view&id=1416&Itemid=2 (accessed 13.05.07).

Shaoul, Jean (2006) 'Blair Cancels British Aero-Space Saudi Arms Inquiry' http://www.wsws.org/articles/2006/dec2006/bae1-d29.shtml, (accessed 29.04.07).

Subair, G, Probe Panel Recommends Removal Of NAICOM Boss, Saturday Tribune, 12.05.07
http://www.tribune.com.ng/12052007/news/news15.html (accessed 12.05.07)

Sykes, G and Matza, D. (1957) *Techniques of Neutralization: A Theory of Delinquency.* American Sociological Review. 22 (6), pp. 664-670.

Storey, B (1953) *Report of the Commission of Inquiry into the Administration of the Lagos Town Council.*

Tignor, R.L. (1993) 'Political Corruption in Nigeria before Independence', in *The Journal of Modern African Studies*, 31, 2.

The News (2005) 'I won't Step Down: Justice Uwais' *The News*, 4 July, pp 18-20.

Transparency International (2007) 'TI's National Integrity System Approach' http://www.transparency.org/policy_research/nis (accessed 12.05.07).

Transparency International (2006), 'Corruption Perception Index' http://www.transparency.org/policy_research/surveys_indices/cpi/2006 (accessed 12.05.07).

Tremlett, G. (2006) *Ghosts of Spain*, London, Faber and Faber, ch. 5.

UNODC (2001) United Nations Manual on Anti-Corruption Policy, Vienna, Austria (http://www.unodc.org/pdf/crime/gpacpublications/manual.pdf, p. 7, (accessed 29.04.07).

Wali, A 'Review of Needs and Development of Needs 2' http://www.nigerianeconomy.com/downloads/needsreview.ppt#257,1, Review of NEEDS & Development of NEEDS 2 (accessed 17.05.07).

Wenar, L. (2007) 'On the ground in Africa' Punch on the web, 11.05.07 http://www.punchontheweb.com/Articleprint.aspx?theartic=Art200705 11035978 (accessed on 11.05.07).

World Bank (2006) Worldwide Governance Indicators: 1996-2005 http://web.worldbank.org/WBSITE/EXTERNAL/WBI/EXTWBIGOVAN TCOR/0,,contentMDK:20771165~menuPK:1866365~pagePK:64168445~p iPK:64168309~theSitePK:1740530,00.html (accessed 17.05.07).

Wrong, M. (2001) In the Footsteps of Mr. Krutz: Living in the Brink of Disaster in Mobutu's Congo. New York: Harper Collins

Zero Corruption Coalition (2006) Citizens Handbook on ICPC & EFCC: Corruption Makes us poor: Stop it, Lagos: Nigeria.

Chapter 11

The Human Security Deficits:
Challenges of Peacebuilding and Sustainable
Development in Nigeria

Habu S. Galadima

Introduction

Nigeria is an ethnically heterogeneous and culturally diverse country with a population of about 140 million people divided into well over 250 ethnic groups. It is the largest country in Africa, and the largest concentration of black people in the world. Indeed, Nigeria accounts for approximately 20 per cent of sub-Saharan Africa's people. The country is characterized by a multitude of religious, ethnic and political faultlines that periodically erupt into communal violence.

It is presumably the second largest economy in Africa. The country is well endowed with enormous natural resources, renewable and non-renewable, as well as biological and physical resources. With the production of about 2.2 million barrels of oil per day (mbd), Nigeria is the sixth largest producer in the Organization of Petroleum Exporting Countries (OPEC). Nigeria provides about 11 per cent of overall U.S. oil imports and ranks as the fifth-largest source for U.S. imported oil. Nigeria has an estimated 187 trillion cubic feet (Tcf) of proven natural gas reserves, giving the country one of the top ten natural gas endowments in the world. Agriculture is the dominant economic activity in terms of employment and linkages with the rest of the economy. The Capital Market is one of the most profitable in the world with about 105 per cent Rate of Return (ROI) and market capitalization of about $4 billion.

Unfortunately, economic mismanagement, endemic corruption and lack of accountability and transparency by successive governments have been the main reasons for the poor economic performance and rising poverty in the country. Despite the country's relative oil wealth, its basic social indicators place it among the 20 poorest countries in the world. Hence, in spite of her large oil and gas resources, Nigeria is a poor country with 80-90 million of its people living below the poverty line. Indeed, Nigeria has the third largest concentration of poor people in the world, after India and China. According to the World Bank Statistical data (*World Development Indicators database*, April 2006) seven out of ten Nigerians live on less than US$1 per day. Nigeria has experienced negative and slow growth and is one of the weakest growing economies in the world on a per capita basis. Since independence the economy has never had a growth rate of 7 per cent for more than three consecutive years. The housing situation has worsened and the number of homeless people has increased, while urban slums have been increasing progressively in number and size. Physical infrastructures have degenerated considerably due to lack of adequate maintenance, coupled with a rapidly growing population.

Nigeria, in recent times, has recorded unprecedented deficits in its human security profile arising from decades of authoritarianism and bad governance. The country's recent political and economic history is characterized by corruption, lack of accountability and transparency, kleptomania, deprivation, abuse of human rights, environmental pollution and degradation; poor macro-economic management and the contraction of the democratic space. These have combined to produce malignant expressions of violent conflicts in the country, mutating from ethno-religious conflicts to sectarian, indigene-settler and resource conflicts.

The recent episodes of inter-ethnic warfare in Nigeria, exemplified by the carnage and rabid killings in the 2001 Jos riot, the 2000 Kano/Kaduna Sharia riots, the countless Tiv-Jukun clashes in Benue and Taraba states, the 2001 Tiv-Hausa riot in Nasarawa state, the 2004 conflicts in Plateau state, including the numerous OPC (the Yoruba sectarian group) - Hausa clashes, the Aguleri/Umuleri war and the Ijaw-Itsekiri riots, among others, are indications of how terrible the political situation has suddenly degenerated in Nigeria. The conflict in the Niger Delta has remained one of the most intractable conflicts in the country since the Biafran civil war with no clear solution in sight.

Conservative estimates put the number of people killed in communal violence across Nigeria since 1999 at around 10,000; some government figures stand at more than 50,000 for central Plateau state alone (BBC October 7, 2004). A credible response to these threats to human security lies in peacebuilding.

The following are some key pertinent questions to guide the analysis in this chapter. What is human security? What is sustainable peacebuilding? What is the human security situation in Nigeria? What is the Nigerian Experience in peacebuilding? What lessons are there from the Nigerian experience? In our attempt to answer these questions we suggest that:

a) The relationship between human security and peacebuilding is dynamic and interdependent, especially as they both focus on addressing the deep rooted and multi-factorial problems inherent in the country, and offers more long term resolutions.

b) Nigeria, since 1999, has been experiencing conflicts arising mainly from deeply rooted threats to human security.

c) The threats to human security have been exacerbated by a long period of economic mismanagement; endemic corruption and lack of accountability and transparency experienced, especially within the thirty years of military rule in Nigeria.

d) To enhance the constructive transformation of the existing conflicts in the country, Nigeria should develop sustainable infrastructure of human security that is guaranteed through packages of peacebuilding measures.

e) A number of lessons can be derived from the Nigerian experience for other countries in Africa.

Understanding Peacebuilding and Human Security

First, what is peacebuilding? Peacebuilding is a process that facilitates the establishment of durable peace and tries to prevent the recurrence of violence by addressing root causes and effects of conflict through reconciliation, institution building, and political as well as economic transformation (See Boutros-Ghali, 1995). The root causes of conflicts are frequently complex, and hard to identify and understand for would-be peacebuilders. In developing countries, they often include skewed land property structures, environmental degradation, and unequal political representation on state level (See Zartman 1995:5; Markakis 1998: 4).

Peacebuilding constructs networks of peace between the ordinary people by deconstructing the structures of violence and re-engineering the structures of peace. Efforts are made to open channels of communication, get people involved in joint projects, work with the media and the educational system to try to break down sentimental walls as well as stereotypes and reduce prejudice and discrimination.

The goal of all of these efforts is to create a sustainable peace environment – characterized by the absence of physical violence, and reconciliation--getting the people to accept each other as part of their own group or be reconciled to mutual co-existence and tolerance. Galtung (1996:1-3) suggested two different concepts of peace: negative peace, and positive peace. He called the mere absence of violence, negative peace. On the other hand, positive peace is a stable social equilibrium in which the surfacing of new disputes does not escalate into violence and war. Peacebuilding initiatives try to fix the core problems that underlie the conflict and change the patterns of interaction of the involved parties (see Reychler 2001:12). Peacebuilding measures also aim to prevent conflict from reemerging. Through the creation of mechanisms that enhance cooperation and dialogue among different identity groups, these measures can help parties manage their conflict of interests through peaceful means. This might include building institutions that provide procedures and mechanisms for effectively handling and resolving conflict. Peacebuilding is a very long, slow process.

The structural dimension of peacebuilding focuses on the social conditions that foster violent conflict. Stable peace must be built on social, economic, and political foundations that serve the needs of the populace (see: *http://cmtoolkit.sais-jhu.edu/*). In many cases, crises arise out of systemic roots. These root causes are typically complex, but include skewed land distribution, environmental degradation, and unequal political representation. If these social problems are not addressed, there can be no lasting peace.

Political structural changes focus on political development, state building, and the establishment of effective government institutions. This often involves election reform, judicial reform, power-sharing initiatives, and constitutional reform. It also includes building political parties, creating institutions that provide procedures and mechanisms for effectively handling and resolving conflict, and establishing mechanisms to monitor and protect human rights.   To   provide fundamental services to its citizens, a state needs strong executive, legislative, and judicial institutions. Many point to democratization as a key way to create these sorts of peace-enhancing structures. Democratization seeks to establish legitimate and stable political institutions and civil liberties that allow for meaningful competition for political power and broad participation in the selection of leaders and policies. It is crucial to establish and maintain rule of law, and to implement rules and procedures that constrain the powers of all parties and hold them accountable for their actions (see Kritz, 2000:591). This can help to ease tension, create stability, and lessen the likelihood of further conflict. For example, an independent judiciary can serve as a forum for the peaceful resolution of disputes and post-war grievances. In addition, societies need a system of criminal justice that deters and punishes banditry and acts of violence. Fair police mechanisms must be established and government officials and members of the police force must be trained to observe basic rights in the execution of their duties.

Economic peacebuilding targets both the micro- and macro-level and aims to create economic opportunities and ensure that the basic needs of the population are met. On the microeconomic level, societies should establish micro-credit institutions to increase economic activity and investment at the local level, promote inter-communal trade and an equitable distribution of land, and expand school enrollment and job training. On the macroeconomic level, the post-conflict government should be assisted in its efforts to secure the economic foundations and infrastructure necessary for a transition to peace.

Integral part of building peace is reducing the effects of war-related hostility through the repair and transformation of damaged relationships. The relational dimension of peacebuilding centers on reconciliation, forgiveness, trust building, and future imagining. It seeks to minimize poorly functioning communication and maximize mutual understanding (see Lederach, 1997:82).

Building peace, for Assefa (2001:342) requires attention to these psychological and emotional layers of the conflict. The social fabric that has been destroyed by war must be repaired, and trauma must be dealt with on the national, community, and individual levels. Peacebuilding is therefore the effort to promote human security in societies marked by conflict. Ernie Regehr has stated that 'peace is built ... on social, political, economic and ecological foundations that serve the welfare of the people' (see, *www.dfait-maeci.gc.ca/peacebuilding/gngoc_report-e.asp*). Let us now take a look at human security.

Human security has come to be an inclusive term that incorporates issues of human rights, humanitarianism, human development, internal conflict, indigenous people's rights, environmentalism, and transnational movements. Human security is the protection from various forms of structural violence. Human security is usually described as the widening of security concerns beyond those of states to include the needs and well-being of people. It means safety for people from both violent and non-violent threats. It is freedom from pervasive threats to people's basic rights, safety, and lives. It was the former Canadian Foreign Minister Lloyd Axworthy (1999), who first defined human security as:

> ...a condition or state of being characterized by freedom from pervasive threats to people's rights, their safety, or even their lives... It is an alternative way of seeing the world, taking people as the point of reference, rather than focusing exclusively on the security of territory or governments ... Human security entails taking preventive measures to reduce vulnerability and minimize risk, and taking remedial action when prevention fails.

He further stated that: "A human security agenda must go beyond humanitarian action, by addressing the sources of people's insecurity. Building human security, therefore, requires both short term humanitarian action and longer term strategies for building peace and promoting sustainable development."

The United Nations Development Programme (UNDP), for example, asserted that: "Human security can be said to have two main aspects. It means, first, safety from such chronic threats as hunger, disease and repression. And second, it means protection from sudden and hurtful disruptions in the patterns of daily life – whether in homes, in jobs or in communities (UNDP 2000). The UNDP report states that human security consists of two basic pillars: the *freedom from want* and the *freedom from fear*. This means the absence of hunger and illness as well as of violence and war. Seven dimensions of human security were identified: economic security, food security, health security, environmental security, personal security, community security and political security.

Economic Security -- Economic Security requires an assured basic income for individuals—usually from productive and remunerative work, or in the last resort, from some publicly financed safety net.

Food Security -- Food Security requires that all people at all times have both physical and economic access to basic food.

Health Security -- Health Security aims to guarantee a minimum protection from diseases and unhealthy lifestyles. In developing countries, the major causes of death are infections and parasitic diseases. Most of these deaths are linked with poor nutrition and unsafe environment (particularly polluted water).

Environmental Security -- Environmental Security aims to protect people from the short- and long-term ravages of nature, man-made threats in nature, and deterioration of the natural environment. Environments such as these generate fear distrust hatred, frustrations, anger, etc. Soil degradation; rapid deforestation; urban air and water pollution; desertification; oil pollution - water, air, and soil; has suffered serious damage from oil spills; loss of arable land; rapid urbanization.

Personal Security –It protects people from physical violence, whether from the state or external states, from violent individuals and sub-state actors, from domestic abuse, from predatory adults. In spite of the government's deploying of troops to maintain peace and order, violence keeps breaking out.

Community Security -- It protects people from loss of traditional relationships and values and from sectarian and ethnic violence. Traditional communities, particularly ethnic groups, come under much more direct attack from each other.

Political Security -- It assures that people live in a society that honors their basic human rights. It suggests the absence of political repression, systematic torture, ill treatment or disappearance of political opponents. Human rights violations are most frequent during periods of political unrest.

Therefore, human security not only includes all basic human needs as well as the right to self-determination and human dignity, but also the protection from physical and mental harm, (such as during armed conflict). It also encompasses the notion of access to resources and services that sustain livelihoods and contribute to overall well-being of individuals, households and communities.

The UN Secretary General, in his 2000 Millennium Report, described this coming together of rights and security as 'freedom from want and freedom from fear.' For Kofi Annan:

> … human security … in its broadest sense, embraces far more than the absence of violent conflict. It encompasses human rights, good

270

governance, access to education and health care and ensuring that each individual has opportunities and choices to fulfill his or her potential. Every step in this direction is also a step towards reducing poverty, achieving economic growth and preventing conflict. Freedom from want, freedom from fear, and the freedom of future generations to inherit a healthy natural environment – these are the interrelated building blocks of human and therefore national security (Anan 2000, SG/SM/7382).

This has led to the emergence of two major schools of thought on how to best implement the human security concept – *'Freedom from Fear'* and *'Freedom from Want'*. While both the *freedom from fear* and *freedom from want* schools agree that the individual should be the primary referent of security, divisions emerge over the proper scope of that protection (e.g. over what threats individuals should be protected from) and over the appropriate mechanisms for responding to these threats.

Freedom from Fear-- This school seeks to limit the practice of Human Security to protecting individuals from violent conflicts. This approach argues that limiting the focus to violence is a realistic and manageable approach towards Human Security. This approach is also called 'Humanitarian' or 'Safety of Peoples' approach.

Freedom from Want-- According to UNDP 1994, 'Freedom from Want' school focuses on the basic idea that violence, poverty, inequality, diseases, and environmental degradation are inseparable concepts in addressing the root of human insecurity. Different from 'Freedom from Fear', it expands the focus beyond violence with emphasis on development and security goals.

The Commission on Human Security (2003:4) accepted this as the basic definition of human security and addressed it through four main components:

1. critical and pervasive threats;
2. human rights;
3. protection; and
4. building on people's strength.

The Commission further identified four priorities for policy action to promote human security:

• encouraging growth that reaches the extreme poor;
• supporting sustainable livelihoods and decent work;
• preventing and containing the effects of economic crises and natural disasters; and
• providing social protection for all situations.

The United Nations Millennium Declaration further outlined the critical elements of human security in the new millennium by highlighting freedom as a fundamental value: "Men and women have the right to live their lives and raise their children in dignity, free from hunger and free from the fear of violence, oppression or injustice. Democratic and participatory governance based on the will of the people best assures these rights" (A/55/L.2, para 6).

The roadmap towards the implementation of the United Nations Millennium Declaration states that:

> The principle of human-centered security, along with the need to protect individuals and communities from violence, is increasingly acknowledged. Human security depends first on the effective application of law and order, which in turn demands a firm adherence to the rule of law. A commitment to human security also demands enhanced international cooperation in conflict prevention, and strengthened capacities to assist countries in building, keeping and restoring peace. A further requirement for ensuring human security is disarmament, which involves a consistent and concerted effort from all. Progress here can both reduce global threats and save resources vital for social and economic well-being (A/56/326, para 13).

Human security is the deepening of the security concept away from a fairly exclusive focus on the state, to include additional referents at various levels—regional, sub-regional and civil society. Human security consequently intersects with a diverse range of social, economic and political issues and problem areas: the violation of human rights by state or non-state actors; homelessness and social dislocation; environmental degradation as the result of ill-considered development. In the human security framework, the ultimate end of the security infrastructure is the protection of people and communities against major threats.

It is our contention that the relationship between human security and peacebuilding is dynamic and interdependent, especially as they both focus on addressing the deep rooted and multi-factorial problems inherent in the country, and offers more long term resolutions. Peacebuilding is the means to secure human security. It solidifies peace by building sustainable infrastructure of human security. The focus of peacebuilding and human security are on the causes of conflict and the transformation of the social and political context of conflict so that human beings can live in a stable and secure social, political, and economic environment. In the human security framework, the ultimate end of the security infrastructure is the protection of people and communities against major threats. Human security deals with all that threatens life, security, integrity and well being of persons. Threats to human security in Nigeria have manifested in conflicts across the country. What is the nature of the human security situation in Nigeria?

The Challenges of Human Security in Nigeria

It is our contention that Nigeria, since 1999, has been experiencing conflicts arising mainly from deeply rooted threat to human security. What is the nature of the threat to human security in the country? Let us now focus our attention to examining some of these. To do this effectively, the chapter is guided by the seven dimension of human security provided by the UNDP.

Economic Security Situation in Nigeria

The economic security situation has been characterized by decades of poor economic management, inconsistent macroeconomic policy, instability and policy reversals, conflicts between different macro-economic policy goals, public sector dominance in production and consumption, pervasive rent-seeking and corruption, inadequate and decaying infrastructure, large debt overhang, among others(see NEEDS document 2004). Nigeria's Gross Domestic Product (GDP) which had risen to an annual average of US$93 billion in the early 1980s had by the 1990s fallen to below US$35 billion. On 1st July, 1973, N1 was issued against US$1.52. However, by May, 1999 N1 was issued against US$0.0113636. This had further deteriorated in 2003 with N1 being issued against US$0.0072875. In other words, N1000 in July, 1973 was US$1,520; the same N1000 was worth US$11.3636 in May, 1999 and in December, 2003, it fetched US$7.2875. Uncontrolled increase in inflation rate has posed the greatest threat to the purchasing power of the Naira. Inflation, which had fallen to 0 per cent in April 2000, reached 14 per cent by the end of 2003. Inflation was estimated at 11.6 per cent by year-end in 2005 (See U.S Department of State, Bureau of African Affairs June 2006).

The inadequate supply and utilization of commercial energy is the major reason for the poor economic development of Nigeria. Lack of investment in the sector for nearly a decade (1990-1999), led to a systematic deterioration of the power generation infrastructure. It has stifled industrial growth and impoverished the citizenry. By 1999, when Nigeria returned to democratic governance, the inadequacy had reached crisis point with only about 15 per cent of the national demand for electric power being met (1,500MW vs. 10,000MW). Between 2000 and 2004, the nation had invested about N150 billion in the electric power sector; but has been able to add only a total of about 1500MW power to the national grid. The problems and hindrances faced by the National Power Holding (NPH) persist in spite of the efforts made by Government to reverse the power situation.

Since 1986 when SAP was introduced, the nation's economy, which by the end of the 1970's was strong enough to expect it to take the country out of poverty by the year 2000, had regressed so far and so fast that by the dawn of the twenty first century, Nigeria is among the poorest of the poor countries. The human security situation in Nigeria has now become characterized by severe poverty condition that cuts across the six geo-political zones of the country. In spite of Nigeria's abundant natural prosperity and oil wealth, the poverty of its people is increasing. It is 'serious and extensive to differing degrees in all parts of the country and within all the states'. The scale of poverty in Nigeria is daunting. Nigeria has a very high incidence of both income poverty (by the $1-a-day poverty line) and human poverty. The greatest problem is that poverty is increasing – both in proportion and in absolute numbers. In 2000, 70.2 per cent of the population fell below the official poverty line from 42.7 per cent in 1992 (see UNDP Report 2001:51-69). Pervasive poverty is a silent threat to human security. Poverty negates human security. It undermines human dignity and self-esteem.

Health Security Situation in Nigeria

Nigeria's Health Sector is in a deplorable state. The World Bank World Development Indicator Database (April 2, 2002) has shown that availability and accessibility to quality health care services in Nigeria is poor. Health facilities are generally inadequate, and in many instances not very functional. Most of the health facilities are mere dispensaries that are staffed by non-professional health auxiliaries. The maternal and infant mortality rates are one of the highest in the world. Secondary Health Care has largely collapsed across the nation while tertiary Health Institutions do not have the diagnostic and investigative equipment and at best can be described to have lost focus. The Referral System is non functional or inefficient. Unregulated traditional medical practice and quackery is all over the place. Nigeria's overall health system performance was ranked 187 out of 191 member States by W.H.O in 2000.

The World Bank Indicator Database (April 2, 2002) also showed that public expenditure on Health of US $8 per capita is much less than the WHO recommendation of 25% of GDP or US$35 per capita and even this is largely misappropriated. The health status indicators in Nigeria, one of the lowest in the world are attributed to many factors including budgetary, institutional, structural, attitudinal inconsistencies. The Health status indicators for Nigeria are far less than the average for sub-Sahara Africa. Life expectancy has increased slowly over the years to reach a level of 53 years in 1991, but by 2000 this figure had dropped to 51.7. The infant mortality rate is 115 per 1000 births; under 5 mortality rate is 210/1000, maternal mortality rate is 800 – 1500 per 100,000 births and HIV/AIDS prevalence of 5 per cent. The infection rate among adults was 1.8 per cent in 1991. The number has radically grown to 4.5 per cent in 1995, 5.4 per cent in 1999 and 5.8 per cent in 2001 and 2002. Aside from HIV/AIDS, Malaria, Tuberculosis, and child health problems (such as diarrhoeal diseases and Acute Respiratory Infections) are the other major health challenges of the country. Nigeria ranks 6th among 22 high burden countries with tuberculosis problem, and accounts for about 25 per cent of global malaria cases. 30 per cent of childhood deaths and 11 per cent of maternal deaths are due mainly to malaria. 53 per cent of the population has access to safe drinking water and adequate sanitation respectively.

Compounding the health challenges in Nigeria is the issue of fake or counterfeit drugs. The fake drug situation in the country was very alarming at one point. Various sources put the percentage of fake drugs on sale to between 50 per cent and 80 per cent, although this is on the downward trend due to the National Agency for Food and Drug Administration and Control (NAFDAC). A lot of treatment failures were attributable to fake drugs. The facts are frightening: paracetamol made with industrial solvent, ampicillin consisting of turmeric, antimalarials and antibiotics with no active ingredients, meningococcal vaccine made of tap water, contraceptive pills made of wheat flour, and the list goes on. Following reports that some patients had suffered intense fever after surgery, NAFDAC in 2003 collected samples of all the brands of water-for-injection it could find and tested them. The results were devastating. Of 149 samples, 147 were found to be contaminated. Only two brands were certified safe for use (*Business Day Magazine*, August 21, 2005).

Poor health – illness, injury, disability, and death – are critical threats to human security.

Food Security Situation in Nigeria

The World Bank (1986) provides a definition of 'food security' as 'access by all people at all times to enough food for an active and healthy life' (World Bank 1986, p69). A more comprehensive definition of food security was given by Forster (1992, p367) with the following equation, where 'hh' is short for 'household:' (hh food consumption requirement – hh food production) × price of food < = income and liquid assets available to purchase. Nigeria, Africa's most populous country, is losing 351,000 hectares of rangeland and cropland to desertification each year (FGN 1999). Agriculture has suffered from years of mismanagement, inconsistent and poorly conceived government policies, and the lack of basic infrastructure. Still, the sector accounts for over 41 per cent of GDP and two-thirds of employment. Nigeria is no longer a major exporter of cocoa, groundnuts (peanuts), rubber, and palm oil. Cocoa production, mostly from obsolete varieties and overage trees, is stagnant at around 180,000 tons annually; 25 years ago it was 300,000 tons. An even more dramatic decline in groundnut and palm oil production also has taken place.

Once the biggest poultry producer in Africa, corporate poultry output has been slashed from 40 million birds annually to about 18 million. Import constraints limit the availability of many agricultural and food processing inputs for poultry and other sectors. Fisheries are poorly managed.

Factors that have hindered food sufficiency over the past 35 years in particular include; the abandonment of the agricultural sector in preference to oil, non-empowerment of the mainly rural farmers who produce the bulk of the food, poor funding of agriculture and its related products, massive corruption within government circles, inadequate fertilization, weak and poor funding poor infrastructure, including the absence of road networks to move goods to the markets.

Environmental Security Situation

The environmental security situation in Nigeria has been characterized by problems such as oil spillage, air pollution; the encroaching desertification; unmitigated oil pollution and gas flaring; deforestation; gully and coastal erosion; conflicting, competing uncoordinated environmental governance policies; biodiversity depletion; loss of vital resources such as fresh water among others. Industrialization and large population movements to urban centers have also contributed to the environmental challenges, especially the solid waste management crises in Nigeria, which have not been given adequate attention by Government over the years.

Ever since the discovery of oil in Nigeria in the 1950s, the country has been suffering the negative environmental consequences of oil development. The growth of the country's oil industry, combined with a population explosion and a lack of environmental regulations, led to substantial damage to Nigeria's environment, especially in the Niger Delta region, the center of the country's oil industry. The country also faces environmental challenges from air pollution and desertification, with the encroachment of the Sahara Desert in the north and severe air pollution in overcrowded cities such as Lagos and Abuja.

The Niger Delta's main environmental challenges result from oil spills, gas flaring and deforestation. Oil spills in the Niger Delta have been a regular occurrence, and the resultant degradation of the surrounding environment has caused significant tension between the people living in the region and the multinational oil companies

277

operating there. It is only in the past decade that environmental groups, the Nigerian federal government, and the foreign oil companies that extract oil in the Niger Delta have begun to take steps to mitigate the damage.

Personal Security Situation

The first comes from the high level of violent crime. This can be simple armed robbery (especially of mobile phones), but can also involve car jacking and violent attacks. The risk is especially common when traveling between major cities. Violent robbery has been a major problem in Nigeria since the emerging oil boom of the 1970s raised expectations of quick wealth among different classes of the population.

Over the years the criminals have become increasingly brutal, better armed, audacious and contemptuous of Nigeria's ill-equipped police force; this has been ineffective in stemming the crime wave. Rich and poor communities in urban areas have been terrorized by armed robbers, and households and companies have had to install elaborate security systems to protect themselves against attacks. The police have intensified their campaign against violent crime. According to the crime statistics of the Lagos State Police Command, 287 armed robbers were killed in 2002 in Nigeria's commercial capital, compared with 257 in 2001. The statistics showed that 34 civilians were killed in 2002 compared with 70 in 2001, whereas 45 policemen died in shoot-outs with armed bandits, up from 16 in 2001 (see Nigerian Police Crime Statistics in 2001).

There is roughly one policeman to every 1,300 citizens in Nigeria, compared with the UN-recommended ratio of 1:400. However, the shortage of resources has not been the only constraint on the fight against crime: some police and soldiers have participated in crime themselves, including setting up illegal roadblocks.

In spite of the enormous wealth in the Niger Delta, the communities have little to show for it beyond contamination, repression, and joblessness. An ever more restless younger generation has found violence, hostage-taking and extortion in place of jobs (*Guardian Weekly*, 14-20 September 2000). Kidnapping of staff and vandalism against premises and oil producing infrastructure is commonplace in Delta, Rivers and Bayelsa states (the heart of so-called Delta region), which are the centre of Nigeria's onshore oil industry.

Shell estimates that around 50-70 members of staff are kidnapped every year. Although most are usually released unharmed once a ransom is paid or concessions agreed with the local community, the experience may be traumatic and employers should consider training staff on how best to cope with being abducted.

Although expatriates in Nigeria have traditionally only been the target of kidnappings in the Niger Delta, and to date have been released without harm, the shooting dead of two US citizens working for Chevron Texaco in an ambush in the Delta in April 2004 was a worrying development. The incessant and rampant kidnappings of expatriates' by the youths of the Niger Delta have become a very serious challenge to Nigeria.

There was a major upsurge in clashes between various gangs and ethnic groups in the crucial oil producing Delta region following the disputed April 2003 elections and this now seems set to increase sharply in the run up to the April 2007 elections. Although many gangs claim to be fighting for the rights of the poor and indigenous inhabitants in the region, many are little more than criminal groups. Inter-gang fighting has led to an increase in violent clashes, which often spill over into wider violence.

The situation has been compounded by the high global oil price which has made stealing oil more lucrative and because the government has increased its battle against corruption in the Delta region which has raised the political stakes. The situation has also become more worrying in the last year with the recent emergence of a new group, the Movement for the Emancipation of the Niger Delta (MEND). This seems to be more organized than many previous groups, as shown by its ability to detonate a number of car bombs and the kidnapping of larger groups of expatriate workers.

Another side of the growing lawlessness is the problem of piracy in Nigerian waters. Most attacks on vessels are in the area around the mouth of the Niger River and are related to the illegal trade in oil.

In the Niger Delta communities, militant youths from disgruntled communities now target oil facilities and their personnel to squeeze money, jobs and social amenities from wealthy, though vulnerable, oil multi-nationals. An increasing number of oil workers have been kidnapped, including foreigners who work in isolated areas in the difficult-to-police swampy terrain of the Niger Delta. Oil workers are usually seized in large groups from isolated locations, held for short periods and freed unharmed. Such attacks are just one facet of violence in the Niger-Delta, where poverty fuels resentment against the oil industry. Sabotage of pipelines and flow stations, abductions of expatriate oil workers, theft of barges full of crude oil and turf wars between militias are also common place.

In the case of Shell, the number of community-related disruptions (which include the closure of production facilities, seizure of assets, blockade of access and disruption of drilling activities) increased by 10 per cent to 176 in 2004, compared with 2003. Nigeria has lost 500,000 bpd in crude production since February 2006.

Community Security Situation

Community solidarity and relationships have fractured and fragmented in many communities in Nigeria. It is our contention that much of the communal violence in the country, which took the form of ethnic, religious or indigene versus settler conflicts, was as a result of economic inequalities and resource scarcity, not ideological or communal differences. Inter-communal violence remains a serious concern in Nigeria. Ethnic nationalist groups have sprung up in recent years, reflecting a growing feeling of frustration with central government and the perceived political domination of the numerically superior north. The explosion of ethnic consciousness and the emergence of ethnic militia that heralded the democratic process constituted a threat to governance in Nigeria.

The activities of ethnic militias like the Oodua People's Congress, the Igbo People's Congress, the Arewa People's Congress, the Movement for the Actualisation of the Sovereign State of Biafra (MASSOB) and the explosion of the extended Sharia law in the North signalled an initial loss of faith in the Nigeria project. Nigeria experienced an avalanche of bloodletting and blood shedding never witnessed in Nigeria's political history since the civil war. Since the end of military rule in 1999, fighting in several regions of the country claimed thousands of lives.

The authorities have been unable to contain militant nationalist groups, such as the Yoruba separatist movement, the Oodua Peoples Congress, the Ijaw Egbesu in the Niger Delta, the Bakassi Boys in the south-east and the Arewa Peoples Congress in the north, all of whom are linked to ethnic disturbances and anti-government activities. Many of these groups are well armed. It is estimated that at least 50,000 people have been killed in various incidents of ethnic, religious and communal violence since the return to civilian rule in May 1999. This gives Nigeria a casualty rate from internal conflict that is one of the highest in the world--and the country is not fighting a civil war. Although most of the conflicts have been between civilians, there have also been some serious clashes between security forces and civilians and militants. Depending on the outcome of the 2007 elections, many of these groups could trigger violence that might engulf the entire country.

Political Security Situation

In the face of intensified ethnic and religious violence, the government continued to employ extreme measures to respond to social unrest and violence. A recent report by the World Organisation against Torture (OMCT) claimed that security forces, operating with orders from the government, were responsible for over 10,000 Nigerian civilian deaths. According to the report, in addition to committing extra-judicial executions of alleged criminals, the state and its security agencies instigated and exacerbated communal conflicts, and failed to react to early warning signals of pending violence. In other developments, allegations of unfair voting registration procedures served to fuel political tensions.

Probably the most serious challenge to the governments' authority has come from rebellious groups in the oil-producing Niger Delta. Since the mid-1990s a number of militant groups, angry at their people's political alienation and economic exploitation, have waged an increasingly violent struggle against the state and multinational oil companies operating in the area. The most high profile of these is probably the Niger Delta Peoples Volunteer Force. Fighting between the various groups and with the Nigerian military has led to the deaths of thousands of people. In 2004, with the fighting between various gangs escalating, the government substantially increased its military presence in the region.

A further cause of the violence in the Niger Delta is Nigeria's oil-related and environmental protection legislation which protects the interests of the oil and gas producing companies over the community needs and interests. Nigerian Federal Government or its authorities, expropriate land for mining or oil purposes, usually without adequate compensation. Furthermore, there is no statutory provision or mechanisms for defining fair and adequate compensation. The environmental impact assessment (EIA) legislation does not make consultation with the concerned communities mandatory and in practice discriminates against local communities due to the inaccessibility of the EIA documents and the short time allowed for consultation. In addition is the lack of adequate and fair compensation for environmental damage.

Communities seek jobs from companies which they are not in a position to provide easily, as the jobs require professional skills and specialized education, which workers in communities often do not have. Communities also seek infrastructure from companies. Other demands include compensation for loss of land and for environmental damage to crops and fishing ponds due to oil spills. Some communities seek contracts from companies. There are also concerns regarding failure to clean up and the lack of consultation when development is being planned. In some cases perceived breaches of these agreements and demands have led to violence, including abductions and sabotage.

Once again, the frosty relationship between President Obasanjo and Vice President Atiku Abubakar has taken a worst turn. The political machine is overheating and is already threatening the foundation of Nigeria's fragile democracy. The government has resorted to using the Economic and Financial Crimes Commission (EFCC) effectively to intimidate, harass and drown voices of opposition in the deep ocean of authoritarianism. This has serious implications for political security in the country.

The Challenges of Conflicts in Nigeria

Arising from these deep rooted threats to human security were the explosions of violent conflicts across the country. In Nigeria, there have been explosions of violent conflicts in Kaduna, Lagos, Jos, Yelwa-Shendam, Kano, Benue, Taraba, the Niger Delta and many others since the inception of the democratic process. The expressions of many of the violent conflicts took the form of competition over identities, territorial claims, land, political institutions and psychological needs. In the first four years following Nigeria's return to democracy in 1999, at least 10,000 people have been killed in communal violence across the country. In recent months, Nigeria has experienced more frequent clashes. Various ethnic groups are involved in conflicts with one another:

a) Ijaws and Itsekiris in the Niger Delta;
b) Ilajes and Ijaws in the southwest;
c) Yorubas and Ijaws in the southwest;
d) Yorubas and Hausas in the southwest and north;
e) Tivs and Jukuns, Fulani and Kutebs in central Nigeria; (Jibo 2003)
f) Fulani and Berom in the Riyom district, south-west of Jos.

Plateau state in central Nigeria has been particularly affected, and the first half of 2004 saw an escalation of violence around the southern part of the state. Since February 2004, southern Plateau State communities have experienced violent clashes, manipulated by ethnic, political, commercial and religious interests and differences. The crisis peaked when Yelwa, in southern Plateau, was repeatedly attacked and counterattacked by armed gangs, resulting in the complete destruction of the town of 20,000 inhabitants.

Following the violence in Yelwa, a peaceful Muslim demonstration in Kano turned violent, when vigilantes targeted Christian communities. Before the military was able to restore security, lives had been lost, 50,000 people were displaced and homes and household property destroyed and looted. While a strong police and military force maintain calm in Kano, high levels of tension still remain. These tensions have deep roots in Nigeria, stemming from long-standing ethnic and cultural clashes between Christians and Muslims.

Riots based (at least ostensibly) on religious affiliation and religious policies have indeed occurred, the worst such being the two confrontations that took place in Kaduna between February and May 2000.

The oil rich Niger delta, in the south of the country, remains the scene of recurring violence between members of different ethnic groups competing for political and economic power, and between militia and security forces sent to restore order in the area. Intense fighting continued in the Niger Delta region between ethnic groups (especially the Ijaw) and government soldiers and security forces. A state of emergency, declared for a few days at the end of December 1998, lasted into January 1999 after as many as 240 people were killed in clashes between protesting Ijaw youths and government troops in the Niger Delta state of Bayelsa.

The ancient oil town of Warri had exploded in violence between the three ethnic groups that makeup Warri - the Ijaws and Urhobos on one hand and the Itsekiri on the other. The violence is aggravated by the widespread availability of small arms—a problem which exists throughout Nigeria but is particularly acute in the delta. Despite a massive army, navy and police presence in the area, local communities remain vulnerable to attack by the militias, criminal gangs and security forces.

There were also violent conflicts between the Ijaw and Itsekiri groups, between Ijaw and Ilaje groups in the south-western state of Ondo, and between Yoruba and Ijaw in the southwest. Fighting in the south-western and northern regions between Yorubas, who comprise the majority in the southwest, and the Hausa-Fulani who dominate in the north. In the north, occasional fighting between Muslims and Christians claimed almost 100 lives while clashes in the east between local farmers and Fulani herdsmen over cattle herding and access to land resulted in about 100 deaths. Control over land also sparked conflict between different Ibo groups in eastern Nigeria.

In the oil-rich Niger delta region, ethnic armed groups are fighting for greater control of the region's oil resources. Among these is the Niger Delta People's Volunteer Force, led by Mujahid Dokubo-Asari. The rebel Niger Delta People's Volunteer Force in Nigeria is fighting for autonomy in the country's oil-rich Niger Delta (*Reuters*, September 29, 2004).

It is also our contention that the threats to human security and the violent conflicts experienced so far in Nigeria have been exacerbated by a long period of economic mismanagement; endemic corruption and lack of accountability and transparency experienced, especially within the thirty years of military rule in Nigeria. Let us now take a look at the role of the military in these.

The Challenges of Military Rule and the Legacy of Corruption

Nigeria tasted her first military intervention in politics on January 15, 1966 when some Army Majors, mainly from the eastern part of the country, executed a very violent coup that resulted in the assassination of some prominent civilian and military leaders from the northern part of the country, including the Prime Minister of the Federal Republic of Nigeria and the Premier of the Northern Region. This coup terminated the five years, two months old experiment with the Westminster model of democracy. This heralded the 30 years of military governance in Nigeria.

What followed was a travesty of governance. Usually the military does not govern with democratic structures as they preferred to rule the country with the mentality of conquest. All voices of opposition were drowned in the deep ocean of authoritarianism as opposition groups were bamboozled, muzzled and crushed. Many prominent Nigerians were detained and tortured for several years and months without trial. Many others were sentenced to various jail terms by kangaroo courts without due process. Ex post facto laws were made to jail the perceived enemies of military regimes. The laws had clauses, which ousted the jurisdiction of the courts. Some Nigerians were hanged for ventilating their grievances while others were simply assassinated by special death squads of the military regime. The rule of law was substituted with the rule of force. In addition was the destruction of networks of relationships built overtime among Nigerians. The values of democracy, especially those of persuasion, negotiation, consultation, consensus and pragmatism were lost to military rule.

All structures of accountability were destroyed or emptied of their content. The institutions of governance became very weak and drained to the extent that they became incapable of bearing heavy strains. The military used its instruments of coercion to suppress, terrorize and intimidate the civil populace repeatedly to such an extent that battalions of sycophants emerged to applaud every misdeed of successive military governments.

The military adopted a strategy of selective recruitment or cooptation of civilians and schooled them in the art of authoritarianism and then rewarded them with appointments into the conspiratorial club. Together, they almost looted the country to a halt. Much of the country's wealth remained concentrated in the hands of small elite. Corruption, nontransparent government contracting practices, and other practices favored the wealthy and politically influential, including a banking system that impeded small and medium investor access to credit and regulatory and tax regimes that were not always enforced impartially. In the process, work ethics were destroyed as the reward system became deregulated and controlled by 'invincible hands'. The public service was destroyed in the process. The executive machine, the public service, lost the traditional values of the public service – neutrality, impartiality, anonymity and security of tenure, during the years of military rule. The situation has not changed. The capacity of the public service to formulate and implement basic policies is greatly constrained and its image of an agent of development seriously compromised. This has serious impact on the governance framework in the country. The Civil Servants still connive with their chief executives to cart away enormous resources from their ministries and parastatal. Corruption and get-rich quick mentality has become the order of the day in the service.

Corruption became the way of life of many Nigerians. They country unfortunately acquired the indelible reputation of a country that is blatantly corrupts and whose officials have little concern for accountability, probity, and transparency, especially under the democratic process. The situation in the country has been characterized by poor government of public money and assets; shoddy system planning and project preparation work leading to inaccuracy of costing, cost/benefit analysis and prioritization in deciding the spending pattern and plan for any given year; Sloppy fiscal management through ineffective expenditure management, institutions, processes and control mechanisms; poor resource allocation decisions and non identification of the costs and benefits of alternative expenditure decisions; Haphazard liquidity management of public funds; Technical inefficiency in managing and utilizing resources; and lack of transparency and accountability of government.

So corrupt is the country now that it has continued to top the list of the Transparency International, a Berlin based NGO, since the year 2000. UK's Department of Foreign and International Development (DFID) reported that 55 per cent of corruption in Nigeria is perpetrated in the presidency (Daily Trust, April 8, 2002). The preliminary interim reports of the value-for-money audit of government expenditures in 2000 showed frequent neglect of the established procedures governing the use of public resources. The Auditor-General of the Federation submitted a 296-page report detailing mind-boggling instances of financial recklessness and indiscipline in all sectors of public service (*This Day* Newspaper, January 19, 2003). Corruption has destroyed the respect for merit, honesty, sincerity and dedication to duty.

Corruption has become so pervasive in government circles to the extent that very few government officials in Nigeria can be said to be free of corrupt practices. The categories of corruption in Nigeria are largely Governmental (including corruption in the Executive, Legislative, Judicial branches of Government), corruption in the Public Service, Political Corruption, Moral Corruption, corruption in various institutions, academic or traditional, and corruption in the private sector of the economy.

These were identified to include, decay or collapse of the family and societal value systems where the public sees no shame in immoral "get rich quick" malady; the lack of exemplary leadership; Nigerian's general and insatiable craze for titles and paper qualifications, inadequate punishments for corrupt persons, high level of unemployment and job insecurity with high cost of living, the high premium placed on governance and politics as a lucrative business for investment and eventual returns with maximal profits, the attitudinal aspect referred as the "Nigerian factor", where the average Nigerian always wants to cut corners, and avoid rules and regulations to secure an unwarranted advantage. The current laws against corruption are largely inefficient and perhaps corrupt. And there is no way the operations of the current anti-corruption outfits in Nigeria - the ICPC and EFCC, could have any credibility in a situation in which those who should have been their prime targets are being shielded from prosecution by a corrupt statute.

It is not surprising that the conditions of life of many Nigerians have been deteriorating, characterized by limited access to health services, poor and inadequate housing, limited access to safe water, limited access to education, limited access to epileptic supply of electricity in urban and rural areas, bad roads and poor road networking, limited access to agricultural inputs and implements, limited access to income generating activities among many others. The country is now confronted with many social, economic and political problems, such as poverty, high-income disparities, crimes, proliferation of small arms and light weapons, communal conflicts, collapse of social and economic infrastructure and problems of rural development among many others.

The long absence of democracy in Nigeria is obviously affecting the political elites and the current democratic process. Indeed, Many Nigerian political elites still see democracy in instrumental terms. They still see democracy as a means to an end – their selfish ends. Thus, the reasons for which the electorates voted them into power no longer matters. The rules of the game of politics are still hardly understood. Certainly, quite a number of the political elites have served at various times and in various capacities under the military. These political elites, having been thoroughly schooled and oriented in the values of militarism, still exhibit militaristic attitudes.

Most of the institutions and organisations have not changed their operations which were structured along the military mode of operations through chains of commands leading to internal conflicts and instability within the organization. It will take some time to get out of this hangover. However, it does appear that the political elites are gradually imbibing the values of tolerance, pragmatism, cooperation and compromise, especially with their collective opposition to the third term bid of President Obasanjo.

The Challenges of Democracy, Human Rights and Peacebuilding

Governance in Nigeria has been largely under authoritarian regimes; 60 years of colonialism as well as 30 years under military rule and only 17 years of civilian regimes in between two military interventions. Many of the pervasive conflicts in Nigeria are consequences of the nature of authoritarianism under which Nigeria was governed for a long time. Systems of corruption, political instability, inadequate infrastructure, and poor macroeconomic management along with attendant lack of accountability and transparency have combined to create various the threats to human security in the country. It is within this context that threats to human security in Nigeria are expressed in conflicts by competing social, cultural, economic, religious, and political frameworks. Almost every ethnic group or geopolitical area of Nigeria complains of marginalization. Among the reasons for the cries of marginalization and other perceived in-equities are the unmet needs of many Nigerians. These are acceptance needs (recognition of identity and culture), access needs (political and economic participation) and human security needs. These complaints at the national level are mirrored at the state level. Whether the complaints are justified or not, it is desirable and necessary to device confidence building mechanisms to ensure peace, stability and progress.

288

In an attempt at transformation, the government under President Obasanjo has embarked on a number of reforms. These are:

Accelerated Privatization, Liberalization and Private Sector Development

The telecommunication sector has been liberalized. The government is focused on strengthening, and unbundling key aspects of power generation, transmission and distribution so that privatization can be enabled. The government claimed that it is focused on its core business of providing public goods whilst letting the private sector alone or, in partnership with public sector deal with production. The government is also making effort at strengthening the regulatory functions and frameworks in telecommunications, power, petroleum, transport and aviation so that citizens and businesses are given a fair deal and their rights protected. The government is concessioning the railway, ports and airports, and privatizing other necessary enterprises.

During 2003 the government began deregulating fuel prices, announced the privatization of the country's four oil refineries. In 2004, the federal government unveiled the National Economic Empowerment and Development Strategy (NEEDS) and its state level counterpart, State Economic and Empowerment Development Strategy (SEEDS), a domestically designed and run program modeled on the IMF's Poverty Reduction and Growth Facility for fiscal and monetary management. The economic reform process encompasses strategies to achieve the Millennium Development Goals (MDGs).

Government plans to achieve this mission through the strategy called "The National Economic Empowerment and Development Strategy (NEEDS) at the Federal level; "The State Economic Empowerment and Development Strategy" (SEEDS) and "The Local Economic Empowerment and Development Strategy" (LEEDS) at the State and Local government levels respectively.

The goals of NEEDS, SEEDS, and LEEDS differ from previous strategies for the development of Nigeria, and included the following:

(i) Wealth creation,
(ii) Employment generation,
(iii) Poverty Reduction, and

(iv) Value Re-orientation

It is hoped that these goals can be achieved by creating an environment in which business can thrive, government re-directed to providing basic services, and people re-directed and empowered to take advantage of the new livelihood opportunities the plan will stipulate.

NEEDS also hopes to:

(i) punish corruption and graft;
(ii) campaign to instill the virtues of honesty, hard work, selfless service, moral rectitude and patriotism;
(iii) involve NGOs and Civil Society organisations in the crusade.

With specific reference to Public Service Reforms, NEEDS hopes to restructure the government to make it smaller, stronger, better skilled and more efficient at delivering essential services. It seeks to transform the government from a haven of corruption to an institution that spurs development and serves the people. The number of government jobs will decline and the cost of running the government will fall dramatically, as in-kind benefits for civil servants, such as subsidized housing, transportation and utilities are monetized. Reforms and Regulations will be implemented to ensure transparency and accountability, and corrupt practices will be outlawed.[xliii]

The NEEDS strategic plan was circulated for comments to the public before the plan was launched on 1st April, 2004 and later by the States at various dates. The NEEDS strategy for development envisages the Nigerian government in the 21[sty] century accepting, as a matter of policy, the following principles:

a) Free enterprise economy;
b) Democracy;
c) Private sector-driven economy and gradual reduction of government interest in economic ventures that could be better performed by the private sector investment;
d) Introduction of modern communication and information technology;
e) Capacity building and the development of highly skilled and professional manpower and
f) Concentration of government in the art of governance.

The acceptance of these principles as development policies for Nigeria, connotes that the present Public Service modeled on old rules and regulations, red-tapism and archaic technology with ill-trained and ill-motivated corrupt-prone public officials, cannot deliver services and play the crucial role expected of it.

The federal government has pursued the strategy of recapitalizing the banks and in the process has squeezed the number of banks from 89 to 25 with a minimum capitalization of N25 billion each. In the process, about N406 billion was raised from the capital market while N652million worth of Foreign Direct Investment (FDI) was generated from outside the country. This has helped in the stabilization of the exchange rate and the removal of the premium in the official and parallel markets. Similar reform is currently sweeping through the Insurance sub-sector with the capitalization threshold increasing to N2 billion for Life business and N3 billion for Non-life business. Re-insurance companies must recapitalize to N10 billion.

The government secured a historic $18 billion debt relief from the Paris Club from its $34 billion debt portfolio. Nigeria finally exited the debtor league on April 2006 with the payment of the outstanding $6.4 billion commitment to the Paris Club. The consistent rise in the oil prices in the international market has ensured an increase in the external reserves which was $28.3 billion by the end of December 2005 and $36.6 billion by the end of June 2006. Inflation fell from 15% in 2004 to 12% in December 2005.

Reform of the Agricultural Sector

The government has taken the following measures to enhance agricultural production as well as promote food security:

i   The National Cocoa Development Committee (NCDC) was established to address the problem of declining coca production;
ii. The Root and Tuber Expansion Programme (RTEP) was designed to bring about sustainable increase in the production of cassava, yam, cocoyam and potatoes, and to promote the processing, marketing and utilization of these crops;
iii. Committees involving various stakeholders have been established to seek effective and practicable ways for increased production and export within the shortest possible time;

iv. Special Programme of Food Security is bringing improved technology, improved water control and improved seeds and cultural practices to 109 sites in all the 36 States and the Federal Capital Territory (FCT);

v. South–South Cooperation Initiative is an initiative within the framework of the Special Programme on Food Security (SPFS). Its focus is on the building and rehabilitation of small–scale water control infrastructure in all the states. The aim is to reduce the total dependence of our agriculture on the vagaries of weather and ensure all–year round adequate water supply for adequate food   production;

vi. The Nigeria–France Project on Agricultural Development is funded with a French grant of €1.13million. It is aimed at improving the productivity and access to markets of low – level farmers in different farming systems in Jagawa, Kano, Katsina and Bauchi States;

vii. Drug administration and control in the livestock sub-sector.

viii. New National Policy on Agriculture and Integrated Rural Development to evolve new strategies for sustained increase in agricultural productivity, a new agricultural policy has been designed to develop this sector;

ix. Federal College of Horticultural Studies to train students in all fields of horticulture and irrigation technology at Certificate, National Diploma (ND) and Higher National Diploma (HND) levels. In addition, the College will also train farmers, processors and other agro-allied groups for vocational skill acquisition; and finally,

x. Fish farm estate development, which involves the establishment of a 50-hectare fish farm in all the states and the FCT. The project has taken off in Kano and Ogun States where more than 30 private fish farmers are involved.

Anti-Corruption, Transparency and Accountability

The reform focuses on specific measures that confront corruption, improve transparency and reduce economic crimes. The passing of the anti-corruption bill, the establishment of the Independent Corrupt Practices Commission along with respect for the rule of law and adherence to the tenets of contract enforcement are intended to make Nigeria more attractive to investors in real sectors of the economy thereby creating remunerative employment opportunities for all. An Economic and Financial Crimes Commission began operations in April 2003 and has made several arrests including of well known and influential personalities-for financial crimes. In recognition of the results recorded by the country in fighting money laundering and the narcotics trade, the Financial Action Task Force (FATF) delisted Nigeria from its list of Non Co-operative Countries and Territories (NCCTs). These ratings increased the country's attractiveness for Foreign Direct Investments (FDIs) and dropped the investment and country risk index significantly.

As part of the reform government has continued and expanded the scope of its Due Process Mechanism to encompass procurement reform in government contracting. This process aims to improve the quality and effectiveness of capital spending by ensuring that only projects, which have been adequately prepared financially and technically, are included in the federal budget. The Due Process Compliance (DPC) Mechanism is an instrument designed to enforce compliance with due process in budgeting and expenditure by all federal spending units. The goal of BMPIU is to ensure full compliance with laid down guidelines and procedures for the procurement of capital and minor capital projects as well as associated goods and services.

Public Sector Reform

Reform of Public Expenditures, reduction of waste in government and improvement of public revenues is a key aspect of the reform programme. Fiscal indiscipline has been a problem and the government has run substantial budget deficit averaging 4.7 per cent of GDP in the past five years. The public sector absorbs too large a proportion of Federal Government revenues. This, the government wants to change.

The implementation of the monetization initiative which gets government out of the business of providing fringe benefits such as housing, utilities, transport, in kind, and gets the benefit to beneficiary civil servants in cash is intended to reduce waste. Civil service reforms aimed at re-professionalization, ensuring merit and raising morale is also an important aspect of the reforms. Other aspects of the public expenditure agenda are pension reforms.

The present PAYG pensions system has become unsustainable, and government has built up sizeable arrears which have yet to be fully quantified. The reforms involved a move away to new contributory pensions system that will also provide a source of long term invisible resources in an economy where this is sorely lacking.

Governance and Institutional Reforms

We have received Report on reforms of the Local Governments to make them more effective and efficient deliverers of services to the people given their proximity to the ordinary people. We are also reforming our tertiary institutions. Universities now have autonomy to choose their leaders and managers and to raise additional resources through various means including charging more fees for non-academic service like bed space. The high level of support given to education in this budget will result in higher subventions from the capital budget to enable completion of projects, upgrade of facilities, repair and rehabilitation. This will complement universities efforts at generating incremental operating resources.

The Niger Delta Development Commission (NDDC)

This was formed through an act of the parliament in 2000 (the Niger Delta Development Commission Act 2000), in response to long-standing demands from the states in the Delta region for a more equitable distribution of the wealth generated by the exploitation of resources found in the states. The NDDC is funded by the federal government, other levies, and contributions from oil companies operating in the region (based on an agreed formula). According to Article 7(1) of the Act of 2000, the Commission has the following powers, to:

(i) formulate policies and guidelines for the development of the Niger-Delta area;

(ii) conceive, plan and implement, in accordance with set rules and regulations, projects and programmes for the sustainable development of the Niger-Delta area in the field of transportation including roads, jetties and waterways, health, education, employment, industrialization, agriculture and fisheries, housing and urban development, water supply, electricity and telecommunications;

(iii) cause the Niger Delta area to be surveyed in order to ascertain measures which are necessary to promote its physical and socio-economic development;

(iv) prepare master plans and schemes designed to promote the physical development of the Niger Delta area and the estimates of the costs of implementing such master plans and schemes;

(v) implement all the measures approved for the development of the Niger-Delta area by the Federal Government and the member states of the commission;

(vi) identify factors inhibiting the development of the Niger-Delta and assist the member states in the formation and implementation of policies to ensure sound and efficient management of the resources of the Niger Delta;

(vii) assess and report on any project funded or carried out in the Niger Delta area by oil and gas producing companies and any other company including NGOs and Ensure that funds released for such projects are properly utilized;

(viii) tackle ecological and environmental problems that arise from the exploration of oil mineral in the Niger-Delta area and advise the Federal Government and the member states on the prevention and control of oil spillage, gas flaring and environmental pollution;

(ix) liaise with the various oil mineral and gas prospecting and producing companies on all matters of pollution prevention and control;

(x) execute such other works and perform such other functions which, in the opinion of the Commission, are required for the sustainable development of the Niger-Delta area and its peoples.

Poverty

The National Millennium Development Goal Report (2003) indicates that the poverty situation in Nigeria has been on the increase in both rural and urban areas over the period 1980 to 1996. Rural poverty increased from 22 per cent to 69.8 per cent, while urban poverty increased from 17.6 per cent to 55.2 per cent over the period. The poverty situation in Nigeria is precarious not only in income poverty but also in terms of food poverty. The Obasanjo administration, worried by the exponential rise in poverty, has also established institutions and processes of poverty reduction. Indeed, the administration established the National Programme for the Eradication of Poverty (NAPEP) in 2001 to address the challenge of poverty in Nigeria. An important objective of NAPEP is to help eradicate extreme poverty by the year 2010 in line with the United Nations Millennium Development Goal (MDG) of halving the proportion of people living in poverty by the year 2015. There are signs that these lofty ideals may not be achievable. There appears to be a number of problems with the nature of the institutions of poverty reduction, as well as the processes and funding of poverty alleviation programmes in Nigeria since 2000.

Building Relationships

Attempts are being made to build networks of horizontal and vertical relationships in Nigeria. The contracted democratic space is gradually expanding as the political process becomes more liberalized. Nigerians are having increased access to decision-making centers than before. People now have more opportunity of joining a host of political parties, private organisations, associations and the process of debates; conflicts, compromises and consensus are gradually being built. The democracy has been tested by protests across the country and has been given a fairly good mark. Citizens now have a right to gather peacefully and protest the policies of their government or the actions of other groups with demonstrations, marches, petitions, boycotts, strikes and other forms of direct citizen action with little molestations from the security agencies. Institutions of governance are gradually showing goods sign re-awakeness from their near comatose state.

In otherwords, the government appears to be constructing bridges for the transformation of the existing conflicts through packages of peacebuilding measures in the country by attempting to deal with those deep rooted factors that are frustrating the development of the necessary infrastructure for sustainable human security. This requires the broadening and deepening of the new democratic order to make it long lasting and cost effective as well as preserve and guarantee freedom of religion, association, speech, civil rights and liberty, justice, respect for the rule of law, equity and fairness. It also involves the building of a system of government that encourages popular participation by all members of the society; a system that encourages responsive and good governance that is capable of preventing military or any other unconstitutional intervention; a system that will ultimately accommodate, reconcile and manage Nigeria's diversity within an overarching polity.

Conclusion

In this paper, we have attempted to the relationship between human security and peacebuilding and argued that the relationship is dynamic and interdependent, especially as they both focus on addressing the deep rooted and multi-factorial problems inherent in the country, and offers more long term resolutions. We argued also that Nigeria, since 1999, has been experiencing conflicts arising mainly from deeply rooted threats to human security. It is our contention in the chapter that the threats to human security have been exacerbated by a long period of economic mismanagement; endemic corruption and lack of accountability and transparency experienced, especially within the thirty years of military rule in Nigeria. Finally we argued further that in order to enhance the constructive transformation of the existing conflicts in the country, Nigeria should develop sustainable infrastructure of human security that is guaranteed through packages of peacebuilding measures. It is our hope that the Nigerian experience would provide lessons for other countries, especially in Africa.

References

Assefa, H. (2001) 'Reconciliation,' in *Peacebuilding: A Field Guide*, Luc Reychler and Thania Paffenholz, eds. Boulder, Colorado: Lynne Reinner Publishers, Inc.

Axworthy, L. (1999) *Human Security: Safety for People in a Changing World*, Canadian Department of Foreign Affairs and International Trade.

Boutros-Ghali, Boutros (1995) *An Agenda for Peace*. New York: United Nations 1995.

Crocker, C. A. and Fen Osler, (2000) (ed.) *Managing Global Chaos: Sources or and Responses to International Conflict*, 5th edition, Washington: USIP.

Foster, P., (1992) *The World Food Problem*, Boulder: Lynne Rienner Publishers.

Galtung, J. (1996) *Peace by peaceful means: Peace and conflict, development and civilization*. Sage, London, pp. 1-3.

Haugerudbraaten, H., 'Peacebuilding: Six Dimensions and Two Concepts,' Institute For Security Studies. [available at: http://www.iss.co.za/Pubs/ASR/7No6/Peacebuilding.html.

See Jibo, Mvendaga, (2003) *The Middle Belt and the Federal Project in Nigeria*, Ibadan: JODAD; Jibo, Mvendaga; Simbine A.; and Habu Galadima, 'Ethnic Groups and Conflicts in Nigeria: The North-Central Zone of Nigeria', Ibadan: The Lords Creation.

Kritz, N. J. (2000) 'The Rule of Law in the Post-Conflict Phase: Building a Stable Peace,' in *Managing Global Chaos: Sources or and Responses to International Conflict*, eds. Chester A. Crocker and Fen Osler

Lederach, J. P. (1997) *Building Peace: Sustainable Reconciliation in Divided Societies*. Washington, D.C., United States Institute of Peace.

Markakis, J. (1998) *Resource conflict in the Horn of Africa*, Sage, London, p. 4.

Reychler, L (2001) 'From Conflict to Sustainable Peacebuilding: Concepts and Analytical Tools,' in *Peacebuilding: A Field Guide*, Luc Reychler and Thania Paffenholz, eds. (Boulder, Colorado: Lynne Rienner Publishers, Inc., 2001), 12.

Zartman, I. W. (ed.), *Elusive peace: Negotiating an end to civil wars*, The Brookings Institution, New York, 1995.

Official Documents and Publications

DFAIT, *DFAIT/NGO Peacebuilding Consultation*, Department of Foreign Affairs and International Trade, December 1996, <u>www.dfait-maeci.gc. ca/peacebuilding/gngoc report-e.asp</u>

Government of Nigeria, *Combating Desertification and Mitigating the Effects of Drought in Nigeria*, National Report on the Implementation of the United Nations Convention to Combat Desertification (Nigeria: November 1999).

National Economic Empowerment and Development Strategy (NEEDS), National Planning Commission Abuja 2004.

SAIS, 'The Conflict Management Toolkit: Approaches,' The Conflict Management Program, Johns Hopkins University [available at: http://cmtoolkit.sais-jhu.edu/

UNDP (2001) *UNDP Human Development Report Nigeria 2000/2001*, Millenium Edition Lagos, Nigeria, 2001 pp51-69.

United Nations Development Assistance Framework (UNDAF), Nigeria, 2002-2007 from the World Bank World Development Indicator Database April 2, 2002, US Library of Congress.

World Bank, 1986. *Poverty and Hunger: Issues and Options for Food Security in Developing Countries*. The International Bank for Reconstruction and Development (The World Bank), Washington, D.C. 69 pp.

Editorial Note

African Renaissance

Book Series: No.1

This is the first in a book series from *African Renaissance*, a multidisciplinary journal published since 2004. The journal, which is a cross between an academic periodical and any high-quality features publication, started as a bi-monthly, and became a quarterly this year (2007) after 15 consecutive issues without missing a deadline, and after launching a book series early this year.

The book series augment the journal in its objectives of advancing both theoretical and empirical research, informing policies and practices and improving our understanding of the interplay of forces that shape the African condition.

This volume was inspired by some of the articles on Nigeria published in the journal. I thank all contributors previously published in AR for re-working their original contributions to fit into the framework of the book project, as well as new authors that submitted solicited contributions to the project.

African Renaissance has emerged as one of the leading platforms for the analysis of the African condition, hopes and aspirations. The journal accepts papers that cover Africa as a whole, as well as those which focus on specific countries on the continent.

For details of submission guidelines for the journal or the book series, please visit the website (www.adonis-abbey.com). Alternatively please email the journal's editor,

Dr Jideofor Adibe at: editor@adonis-abbey.com

For sales enquiries, please email: sales@adonis-abbey.com

Dr Jideofor Adibe
Editor
African Renaissance.

Contributors' Biographical Notes

1. **Kenneth Omeje** is Research Fellow in African Peace & Conflict Studies at the University of Bradford. He holds a Master's degree in Peace & Conflict Studies from the European Peace University in Burg/Schlaining, Austria and a PhD in Peace Studies from the University of Bradford. He was previously a Research Fellow in Development Studies & Lecturer in Political Science at the University of Nigeria, Nsukka, and has held visiting research fellowship positions at the Centre for African Studies, University of Florida, Gainesville, USA (1992); Institute of Higher Education, Comprehensive University of Kassel, Germany (2000), the Law Department, Keele University, UK (2000) and Department of International Politics, University of Wales, Aberystwyth (2001). Kenneth has published in many peer-reviewed journals and is the author of *High Stakes and Stakeholders: Oil Conflict and Security in Nigeria* (Ashgate, 2006).

2. **Ukoha Ukiwo** is Research Fellow at the Centre for Advanced Social Science (CASS), Port Harcourt, Nigeria. He was CRISE Scholar (2003-2006) at St Cross College, University of Oxford where he earned his D. Phil in Development Studies. He holds a Master of Science degree in Political Theory from University of Port Harcourt. Dr. Ukiwo's articles on democratization, ethnicity, social movements, vigilantes and African development have been published in reputable journals, including *The Journal of Modern African Studies, International Journal of Educational Development, Polis* and *Oxford Development Studies.*

3. **Usman A. Tar** received a PhD in Peace Studies from the Department of Peace Studies, University of Bradford, and M.Sc. in International Relations from the School of Graduate Studies, University of Maiduguri, Nigeria. He holds a Lectureship position in Politics at the University of Maiduguri but presently on leave of absence. Until recently, he was an Associate Research Fellow at the Africa Centre for Peace and Conflict Studies, University of Bradford. He sits in the Editorial Boards of the *Review of African Political Economy* (Sheffield); *Information and Democracy* (London) and has previously served as

contributing editor to *Peace, Conflict and Development* (Bradford). He has published in a number of peer review journals and contributed chapters in edited books. His book, *The Politics of Neoliberal Democracy in Africa: State and Civil Society in Nigeria* (London/New York: I.B. Tauris), is expected in early 2008.

4. **Gani Yoroms** holds a PhD in International Relations from the Ahmadu Bello University, Zaria, Nigeria and is the Head of Department of Defence and Security Studies, African Centre for Strategic Research and Studies, National War College, Abuja, Nigeria. He was formerly a senior staff at the defunct Centre for Democratic Studies, Abuja and also worked briefly in the Presidency as an administrative officer before joining the National War College, Abuja as one of the pioneer academic staff of the College. He has published in different international journals and edited books. His current research interest includes Security, Conflict and development in Africa.

5. **Oshita O. Oshita** is Director of Research and Policy Analysis at the Institute for Peace and Conflict Resolution, The Presidency, Abuja, Nigeria. He holds an M.A. degree in Peace and Conflict Studies from the University of Bradford and a Doctorate degree in the Philosophy of Social Science from the University of Ibadan, Nigeria. He attained Senior Lectureship position at the University of Calabar, Nigeria, in 1997. He was a Chevening scholar at the University of Bradford (2002-2004) and Visiting Scholar, Institute of African Studies, University of Bayreuth, Germany (Spring 2007). He has published in many international peer-reviewed journals and has written/edited 7 books. His most recent book, *Conflict Management in Nigeria: Issues and Challenges*, was published by Adonis & Abbey, London (April 2007). He is a Resource Person and Visiting Lecturer at the Abdusalami Abubakar Centre for Peace and Development Studies, Minna, Nigeria.

6. **Omotayo Adeniyi Adegbuyi** holds a B.Sc. degree (Second Class Upper Division) in Marketing from Enugu State University of Science & Technology and a Master's degree in Marketing from the University of Lagos, Nigeria. He is a Lecturer in Marketing at the College of Business and Social Sciences, Covenant University, Ota, Nigeria – a position he has held for the past four years. A widely published scholar, his contributions have appeared in many scholarly journals

and proceedings of major national and international conferences. He is a 2007 recipient of the F.S Idachaba Foundation grant for research and scholarship. He is currently pursuing a doctorate degree in Marketing at Covenant University. He is an associate member and examiner of the National Institute of Marketing of Nigeria. He is married with three children.

7. **Chukwuemeka U. Okoye** holds a PhD in Agricultural Economics and is a Senior Research Fellow at the Centre for Entrepreneurship and Development Research / Senior Lecturer in the Department of Agricultural Economics, University of Nigeria, Nsukka. He is an Associate Fellow of the African Institute for Applied Economics, Enugu, Nigeria and a fellow of Lead International Institute, London. He holds the Support Africa International 2001 first price for research on sustainable agriculture. He has published in many reputable local and international journals and has consulted for the World Bank, UNDP, IITA, DFID-SLGP, among other notable institutions. His current research interest is in the area of poverty, environment and development.

8. **Onyukwu E. Onyukwu** is Senior Lecturer in the Department of Economics, University of Nigeria, Nsukka and Development Policy expert. He holds an M.Sc. degree in Economics from the University of Nigeria, Nsukka and an MA degree in Development Studies from Leeds University, UK. He was previously a Research Fellow at the Institute for Development Studies, University of Nigeria, Nsukka. He has published many book chapters in edited readers, monographs and articles in international journals. He has severally served as consultant to the World Bank, UNDP, DAI and DFID and has participated in many high profile conferences and professional programmes. He is a fellow of the African Institute for Applied Economics and a member of the International Development Economics Associates.

9. **Stan Ukeje** is currently a Principal Economist at the External Sector Division of the Monetary Policy Department, Central Bank of Nigeria Headquarters in Abuja. He holds an MSc. in Economics from the University of Nigeria, Nsukka and an MBA from the University of Lagos. Before joining the Central Bank of Nigeria, he was a Senior Lecturer and Head of the Department of Economics, Anambra State

University, Uli. Between 1992 and 2001, he was a Principal Lecturer and Head of the Department of Business Administration and Management, Institute of Management and Technology, Enugu. He had earlier worked with the Federal Ministry of National Panning, Lagos and the Federal Savings Bank. He has several journal and (joint) book publications to his credit.

10. **Chukwuma Agu** is the Coordinator of Research at the African Institute for Applied Economics, Enugu, Nigeria. He holds a PhD in Economics from the University of Nigeria, Nsukka, specializing in Open Economy Macroeconomics. He is an alumnus of the Global Economic Modelling School, Brussels, and has participated in several specialized trainings including the Cambridge Advanced Programme on Rethinking Development Economics. In 2006, he was a Visiting Fellow at the Centre for the Study of African Economies, University of Oxford. He has been deeply involved in the design of reform programmes, first as part of the technical team that prepared the National Economic Empowerment and Development Strategy (NEEDS) of the Federal Government of Nigeria and later providing support to several state governments in the preparation of their policy documents. He also works as consultant to a number of development partners. He has several publications including articles in international peer-reviewed journals and has authored / co-authored a number of book chapters.

11. **Paul Okojie** teaches law at Manchester Metropolitan University. He is also the Chair of the Board of Trustees, Ahmed Iqbal Ullah Race Relations Archives, Manchester University. He studied Law at the University of London and Keele University. He has written widely in the areas of race, immigration, policing and civil liberties. He wrote the section on international humanitarian law and human rights in Forsyth T.J. (ed.) (2004) *The Routledge Encyclopedia of International Development.* London: Routledge.

12. **Abubakar Momoh** is Senior Lecturer, Department of Political Science, Lagos State University. He holds a Ph.D. in Political Theory. He is currently Vice President, African Association of Political Science

(AAPS). He has done research on pan-Africanism, democracy and urban youths in Africa.

13. **Habu S. Galadima** is Senior Lecturer in the Department of Political Science and Deputy Director, Academic Planning Division, University of Jos, Nigeria. He was previously Assistant Director, Defence and Security Studies, Institute for Peace and Conflict Resolution, the Presidency, Abuja and Research Fellow at the National Council on Intergovernmental Relations, Abuja. He holds a Ph.D degree in International Relations and Strategic Studies (Jos, Nigeria). He has a number of articles in peer-reviewed journals. In addition, he has co-authored a book chapter with Ricardo Rene Laremont entitled: "Lessons for the Transition to Democracy in Africa: The Experience of the Military in Argentina, Brazil, Chile, Nigeria, and Algeria" in Ricardo Rene Laremont (ed.) *The Causes of War and the Consequences of Peacekeeping in Africa* (Portsmouth, NH: Heinemann: 2002).

Index

A

Abacha, Gen Sani, 18, 113, 114, 153, 205, 233, 260

Abia, 13, 57

Abiola, Alhaji M.K.O., 113, 114, 183

Abubakar, Gen Abdusallami, viii, 16, 31, 34, 83, 86, 93, 101, 113, 118, 125, 166, 230, 282

Action Group, 49, 53, 56, 111, 149, 238, 239

Adamawa, 13, 262

Adegbuyi, Adeniyi Omotayo, viii, 28, 29, 163

African Continental Bank, 211, 235, 236

Aguleri-Umuleri community crisis, 23

Akunyili, Dora, 18, 19

All Peoples Grand Alliance, 34, 258

Amanyanabo of Nembe, 51

Anambra, 13, 14, 117, 118, 121, 143

Anglo-Nigerian Defence Pact, 149

Arabian Gulf, 12

Awolowo, Chief Obafemi, 111

Azikiwe, Nnamdi, 49, 111, 236, 237

B

Babangida, Gen. Ibrahim, 21, 28, 115, 125, 151, 165

Bakassi Boys, 24, 148, 154, 161, 162, 280

Bakassi Peninsula, 51

Balogun, Tafa, 241, 260

Bayelsa Forum, 52

Bayelsa State, 52, 59, 63, 65, 100

Benin River, 54, 62, 64

Biafran secession, 56

Buhari/Idiagbon, 20, 240, 242

Bureau of Public Enterprises, 166

C

Calabar Ogoja Rivers (COR) State, 49

Cameron, Sir Donald, 45

Carter, Jimmy, 114

Central Bank, 30, 202, 205, 208, 211, 212, 213, 214, 216, 217, 218, 219, 220, 221, 222, 223, 233

Centre for Democracy and Democracy, 87

Centre for Democracy and Development, 90, 97, 101, 102

Centre for Economic Development, 231

Chatham House, 19, 38

Christian communities, 283

Citizens Forum for Constitutional Reform, 82, 83, 87, 102

Civil Liberties Organisation, 82

Coker Commission of Inquiry, 238, 261

Conference of South South Governors, 58

consequential power brokers, 13

Corrupt Practices Commission, 117, 292

CPBs, 13, 14

Cross River basin, 43

D

Delta State, 54, 55, 57, 62, 63, 256

305